Visions, Images, and Dreams
Yiddish Film Past and Present

Studies in Cinema, No. 24

Diane M. Kirkpatrick, Series Editor

Associate Professor, History of Art
The University of Michigan

Other Titles in This Series

No. 13	*Bertolt Brecht,* Cahiers du Cinéma, *and Contemporary Film Theory*	George Lellis
No. 14	Casablanca *and Other Major Films of Michael Curtiz*	Sidney Rosenzweig
No. 15	*Old Hollywood/New Hollywood: Ritual, Art, and Industry*	Thomas Schatz
No. 16	*Donald Duck Joins Up: The Walt Disney Studio During World War II*	Richard Shale
No. 18	*The Spanish Civil War in American and European Films*	Marjorie A. Valleau
No. 20	*Cinema Strikes Back: Radical Filmmaking in the United States, 1930-1942*	Russell Campbell
No. 21	*Third Cinema in the Third World: The Aesthetics of Liberation*	Teshome H. Gabriel
No. 22	*Women's Reflections: The Feminist Film Movement*	Jan Rosenberg
No. 23	*The Samurai Films of Akira Kurosawa*	David Desser

Visions, Images, and Dreams
Yiddish Film Past and Present

by
Eric A. Goldman

UMI RESEARCH PRESS
Ann Arbor, Michigan

Copyright © 1979, 1983
Eric Arthur Goldman
All rights reserved

Produced and distributed by
UMI Research Press
an imprint of
University Microfilms International
Ann Arbor, Michigan 48106

Library of Congress Cataloging in Publication Data

Goldman, Eric A. (Eric Arthur)
Visions, images, and dreams.

(Studies in cinema ; no. 24)
Revision of thesis (Ph. D.)–New York University, 1979.
Bibliography: p.
Filmography: p.
Includes index.
 1. Yiddish films–History and criticism. I. Title.
II. Series.

PN1995.9.Y54G64 1983   791.43'09'0935203924   83-15565
ISBN 0-8357-1515-9

This book is dedicated to three persons who influenced me to undertake this project: Ephraim L. Goldman ז״ל, my father, whose love for Judaism and Yiddishkayt left an indelible mark; Jay Leyda, who made cinema history come alive; and David Matis, who first recognized the need for research on aspects of Jewish cinema and who brought together Yiddishkayt and cinema history.

Contents

Preface *ix*

Acknowledgments *xiii*

A Note on Transliteration *xv*

Introduction: What is a Yiddish Film? *xvii*

1 Precursors, 1910-1918 *1*

2 Postwar Silent Pictures: Austria, Poland, and the United States, 1919-1928 *11*

3 The Soviet Yiddish Film, 1925-1933 *33*

4 The American Yiddish Sound Picture, 1929-1937 *55*

5 The Golden Age of Yiddish Cinema Part I: Poland, 1936-1939 *83*

6 The Golden Age of Yiddish Cinema Part II: United States, 1937-1940 *111*

7 After the War: Limited Success, 1946-1950 *143*

Epilogue: A Rebirth of Interest *157*

Notes *167*

Filmography *173*

Bibliography *207*

Listing of Yiddish Films Available for Rental *213*

Index *215*

Preface

I first learned of the existence of a film form called Yiddish cinema in the late 1960s. While visiting friends in Boston, I was told of a screening of the Yiddish film *Der Dibuk,* but I was unable to attend. For all I knew, there was no other Yiddish film. However, in 1972, I learned that a series of Yiddish films had been shown at the University of Massachusetts in Amherst. What were these Yiddish films? Who produced them? When and where were they made?

I first looked at a Yiddish picture in 1974, when I ventured out to the borough of Queens to watch *Yidl Mitn Fidl.* Though my knowledge of Yiddish was limited at the time, I was intent on seeing a Yiddish film. To my amazement, I was the youngest person in the audience; the next youngest must have been seventy. I felt very conspicuous. What was I doing there? It was at this point that I decided to undertake an exploration of what Yiddish cinema was, to find out more about this cinematic expression and seek out Yiddish films. I also realized that were I to wait too long, there would be no living participants to relate their personal experiences with this work. What I have therefore attempted to do is fix a factual history and provide a chronicle of an expression of cinematic creativity. I have placed emphasis on production history and how this was affected by the cultural life and situation of Jews in a number of countries.

The Yiddish cinema transcends territorial, political, and aesthetic boundaries. This film form evolved within the converging radicalism of Eastern Europe in the Twenties and Thirties and the "traditionalism" of Hollywood. The plots and subplots touched on social and religious questions, and reflected Jewish life in transition. Yiddish cinema contains a richness that envelops Jewish theater, music, and folklore.

There is no study that provides a full account of the history of world Yiddish cinema. David Matis, an editor for the *Jewish Daily Forward* was the pioneer advocate for a Yiddish cinema history. In 1961, he wrote an article in Yiddish, "Tsu Der Geshikhte fun Yidishe Films" (Toward a

History of Yiddish Cinema) in *Ikuf-Almanak,* in which he provided a basic listing of Yiddish pictures including some criticism of the films, gleaned from Yiddish sources. In 1973, Stuart Fox completed a filmography of Jewish subject films as part of his master's degree at the University of Southern California; this included a partial list of Yiddish films. In 1976, Patricia Erens wrote a piece in *Film Comment* on Yiddish cinema in America, partly stimulated by an interview conducted by Peter Bogdanovich with Edgar G. Ulmer published in *Film Culture* in 1974. Since that time a few more articles have appeared, each focusing primarily on pictures made in America between 1936 and 1939.

It is most shocking that I could find no general film history that even mentions the production of Yiddish films, with the exception of a paragraph in Georges Sadoul's *Histoire du Cinema Mondial;* not even film histories written in Israel touch on the subject. No study of Jewish cultural life, Jewish intellectual history, and with the exception of Nahma Sandrow's *Vagabond Stars: A World History of Yiddish Theater,* no Yiddish theater work reveals that Yiddish pictures were made. Zylbercweig's *Leksikon fun Yidishn Teater* (Lexicon of Yiddish Theater), a source guide for Yiddish theater researchers mentions the appearance of film actors in rare instances and includes no references to any person who was involved solely in film production. Producers, directors and actors in Yiddish cinema are also not credited in any film lexicon, unless they have done extensive non-Yiddish film work.

Many of the Yiddish films are either not in circulation at the present time or are to be found in a limited number of film archives around the world. Films finally being preserved in the United States which have been deposited with the Library of Congress and the American Film Institute cannot be seen, but I was fortunate to see prints of many of these films through private sources. An additional hardship is that many of the films have disappeared, either through nitrate disintegration or war.

The various problems of little previous research in my field, little interest, and lack of screenable prints made the preparation of this book most difficult. Fortunately, I was able to locate and interview many of the persons who participated on various levels in Yiddish filmmaking; their oral histories are an essential part of this study. I was also able to do research in Europe and Israel, and film archivists and librarians in the various film archives and libraries which I visited were most willing to assist me with my work and screen prints whenever possible. A wealth of material was available in New York; in the Theater Research Division of the Library for the Performing Arts, the Museum of the City of New York, and most especially in the archives and library of the YIVO Institute for

Jewish Research. I can truly say that had I not been able to do research at YIVO, the bulk of this study could not have been written.

This book is a history of the beginning, evolvement, and dubious fate of Yiddish cinema and the persons and events that affected its development. I deal with its relationship to and development from Yiddish theater in historic terms. Wherever possible I focus on individual films, but I have not intended to provide a specifically aesthetic, stylistic, or critical work. I give attention to the work of various filmmakers and the reasons why they made Yiddish pictures. Method of production and the influences that affected their work serve as the focal point of this study.

In the introduction I have attempted to provide an understanding and definition of Yiddish cinema. This is most important as it states the criteria for inclusion or non-inclusion of many films in this study. In the first chapter I deal with the precursors to Yiddish cinema: filmed theater and certain Jewish subject films. Following this, I examine Yiddish silent pictures; I do not include Soviet-made pictures in this chapter, for this wealth of creativity warranted separate exploration. The chapter on Soviet Yiddish cinema concentrates on various periods of filmmaking between 1925 and 1933, each affected by the changing political and artistic atmosphere of the post-Revolution years.

In the last four chapters, I explore sound pictures. The first of these chapters concentrates on the low-budget pictures made in America through the thirties and deals primarily with the work of Sidney Goldin, Henry Lynn, and Joseph Seiden. The following two chapters deal with a phenomenon that I have termed "The Golden Age of Yiddish Cinema," for during a short period of five years, Yiddish cinema reached its highest artistic level, bringing with it financial success. The "Golden Age" took place simultaneously in Poland and America and although the Polish films provided the impetus for the high quality American pictures, I have treated the films of each country in two separate chapters. The final chapter touches on a brief revival in Poland and America after the War. The epilogue is an account of my personal involvement in Yiddish cinema. It provides a brief history of the rebirth of interest in Yiddish pictures, both for the spectator and producer.

Acknowledgments

I wish to express my gratitude to numerous persons who have helped me with this work: to Jay Leyda, Gottesman Professor of Cinema Studies at New York University for his constant encouragement and enormous help; to David Matis of the *Jewish Daily Forward* for his assistance and generosity; to Dr. Evelyn Lapin and Dr. Irena Klepfisz of the Max Weinreich Center of the YIVO Institute for Jewish Research for opening up the wealth and beauty of Yiddish language and culture and to Yadja Zeltman, former assistant dean of the Center for her support and stimulation; to Professor David Roskies of the Jewish Theological Seminary for his insights and direction; to Deborah Franklin, formerly of the Rad Jewish Film Archives, for her continuing assistance; and to Harold Seiden for his graciousness and support.

I am grateful to the librarians and archivists who assisted me with my work. At the YIVO Institute for Jewish Research: Dina Abramowicz, chief librarian, who gave unstintingly of herself and her time; Bella Weinberg, Zachary Baker and Mark Padnos, assistant librarians; and Marek Web, archivist. At the Museum of the City of New York: Esther Enzer and Diane Cypkin, Yiddish theater consultants. At the Theater Research Division of the Library for the Performing Arts of the New York Public Library: Monty Arnold. At the Museum of Modern Art—in the Film Study Center: Charles Silver and Emily Sieger; in the Archives: Eileen Bowser, curator; Jon Gartenberg, assistant curator. At the American Film Institute: Audrey Kupferberg, motion picture archivist; and the staff of the Rutenberg and Everett Yiddish Film Library of the National Center for Jewish Film.

In Israel much thanks go to Lia Van Leer and her gracious staff at the Israel Film Archives. At the Hebrew University—in the library: Avraham Wolfson; at the Abraham F. Rad Jewish Film Archives: Dr. Geoffrey Wigoder, and Yaacov Gross. At the Israel Broadcasting Authority: Nili Kaplanski.

xiv   Acknowledgments

For their generous assistance I wish to thank Leszak Armatys of Filmoteka Polska, Warsaw; Dr. Walter Fritz of the Oesterreichisches Filmarchiv, Vienna; Moishe Rosenfeld of the Workman's Circle; Professor Susan Slotnick of Ohio State University; Professor Nahma Sandrow of the Max Weinreich Center; Yossi Lapid, Lejb Fogelman, James and Masha Khlevner, William Wollheim, Joanne Nussbaum, Hugh Denman, Seymour Rechtzeit, Leon Liebgold, Asher Tarmon, Israel Becker, Yehuda Stav, Lucjan Dobroszycki, Betty Posnansky, Russ Karel, Belle Goldman, Bobbi Zylberman, Morris Borger, and Marsha Bernstein. I also wish to thank Professors William G. Simon and William K. Everson of the Cinema Studies Department of New York University for their encouragement.

My special thanks to the numerous film actors, directors, producers, and technicians whose names are listed in the filmography for generously sharing their experience.

Research for this book was funded in part by the YIVO Institute for Jewish Research, the National Foundation for Jewish Culture, and the Memorial Foundation for Jewish Culture. I am grateful to these institutions for their generous support.

Lastly, above all, I wish to thank my wife, Susan, my best reader and severest critic, for her patience, encouragement and assistance.

A Note on Transliteration

Transliteration always presents a problem. There are a number of ways to spell a variety of words. For the purpose of this study, I have followed a clear, standard system provided by the YIVO Institute for Jewish Research for direct phonetic transliteration of Yiddish.

> i = as in English *bee*
> e = as in English *yet*
> ey = as in English *bay*
> ay = as in English *fly*
> tsh = as in English *catch*
> kh = gutteral h, commonly used in English as "ch," as in Sholom Aleichem or Lechaim

I have adhered to this when transliterating all film and literary titles, as well as footnotes and bibliography.

In the case of personalities, I have chosen instead to use the popular spelling of names. In this way Sholom Aleichem is not spelled Sholem Aleykhem and Itzik Manger does not become Itsik. I have also used popular spellings of words that have become part of English usage; Bar Mitzvah is not spelled Bar Mitsva, except as a film title.

For Hebrew words used in the notes and bibliography, I have used ch rather than kh and tz, not ts in order to differentiate the two languages. I hope that this serves to aid rather than complicate the reading of this work.

Introduction:
What is a Yiddish Film?

Sound Yiddish Pictures

When one attempts to provide a definition for what makes a film production Yiddish, the simplest common denominator is language. The picture may be made in Poland, America, or Russia, but if the language of expression is Yiddish, it falls within the purview of this study. Yiddish is not a nationality, nor a religion, so even though a film may be totally Jewish in character, if it is in French, English, or Hebrew, or any language but Yiddish, I have not considered it.

One may argue that if a picture contains some Yiddish, it could be deemed a Yiddish film; I do not accept this. A comedian might include some Yiddish words in his/her sketch, or someone might give a brief Yiddish soliloquy as does James Cagney in Roy del Ruth's *Taxi* (1932), but this does not make a film Yiddish. A picture might even contain a large amount of Yiddish as does Joan Micklin Silver's *Hester Street* (1976), but English is the main language of the film. For the purpose of this work, I have defined a Yiddish picture as a film which has Yiddish as its primary language of expression.

Silent Yiddish Pictures

A problem arises with pictures made before sound was introduced. With no audible language, how can one determine what a Yiddish film is? The presence of Yiddish inter-titles is not a distinguishing factor as they were often inserted on a variety of non-ethnic pictures which reached Yiddish-speaking audiences. I have therefore turned to other criteria in my definition of "silent" Yiddish cinema.

The first and most important criterion is audience. If the film was made specifically for a Yiddish-speaking audience then it is reasonable to consider it a Yiddish film. However, this category can also include racist and anti-Semitic films made expressly for Jewish audiences, which I cannot consider Yiddish. Audience is an important consideration, but it is by no means a sole determining factor.

A second question concerns subject matter. As I see it, the intent of Yiddish cinema has always been to stimulate and reinforce Jewish identity. If a film treats pogrom, anti-Semitism or expulsion as positive acts, then it defeats that purpose. If intermarriage and assimilation are sanctioned, it is not a Yiddish film because the future of Jewish life is threatened. Yiddish cinema intended to insulate Jews from assimilation and external change; it attempted to keep Jewish culture and peoplehood intact. If it does not do this, then it is not a Yiddish picture.

Another factor might be whether the filmmakers and actors are Jewish. If Yiddish cinema is to be considered as an expression of Jewish creativity, then most of the persons involved in its development should be Jewish. There were some non-Jews connected with Yiddish cinema, as directors, technicians and minor actors, but the major part of production was handled by Jews. Films executed primarily by non-Jews would not be Yiddish pictures.

Taking all of the criteria I have listed into account, I can define silent Yiddish cinema as *a Jewish cultural expression on film aimed primarily at Yiddish speaking audiences which works toward strengthening Jewish identity and survival.* These films, had they been made with sound would have been produced in Yiddish. For the purpose of this book, I have termed other films, with Jewish themes or characters, as "Jewish subject pictures."

1
Precursors 1910–1918

Beginning in 1794 by an edict issued by Czarina Catherine, Jews living under Russian rule were to be confined within a "Pale of Settlement." The government sought to restrict mobility and control Jewish life and forced Jews systematically to leave their rural surroundings and live in the towns and shtetls[1] of the Pale. There, bunched together, they were deprived of civil rights and limited in economic growth.

Shortly after Alexander III became Czar in 1881, a series of pogroms broke out across the Pale. Hundreds of Jews were murdered; thousands lost their property. "May Laws" placing strong restrictions on mobility were put into effect in 1882 forcing the relocation of thousands of Jews and setting into motion a mass exodus of Jews to America. During the next thirty years, government directed pogroms and strong anti-Jewish legislation made Russian Jewish life intolerable.

After the 1905 Revolution, conditions worsened as the Black Hundreds,[2] who fought the revolution with anti-Jewish pogroms, came to power. New atrocities were perpetrated and additional restrictions were levied on Jews. In 1910, 1200 Jewish families were deported, with unmitigated cruelty, from Kiev; this drew sharp negative reactions from the capitals of Europe. In response to this, a short film was commissioned through the Pathé Film Company, apparently by the Czarist government, to demonstrate how well Jews "really" lived under Czarist rule. That short film, *Jewish Types in Russia* purported to provide as *Moving Picture World* put it, "an opportunity to see the people that are heard to be so oppressed."[3]

Having already "documented" Jewish life, Pathé was spurred by the efforts of one of its scenarists, Alexander Arkatov, to prepare a short narrative film on a Jewish theme. Using "its regular staff of non-Jewish actors with a few Jewish 'types' in the background,"[4] Pathé made *Lekhaim* (To Life), a 10-minute film from an original story by Arkatov, about a Jewish woman who breaks with tradition by eloping with the man she loves

2   Precursors

Photo: Jay Leyda.

One of the earliest films to provide a glimpse of Jewish life in Eastern Europe was *Lekhaim* (To Life) (1911) written by Alexander Arkatov.

rather than the one she is promised to. A second Jewish subject film, *Rachel,* utilizing the same group of actors followed the next year. These films, well received in Europe and America, whet Arkatov's appetite for Yiddish filmmaking. He would become the leading producer of Jewish subject pictures in Russia and precursor of Soviet Yiddish filmmakers.

The United States and Sidney Goldin

Jewish subject pictures had been popular in the United States since the beginning of the century. The early pictures were slapstick ethnic comedies or melodramas with Jewish protagonists, not meant to tackle important Jewish issues. However the Kiev cruelties inspired at least two American producers to respond to the oppression of Russian Jews, setting the stage for later productions. *In the Czar's Name* and *Russia, The Land of Oppression,* both made in 1910, were about oppressed Russian Jewish families who find freedom by reaching American shores through the help of Russian aristocracy. Although they were not Yiddish pictures, as each story revolves around relationships between Jews and their non-Jewish lovers, their intent was to "enlighten" the American public about Russian anti-Jewish policy.

In the spring of 1911 a Jewish factory worker, Mendel Beilis, was accused of having murdered, for ritual purposes, a Russian youth. For the next two years, strong anti-Semitic feeling was felt all across Russia. With Beilis's indictment came a condemnation of Russia's Jews. There were protests across Europe and in America, but Sidney Goldin was the first American cinema director to put his expostulation onto film. Goldin had made a few films on a variety of subjects, but as a Jew, he was stirred to make *The Sorrows of Israel*. Using the same basic themes as the earlier anti-Russian films of 1910, he made the picture, set against a backdrop of pogroms and oppression, about a young Jew who manages to flee Russia for America with the help of a Russian noblewoman. Goldin had himself emigrated from Russia. Shortly afterwards, he directed another picture, *Bleeding Hearts* (also called *Jewish Freedom under King Casimir of Poland*), set in fourteenth-century Poland about Jews who are given refuge from oppression by Casimir the Great.[5] The contrast between the generosity of Casimir's Poland and Czarist Russian anti-Jewish policy was clear.

With *The Sorrows of Israel* and *Bleeding Hearts,* Goldin identified a new potential audience, the Jewish viewer. In order to give his pictures a broader base of appeal, each of his films had used as heroes Jews and non-Jews, with the Jewish hero saved by a Gentile lover. Why not prepare Yiddish pictures—films about Jews, without inter-religious relationships, which would be geared to a specifically Jewish audience? While Goldin toyed with the idea, he decided to get a better understanding of the Jewish community and in September 1913, he approached the executives of some of New York's Jewish institutions to make a one-reel documentary on the work of their agencies. They consented and Goldin, combining both reenacted and documentary sequences, made *How the Jews Take Care of Their Poor*. Shot in some of the Jewish hospitals and agencies of New York, the film showed the work of Jewish philanthropic societies.[6]

Goldin had just finished shooting *How the Jews Take Care of Their Poor,* when word of Mendel Beilis' acquittal reached America. He wasted little time in mounting *The Terrors of Russia* (also released as *The Black Hundreds*), a re-creation of the Beilis case and an indictment of Russian anti-Semitism.[7] The picture was not a Yiddish film; instead, it was a film in defense of Jews made for the broad viewing audience. As a follow-up, Goldin made *Escaped from Siberia* during the spring of 1914, again using inter-racial relationships and highlighting anti-Semitic injustice in Russia as his subject.

In the summer of 1914, Goldin undertook to make a picture about an

Photo: David Matis.

The Grandfather of Yiddish cinema, Sidney M. Goldin (1880–1937) began his career directing gangster films. His love for Jewish life brought him to Jewish film production. Goldin's first Jewish picture, *The Sorrows of Israel* was made in 1913. He died on the eve of the "Golden Age of Yiddish Cinema," never living to see completion of his last film, *Dem Khazns Zundl,* an attempt to bring production quality to the Yiddish screen. Like Moses, he saw "the promise" only from afar.

unusual figure from Jewish history, Uriel Acosta. Acosta, a seventeenth-century apostate, had also been the subject of a play written by Karl Gutskov which was used on the Yiddish stage. Made for general distribution, *Uriel Acosta* was Goldin's last Jewish subject picture made during this period.

After *Uriel Acosta*, no trace of Goldin's work is found until he reemerges in Austria in 1921 to lay claim to his title of "grandfather" or "dean" of Yiddish cinema. He would not yet make a Yiddish picture, nor would he be the first; Yiddish films were already being made in Eastern Europe. Rather, Goldin should be known as the one who seized on the idea of Yiddish cinema, developed it, and carried it into the sound era. This would be his contribution.

Eastern Europe

Within the Pale of Settlement, which stretched from the Baltic to the Black Sea and from Warsaw and Dvinsk to Odessa, Yiddish theater had become an important part of Jewish cultural life. During this first decade of the twentieth century, a number of amateur theatrical clubs and troupes evolved, numbering 360 by 1910.[8] One of these troupes was the Kaminsky troupe, managed by Avrom Yitskhok Kaminsky, but led by his wife Esther Rokhl Kaminska. Esther Rokhl had gained her reputation as a leading actress playing a variety of roles from Goldfaden to Gordin heroines. Her popularity was so great that she was called both "mother of Yiddish theater" and the "Jewish Duse." Together with Avrom Yitskhok—who was not only manager, but actor, writer, and director—she made the Warsaw Company an outstanding Yiddish theater group.

The Kaminsky troupe was approached in 1911 by Mojzesz Mordka Towbin, a producer for the Warsaw film company, Sila (Strength), for permission to film their production of Z. Libin's *Der Vilder Foter*. Influenced by Film d'Art, an effort begun in 1908 in Paris to bring quality stage productions to the mass-oriented screen, Towbin sought to put the great classics of Yiddish theater on film. There were nearly three million Yiddish-speaking Jews in Congress Poland, and Towbin saw tremendous financial and artistic possibilities in this endeavor. Kaminsky, excited by the prospect of filming his company's presentations, quickly gave his consent. Most often, the cameras would be brought directly to the theater to literally record the performance.[9] In this manner, the Sila Company filmed *Der Vilder Foter* (The Savage Father) and Jacob Gordin's *Di Shtifmuter* (The Stepmother) in 1911. In each film Stanislaw Sebel handled the camera, and Andrzej Marek directed; Kaminsky served as artistic coordinator. These and the filmed theater that would follow were the precursors to Yiddish cinema. Here, the camera would merely record the performance; only later would plays, with "stageboundedness" removed, be artistically adapted for cinema.

In 1912, Kaminsky moved his company into its own theater, opening with a production of Jacob Gordin's "Mirele Efros." Esther Rokhl played Mirele, with her daughter, thirteen-year-old Ida, playing her grandson Shloymele. Other members of the cast included Esther Rokhl's daughter Regina, her husband Gershon Weissman, and Jacob Libert. The play was highly successful, and Kaminsky consented to have it filmed. Andrzej Marek was again hired to direct, but by the end of the filming, Kaminsky felt so confident about filmmaking that he took over direction of all future productions. That year, Kaminsky made Jacob Gordin's *Got, Mentsh un Tayvl* (God, Man and Devil) and *Di Farshtoysene* (The Forgotten).

The filming of Kaminsky productions was limited not only to Sila in Warsaw, for as the troupe toured other parts of the Pale, they were approached by other film companies. Nahum Lipovsky filmed the troupe during performances of *Khasye di Yesome* (Khasye the Orphan) in Dvinsk and the Mintus Company recorded their adaptation of Tolstoy's *Masters and Workers* in Riga with Misha Fishzon in the lead. Mintus filmed three other plays in 1912 with various traveling Yiddish troupes: Gordin's *Yom Hakhupa* (The Wedding Day), Isidore Zolatarefsky's *Der Yeshive-bokher* (The Yeshiva Student), and Thomashefsky and Zeifert's *Dos Pintele Yid* (The Essential Spark of Jewishness). That same year, playwright/director Mark Arnstein filmed a second version of *Khasye di Yesome* at the Vilna Circle Theater, the filming being done during the day when the theater was empty.[10] In 1913, Mintus filmed at least two productions mounted by the Kaminsky troupe, *Leybe der Shuster* (Leybe the Shoemaker) and Ossip Dymow's *Shma Yisroel* (Hear O Israel); a third Mintus production was *Vu Iz Emes* (Where Is Truth), a "tragedy of a Jewish seamstress."[11]

While traveling theater troupes were having their repertoires "recorded" for distribution across the Pale, a few original Yiddish film productions were being mounted in Russia. Sholom Asch's *Got Fun Nekome* (God of Vengeance) was being prepared for filming in 1912 by Alexander Arkatov; starring Israel Arko and Misha Fishzon with a Russian cast. Arkatov was devoting almost all his time to the preparation of Jewish subject films. Gaumont in Moscow followed Arkotov's lead by filming *Mirele Efros* with a Russian cast, and the first experiments with Yiddish talking pictures were made in St. Petersburg that April with S. L. Akarski singing Jewish couplet songs in *Vu Iz Mayne Khasye* (Where is My Khasye). A year later, Arkatov wrote and directed a narrative based on Jewish life, *Sorrow of Sarah,* a story about the hardships of a penniless fiancée,[12] using one of the more popular Russian actors of his time, Ivan Mozhukhin, in the lead role.

In 1913 Warsaw, Henryk Finkelstein, owner of Kosmofilm, took over Sila's contract with the Kaminsky troupe. He had just returned from Palestine, where he made a documentary film, *Egypt and Palestine*. He saw tremendous potential in Yiddish "Film d'Art"; within a year he mounted six film productions of Yiddish plays. Business was booming.

However, with the advent of World War I in 1914, production slowed as entire communities were cut off from each other and distribution became difficult. There was also a scarcity of film stock and equipment. With each successive occupation of Poland by invading armies, there was a new sense of uncertainty, but Finkelstein still managed to make one "film recording" a year between 1914 and 1916. By the end of 1916, film stock was too rare, good Yiddish theater even harder to find, and the Warsaw film industry was at a standstill.

A first chapter of Polish Yiddish cinema, "filmed theater," had been forged. It filled a tremendous void in Jewish cultural life, for it allowed small communities which might otherwise not have been able, to have a Yiddish theater presence. They could watch the great actors of their day— Fishzon, Kaminska, Landau, Samberg, and Weissman every week, whereas otherwise they might have had to wait years.

Cinematically, the result of this new experiment was often uneven, static, and uninspired photographed theater, a syndrome which plagued Yiddish cinema at various times throughout its history. It is difficult to evaluate these pictures today for few exist. Yet, by contrasting a filmed theater piece, such as Kaminsky's adaptation of *Mirele Efros* (1912) with another film of the period, *Meir Ezofowicz*, made a year later, we know that a high level of technical quality was attainable in Poland. Where *Mirele Efros* is a continuous indoor, frontal recording of theater, *Meir Ezofowicz*, the Eliza Orzeszkowa Jewishly-oriented story, incorporates a wide variety of camera techniques and some fine exterior shooting.

As had been learned through the experience of Film d'Art, stage acting and film acting were often incompatible. On stage, the great actors would make demonstrative gestures, which when recorded on film would look silly. The camera did not help as it merely recorded, mostly in long shot, the actions from the stage, as the cinema director had yet to forcefully implement the nuances of camera work. In a later film, *Tkies Kaf* (1924), the older actors who had been trained for the theater still played to the crowds, while younger actors with general training acted for the camera. It would only be a matter of time before film acting became incorporated into Yiddish cinema. Warsaw filmmakers would soon develop a new Yid-

Photos: Filmoteka Polska, Warsaw.

An interior and exterior look at *Meir Ezofowicz* (1913). Already there was a high level of technical quality of filmmaking in Poland.

dish film form, removed from the stage, yet still clinging to the traditions of "Yiddishkayt" formed during this period.

The Talking Picture

The Mizrekh company made *The War and the Jew* in the Ukraine in 1914, and sound was added a year later. That same year, a producer in Kursk named Reznikov released *Kiddush Hashem* (Sanctification of God's Name), "the first talking picture of Jewish life filmed in the landscape around Kursk."[13] Exactly what language, Russian or Yiddish, was used, is unclear.

We do know that in September 1911, a filmed recording, *A Brivele der Mamen* (A Letter to Mother). was made of a singer named Smolenski with his troupe, singing in Yiddish. *Vu Iz Mayne Khasye* (Where Is My Khasye) sung by S. L. Akarski was filmed in St. Petersberg in April 1912. The following year, a 100-meter "talking film," *Yidl mitn Fidl* (Yidl with a Fiddle) was made by Filma Company, and *Beser Dem Toyt Eyder Aza Shand* (Better Death Than Such Shame) with N.B. Leonov playing five different characters was made with sound in 1914.

These sound experiments in Yiddish cinema came abruptly to an end with the outbreak of war in 1914. They were not repeated in Russia until the first Soviet Yiddish sound picture, *Noson Beker Fort Aheym* (Nathan Becker is Going Home) was released, almost twenty years later, in 1932.

The 1917–1918 Russian Films

With the Czar's abdication and after three years of war with no Jewish film activity, Jewish filmmakers wasted little time preparing productions. At the forefront again was Alexander Arkatov. In Odessa, he worked with scenarist V. Voldo in adapting Sholom Aleichem's *Der Blutiker Shpas* (The Bloody Jest) for the screen. It is set during the reign of Czar Nicholas II, at a time of strong anti-Jewish feeling. Arkatov used the Sholom Aleichem story to stress that under the Czar, Jew and Gentile would always live in constant stress. With the new regime, no such situation would be present, as Jew and Gentile could finally live together peacefully without the threat of anti-Semitism. That same year, Josef Soifer made the film *The Beilis Case,* showing strong anti-Semitism during Czarist rule, with great hopes placed on the new regime. Both pictures used non-Jewish actors and were produced for wide distribution.

In 1918, Soifer made *Aziade,* and Arkatov made two more Jewish subject pictures based on Yiddish literary sources, *Judge, People* (from an I. L. Peretz folktale), and Sholom Aleichem's *Ven Ikh Bin Roytshild* (If I

Precursors

Photo: Jay Leyda/Alexander Arkatov

Alexander Arkatov filmed the Sholom Aleichem story, *Der Blutiker Shpas* (The Bloody Jest) (1917) to show the severity of Jewish life under Czarist rule. One of a series of films by Arkatov using actors amid real surroundings and non-actors.

were Rothchild); they were filmed with Russian casts. Change was in the air, and Soifer and Arkatov feared for their future. Both filmmakers found themselves in the Ukraine where occupation followed occupation and they finally fled, Soifer to Paris and Arkatov to Hollywood. Neither filmmaker ever made Jewish subject pictures again. With their flight, an era of filmmaking had ended. In Eastern Europe it was left to the theater companies to resurrect Yiddish cinema; in Western Europe and America it was left up to Sidney Goldin.

2

The Postwar Silent Pictures: Austria, Poland, and the United States, 1919–1928

In the postwar period, Yiddish cinema attempted to separate itself from the theater. It had relied too heavily on Yiddish theater not only for its subject matter but for aesthetics. If Yiddish cinema were to succeed as a creative Jewish art form and not merely as a means for recording theater, it had to develop its own style, form, and acting. The early years had proven the awkwardness of extended long-shot recordings from the stage. What was needed now was for Yiddish filmmakers to employ new camera and montage technique as well as to integrate stylized film acting.

Austria

Austria would serve as the setting for the ushering in of this new period of Yiddish filmmaking. This is not surprising as the country was a Jewish intellectual and cultural center, and there was virtually no area of the arts in which Jews were not centrally involved.

Yet Austria was also a hotbed of anti-Semitism. In 1921, three-quarters of the 100,000 Galician Jewish refugees who had fled Russian zones to Austria during the war were expelled. Shortly after these expulsions, the country's anti-Semitic forces took action to restrict Jewish involvement in the arts and sciences by pressuring for the enactment of a quota system on Jewish students in institutions of higher learning.

It was this state of crisis that prompted Austrian filmmakers, most of whom were Jewish, to first work with Jewish themes. Their films were meant to tackle the problem of anti-Semitism in the country by showing the contribution Jews made to Austrian society. One such picture was Otto Kreisler's *Theodor Herzl, der Bannerträges des Judischen Volkes* (Theodor Herzl, Champion of the Jewish People), starring Rudolf and Joseph Schildkraut. Herzl, a Viennese Jew, had defined the Jewish problem some

12   Postwar Silent Pictures

twenty-five years earlier as anti-Semitism, which could not be eradicated as long as the Jew remained stereotyped in the mind of the Gentile. This film, made the year of the expulsions, challenges the future of Jewish life in such a society.

Though message films about anti-Semitism for the broad public continued to be produced, it was a 1923 anti-Semitic rally of 20,000 people in Vienna that prompted the production of films made exclusively for the Jewish community. Filmmaker Sidney Goldin felt that the medium of film could best provide an element of escapism for the Jewish audience in that difficult time. His two films, *Mizrekh un Mayrev* (East and West) with Molly Picon and *Yisker* (Remembrance) with Maurice Schwartz, made in 1923 and 1924 respectively, return the viewer to the comparative comfort of Eastern Europe.

Mizrekh un Mayrev (East and West) — 1923

By 1923, when director Goldin asked Molly Picon to star in *Mizrekh un Mayrev,* she was already a face well known on the Yiddish stage and cabarets throughout Europe. She, along with actor husband Jacob (Yankl) Kalich, charmed audiences with vaudeville skits and songs. Picon's special ability to sing, dance, do vaudeville and gymnastics made her a unique performer.

It was Kalich who first discovered Picon, and brought her to Europe to refine her talents and better her Yiddish. As Molly Picon described it:

> He promised to make a star out of me. He had a very difficult time doing it in America because I was the daughter of a wardrobe mistress, the Picon's "tokhter" (daughter) I was...The managers in New York said "The Picon's Tokhter" a star? And the size of me — I weighed a hundred pounds. All the leading ladies weighed 180. So he took me to Europe, first of all to perfect my Yiddish which was not too good and then to get my "star legs" and not to be inhibited by working with people who knew me. For 3 years, we wandered over Europe.[1]

Picon's film career began, at age 16 with *Little Girl with Big Ideas* (1917), produced in America with Yiddish composer Joseph Rumshinsky. While in Europe, she starred in two Austrian pictures, Otto Kreisler's *Das Judenmädel* (1921) and Sidney M. Goldin's *Hütet eure Töchter* (1922) before making *Mizrekh Un Mayrev* in 1923. Years later she starred in two Yiddish films, *Yidl mitn Fidl* (1936) and *Mamele* (1938), both made by Joseph Green in Poland. Since then, she has had several roles in American films, including *Come Blow Your Horn* (1963) and *Fiddler on the Roof* (1971).

Sidney Goldin had just finished working with Picon on *Hütet eure*

Töchter, which had no Jewish content, when Picon's husband proposed the idea of co-producing a Yiddish picture. Goldin was certainly no stranger, having made a number of Jewish subject films the previous decade in America. For Kalich, it was a novel idea, for he hoped to take the picture back to America with him with the idea that it would greatly enhance his and Picon's careers.

Mizrekh un Mayrev (East and West), set in Russian Poland, is about a talmudist (Kalich) who as a joke plays the role of a groom in a mock wedding and mistakenly becomes legally married to the niece of his benefactor from America. After realizing the severity of the situation, the talmudist agrees to divorce the girl (Picon), but only after five years of separation. During this period, the young man, by means of assiduous study becomes a celebrated writer and joins his wife in America, where they remain together.

Despite the fact that the film was aimed at the Jewish audience, it did extremely well financially. During its 1923 run in Vienna, it even outlasted Chaplin's *The Kid* in theaters. The film is well acted and extremely well filmed.

Yisker (Remembrance) — 1924

In 1924, Goldin asked Maurice Schwartz, who was on tour in Vienna to star in Harry Sackler's *Yisker* (Prayer of Remembrance). It was a play with which Schwartz was acquainted and which had become a staple of his New York Yiddish Art Theater the previous year. Cast with Austrian supporting players, Schwartz plays Leybke, a young Jewish forester who has become a martyr for his people. On the anniversary of his death, a procession of Jews make a pilgrimage to his tomb to recite the prayer for the dead, the Kaddish. There the story is told of how he became a hunter for the duke and after having refused the advances of the duke's daughter, is slandered and imprisoned. Shortly thereafter the duke's daughter poisons herself, and Leybke is buried alive as punishment.

Yisker, labeled a "Judischer Tendenzfilm" (Jewish message film), is clearly a story about Jewry in the face of adversity. It stresses the vulnerability of the Jew in a Christian world. At one point, Tsiml, father of the woman that Leybke loves, is forced to stage a "bear-dance" for the duke — a humiliating activity that Jews at that time were compelled to do. The picture was Schwartz's first picture and left him with an intense love for the medium, one which would last for the rest of his life.

Mizrekh un Mayrev and *Yisker* were Yiddish pictures made for Jewish spectators. Goldin bet that he could distribute the pictures beyond Austria. With well-known talent like Picon and Schwartz, he believed the films would surely be financially successful in America; they were. There was

A fun-loving American-born girl (Molly Picon) finds herself the center of controversy as she goes to the "Old Country" for a family wedding in *Mizrekh un Mayrev* (East and West) (1923). In the center is Molly Picon. On the right is actor/director Sidney Goldin. Opposite page: The American girl got more than she bargained for—a husband and family. In the center is Jacob Kalich. Next to him is his real-life wife Molly Picon. *Mizrekh un Mayrev* (1923).

Photo: Yiddish Theater Collection, Museum of the City of New York.

Photo: Yiddish Theater Collection, Museum of the City of New York.

Photo: YIVO Institute for Jewish Research.

Yisker (1924) was Maurice Schwartz's (far left) first film. This picture left him with an intense love for the film medium, one which would last for the rest of his life.

finally an awareness that Yiddish cinema not recorded directly from the stage was marketable; Goldin left for America to capitalize on it.

The year 1925 brought some stability to the Austrian economy because loans floated by England, the League of Nations, and the United States effected a temporary boom. With the recovery came some quelling of anti-Semitic activity; this in addition to Sidney Goldin's departure west brought to an end an era of Yiddish filmmaking in Austria. It had been a period of creative output which depended greatly on conflict to stimulate production. Once things seemed to settle down, the raison d'être was gone and the industry disappeared.

Poland

As Sidney Goldin was preparing *Yisker* in Austria, a movement was underway to revive production of Jewish pictures in Poland, where no Yiddish picture had been released since the 1916 production of *Zayn Vaybs Man*. Following the showing of that picture much had happened, including the end of a world war and the rebirth of an independent Polish state, after a century and a half of external rule. With the new state, however, came a difficult period for Poland's Jews. Nearly 30,000 Jews were massacred by Pilsudski's soldiers in 1920, and in the years that followed, sporadic pogroms took place in various parts of the country.

The Polish government devised an official policy, soon known as "the cold pogrom," toward the elimination of Jews from economic life. In Austria, this restrictive climate had spurred on production. However, in Poland, Jewish film producers, who a decade earlier had produced many films on Jewish subjects, were too frightened to continue.

Despite the internal situation in Poland, Yiddish theater was again thriving, with the Warsaw Yiddish Art Theater (VYKT) gaining world attention. Writer Henryk Bojm along with producer Leo Forbert felt that there would also be interest in Yiddish pictures. Paying little attention to government pressure, they created their own company. They recruited veteran Yiddish actors like Esther Rokhl Kaminska, her daughter Ida Kaminska, and Ida's husband Zygmund Turkow, all members of the Warsaw Yiddish Art Theater, in preparation for the first postwar Yiddish film to be made in Poland.

Tkies Kaf (The Vow) — 1924

Writer Henryk Bojm, born into a Chassidic family and given a traditional Yeshiva background, became interested in secular literature at sixteen, and shortly thereafter left for Warsaw. While there, he became interested in photography and began traveling from town to town doing portraits. He eventually set up a photography workshop with his brother-in-law in a town near Warsaw and toward the end of the War began writing short literary pieces. His interest in photography expanded to cinema, and he began writing film scenarios. Unsuccessful in his attempts at finding anyone to read his scripts, Bojm finally convinced Leo Forbert, an assimilated Jew and owner of Meteor, the largest photography studio in Warsaw, to meet with him. Forbert was most excited, in part as a "rebuttal" to the government's "cold pogrom" policy, and agreed to join Bojm in creating a Jewish film group, "Leo-Film."

Bojm's script for *Tkies Kaf* (The Vow) attempted to show processes of emancipation within a traditional Jewish framework. The story is about two friends who are unhappy that neither of their wives have borne children, and pledge, with a *tkies kaf* (a handshake signifying agreement), that if one should bear a son and the other a daughter, the children would marry and so bring their families closer together. Years pass, the friends lose contact with each other, and a son is born to one family with a daughter to the other. The children grow up and by accident meet and fall in love, only to have the boy's father, who forgot his pledge, plan another match for his son. The prophet Elijah intervenes and after a series of mishaps, the son marries the girl to whom he was pledged.

Bojm wrote the script with Esther Rokhl Kaminska in mind as the girl's poor mother, at the same time envisioning her real-life daughter Ida as the daughter, with Ida's husband, Zygmund Turkow, cast to play eight different roles. By enlisting the Kaminskas and Turkow in his film, Bojm engaged the best talent that the Polish Yiddish stage of that day had to offer. Turkow had begun his career directing amateur theater productions for "Dos Artistishe Vinkele" (Little Corner for the Arts). With his marriage to Ida Kaminska he brought together, in 1921, two troupes, the Kaminsky company and the Turkows, made up of Zigmund, his brother Jonas, Jonas' wife Diana Blumenfeld, and sometime-member brother Yitskhok. This new group took on the name Varshiver Yidisher Kunst Teater (VYKT — Warsaw Yiddish Art Theatre).

In 1924, Leo Forbert's cousin Seweryn Steinwurcel, who had served as cameraman on Forbert's two previous films for Meteor, was asked to film the picture. A graduate of the School of Mechanics and Technicians, and from a family of photographers, Steinwurcel had quickly gained a reputation as an extremely talented cameraman and film technician. In a chat with Steinwurcel, he told me:

> We began to make Polish films which had nothing to do with Jews and the films did not bring good financial results.... Then a friend of ours, Mr. Bojm, who was well known in Yiddish cultural circles, proposed to make the film *Slubowanie (Tkies Kaf)*. In the past two films there was a Polish director, but he couldn't make a Yiddish film. We arranged for a complex of actors and directors...[2]

Both Bojm and Forbert felt that Bruno Bredschneider, a non-Jew who had served as Forbert's main director was not well enough acquainted with Jewish custom and language. Instead, they decided to hire someone from outside the country, very possibly Goldin, to handle direction. The actors were annoyed at not having a director.

> We agreed to participate in the film on one condition — that the company must bring in an experienced director from outside, who would guarantee the quality of the film as well as direct our acting, which must, as one knows, be different than in theater. The condition was accepted and we began pre-production.[3]

Finally, the first day of filming came and there still was no director. If Forbert had Goldin in mind to direct, Goldin certainly was unavailable as he was working on *Yisker*. Forbert and Bojm still did not feel comfortable

Photo: Seweryn Steinwurcel.

Some of the cast and crew of *Tkies Kaf* (The Vow) (1923). In the far left is producer Leo Forbert. Below him is Zygmund Turkow. To his right is Esther Rokhl Kaminska, Ida Kaminska and David Lederman. Second from the right is director of photography Seweryn Steinwurcel. Third from right is screenwriter Henryk Bojm. Sitting below Bojm (with hand on foot) is production assistant Jacob Fisher.

enough to have a Polish director take charge, so they began to shoot the film with no director. This made leading actor Zygmund Turkow quite disconcerted.

> It dawned on me the first day that technically everything was going well; however artistically, it could not continue without a director. The "specialists"—the producer and scenarist—had no inkling of elementary rules of direction. The cameraman, in contrast, had learned from his work in Polish film, but worried more about camera work than acting, movement or mise-en-scene. As for my "in order" inquiry about the promised director, I finally got an answer that the prospective foreign candidate allegedly could not come and we must continue by using what we had—pulling out from the film was too late.... There was no choice but to take the initiative in hand....[4]

With Steinwurcel handling the technical side of production, Turkow felt comfortable taking over direction of the film. This was the first Yiddish picture made in Poland that was to be completely removed from the Yiddish stage. Aware that this was a historic milestone in Yiddish filmmaking, Turkow took great care in making the transfer from theater to cinema. He

Photo: David Matis.

Photo: David Matis.

Four of the faces of Yiddish film great Zygmund Turkow (1896–1970). In *Tkies Kaf* (The Vow) (1923), the versatile Turkow not only played eight roles, including Elijah the prophet (opposite page, left), but he directed the picture. This was no small feat, considering that he had to direct his mother-in-law, wife, brother and sister-in-law, to name but a few. In the above right picture on the lower right, Turkow is second from right. Also in the picture is Adam Domb (far left) and Moyshe Lipman (right).

clearly had his work cut out for him, for in addition to his own lack of experience in film, he was working with great theater artists including his mother-in-law, Esther Rokhl, who knew nothing about film acting. While Turkow succeeded in giving direction and unity to his actors, he failed to affect the stage manner of the cast. The picture provides a priceless record of great acting, but unfortunately the actors are, more often than not, playing for the "third balcony."

Exteriors for *Tkies Kaf* were shot on location in Vilna and on Warsaw's Nalewek Street. Steinwurcel developed an entire range of shots for exterior shooting. Polish film critic Andrzej Wlast wrote that the camerawork was "done with a great feeling of photogeneity."[5] He also called attention to the cinematic realism the picture conveys juxtaposed with "theatrical mannerisms too close to Russian style."[6] As for interior filming, the filmmakers were limited to Forbert's small photography workshop instead of a large film studio. Writer J. M. Neuman, who had a small acting role, recalled nearly losing his eyesight because of the intense light.[7]

> Instead of filming in a large studio which was used for Polish production, we were shown into a photography workshop which was barely big enough for photography, certainly too small for film work. The sets in which the first scenes had to be shot were conceived and professionally executed with taste, which developed in us a sense of trust....[8]

The picture was prepared for general distribution, instead of setting an eye on just a Jewish market. Inter-titles, written by Bojm, were prepared in Polish, which was felt to be more easily read by the masses. Only later were titles prepared in Yiddish for release in Europe and America. The film was released some ten years later with a sound narration in the United States as *A Vilna Legend.*

What struck me most when seeing the film was the strong difference between the exterior scenes and the interiors. The exteriors are well paced with good camerawork and film acting; especially exciting were the wedding dance segments and a lovely visual sequence where one of the heroes runs after a trolley-car. Turkow and Steinwurcel also used montage to their advantage. In contrast, indoors the acting is very theatrical, with demonstrative gestures and poses. Interior camerawork is often static, recording mostly in long shot a "for theater" performance; editing is practically nonexistent. Yet, despite these obvious flaws, the film narrative is well paced and indeed was well received, both artistically and financially. Wlast at the time called it "the best film done to date in this country."[9]

Der Lamedvovnik (One of the 36 Just Men) — 1925

With the success of *Tkies Kaf,* Bojm, Steinwurcel and Forbert began mounting plans for a second picture, *Der Lamedvovnik* (One of the 36 Just Men), to be filmed the following year, 1925. As Steinwurcel indicated to me, "this *[Tkies Kaf]* showed that one could make money with Yiddish films."[10] This time they turned to Henryk Szaro, an extremely talented film director who had worked with Steinwurcel on the Polish film *Rywale* (1925). Szaro, who changed his name from the Jewish Szapiro (Shapiro), was a graduate of the Moscow School of Drama where he studied with Arbatov and Meyerhold. Russian-born, he gained directing experience in Leningrad with Pavlova and studied with Stanczyk after moving to Warsaw. By the late twenties he had become one of Poland's best directors.

Jonas Turkow and Moyshe Lipman, who had played small roles in *Tkies Kaf,* were given the leading parts in the new film. It was a film about a shtetl that is attacked by the Russians during the Polish uprising of 1830–1831. In the community lives a tsadik (righteous person), one of thirty-six simple people believed to exist secretly, who according to tradition carry on their shoulders the weight of the sins of the world. Turkow plays the tsadik, a "lamedvovnik" (one of the thirty-six), who sacrifices himself in order to relieve the town's misfortune.

The company chose sites in the towns of Kazimierz and Sandomierz for exterior filming. Rather than shoot interiors in Forbert's cramped photography workshop, they filmed at the large Kirschner studios in Warsaw. I know of no existing print of this picture, but according to Polish film historian Jerzy Toeplitz, Szaro was able to preserve a "highly unified atmosphere" in *Der Lamedvovnik* and set new trends in direction. Toeplitz also calls attention to the carefully molded camera scenes, design and sets that "skillfully bring out realistic detail."[11]

Der Lamedvovnik (also released as *The Secret Saint*) was not received as well as *Tkies Kaf,* and Forbert quickly found himself in financial trouble. Although he became known as an enterprising and exciting producer, Forbert, according to Steinwurcel, was not an able business man. Before the year was up, he was forced to turn over control of his company, Leo-Film, which thereafter produced only Polish films. Thus ended the short period of existence of "Leo-Film" as a Jewish filmmaking group.

In Poylishe Velder (In Polish Woods) — 1928

Wild inflation in 1926 did not make it any easier for Bojm and Forbert to prepare another project. However, with Pilsudski's takeover of the govern-

Interior scene from *Tkies Kaf* (The Vow) (1923). Filming was done in a small photography studio. Second from left is Zygmund Turkow. Next to him is Esther Rokhl Kaminska and Ida Kaminska. Second from the right is Jonas Turkow. Opposite page: Shot on location at the Vilna cemetery, Esther Rokhl Kaminska with daughter Ida in *Tkies Kaf* (The Vow) (1923).

Photo: David Matis.

Photo: David Matis.

Photo: Jonas Turkow.

Jonas Turkow as a tsadik (saintly man) in *Der Lamedvovnik* (One of the 36 Just Men) (1923).

ment a new period of calm set in in Poland. One of Pilsudski's first acts was to terminate the official policy of anti-Semitism in Poland. With a new era of good will and nationalism, the two chose Joseph Opatoshu's 1921 novel *"In Poylishe Velder"* (In Polish Woods) as a possible film venture. *In Poylishe Velder* is a down-to-earth historical rendering of Jewish heroes who curse, frolic, steal, fight, drink, and raise hell. Set at a time when Hasidism and Haskala (Jewish Enlightenment) clashed in Eastern Europe, the novel described the decay of the Hasidic Kotzk dynasty founded by Rabbi Mendel of Kotzk as well as Polish-Jewish unity during the uprising of 1861-1863.

Bojm's work was cut out for him. Creating an original story was one thing, even adapting a stage play, but assimilating a current best seller for the screen was much more difficult and had not been done before in Yiddish film except in the Soviet Union (to be discussed in Chapter 3). Bojm had the encouragement of Opatoshu, a Polish born Yiddish novelist and short story writer who had been living in the United States since 1907. Opatoshu sat with Bojm making suggestions and even visited the set during filming. The film concentrates on the adventures of Mordkhe who leaves home to study with a rabbi, then joins up with Polish militia men in their fight against the Russians.

Jonas Turkow, who had a leading role in *Der Lamedvovnik,* was asked to direct the picture. He had worked in Polish films, in addition to his work on the Polish, German and Yiddish stage, and felt quite prepared to tackle the project. In an 1928 interview, he said that he was working from a "realistic base" in making the effort to "artistically present this epic of Jewish life."[12] In the lead roles were Diana Blumenfeld, Turkow's wife and Silven Rich; Forbert himself supervised design and setting. Non-Jewish actors were hired to play Polish parts; this was the first time Jews and non-Jews worked together in Poland on a Yiddish film. The picture was shot on location in Kotzk and surrounding areas, with interiors filmed in a Warsaw studio.

The release of *Poylishe Velder* was delayed due to an unforeseen difficulty. Agudath Israel, a group of ultraorthodox Jews who wielded power as political representatives of large numbers of Jews, protested the forthcoming film on moral and religious grounds.[13] The Polish film censor, in 1928, at a time when pro-Semitic feelings were strong, felt obliged, or rather was persuaded by superiors, to invite the Agudah to view the film. A rabbi was allowed to react to scenes that he felt were improper.

> Truly, in fact, Opatoshu holds a special place—he is the first person in the history of film who had the "good fortune" to have had his film evaluated by a Warsaw Rabbi....[14]

Jewish actors and non-Jewish actors worked side by side in the production of *In Poylishe Velder* (In Polish Woods) (1929), a story of Polish-Jewish unity.

Photo: YIVO Institute for Jewish Research.

On location near Kotzk, Jonas Turkow directing a scene from *In Poylishe Velder* (In Polish Woods) (1929).

Photo: YIVO Institute for Jewish Research.

The segments the Agudah representative found as unacceptable were "orgy" scenes, glimpses of men and women kissing and a shot of a man and woman approaching the rabbi's house together, actions strictly prohibited according to strict interpretation of Halakha (Rabbinic law). The rabbi who had the film cut was of course worried not only about a little "sex," but also about the intent of the story, which dealt with a Jewish youth breaking with traditional ways of life. This greatly threatened him and his fellow rabbis.

> Understand this—that such an "authority" took great care to cut out more from the picture than not. What was left was a patchwork film without any cohesion, without a face.[15]

The critics disapproved of the finished work and though many viewers did come to see it, distribution was limited. It was a valiant effort but with the depression in 1929, there would not be another opportunity. There was no paucity of ideas, Bojm always had another, but there simply was no capital. Forbert and Bojm returned to photography, though Bojm did assist in the sound version of *Tkies Kaf* (1937). Steinwurcel became one of the foremost cameramen in Poland, returning to Yiddish films with *Der Purimshpiler* (1937) and *Mamele* and *A Brivele der Mamen* (both 1938). Zygmund Turkow would be very active in Yiddish "talkies," though his brother Jonas and sister-in-law Diana Blumenfeld were never again seen on the Yiddish screen. It would be seven long years before Yiddish feature film production would again thrive in Poland.

America

The American film industry continued to make pictures geared for universal consumption, and despite the complete dominance of Jews in film production, the industry was uninterested in making pictures aimed at any one ethnic group. Some Jewish subject films with Jewish characters were produced during this period, most often stories of Jews who sought intermarriage and assimilation and upon achieving "the American dream," left behind their Jewishness.

This type of story appealed to a broad audience. Yet, for many Jews these films were objectionable, especially when intermarriage of Jew and Gentile was suggested. There were some Jews who found no problem with the Jewish subject picture; they were integrated into American society. English was their language and intermarriage a fact of life. But for the majority of Jews, Yiddish was still their "mame-loshen," their mother-tongue, English something only learned. They maintained a tradition that encouraged education, upward mobility and acceptance into society, while still remaining a Jew and seeing that one's children would also maintain their Jewishness. They could not accept the Hollywood product.

It was not surprising that in response to the Jewish subject picture, there would be interest in turning out acceptable Yiddish cinema. With the success in America of such Yiddish pictures as the Austrian-made *Mizrekh un Mayrev* (released in the United States as *Mazel Tov*), and *Yisker,* there was hope for a new industry which would produce film entertainment geared for the Jewish audience. Maurice Schwartz, director of the Yiddish Art Theater, decided to be the first to try.

In the early twenties, Schwartz had become the master of the Yiddish stage and Second Avenue. The Yiddish Art Theater under his tutelage had attracted the great talents of the Yiddish stage and quickly became a New York institution that would last for over thirty years; a central meeting place for the theatrical elite, Jew and non-Jew alike. His company had toured the capitals of Europe, playing everything from Sholom Aleichem to Molière. Within a short number of years, Schwartz had quickly proven himself an extremely talented actor, director and producer.

Schwartz had always shown great interest in the cinema and was excited by its vast power to reach the masses. He first fell in love with film when he starred in Sidney Goldin's *Yisker* (1924). Schwartz also spent part of 1925–1926 along with fellow actors from the Yiddish theater under contract to MGM in Hollywood; it was there that Schwartz learned "film technique." He badly wanted to direct film and with Jewish subject pictures being released in Hollywood that endorsed assimilation and intermarriage, it seemed to him that there would be no better time. He reasoned that with his knowledge of the literature, Jewish life, acting, direction and film, he could be the one to revolutionize Yiddish pictures. It was a determined effort, but an unsuccessful one.

Tsebrokhene Hertser (Broken Hearts) — 1926

In 1926, Schwartz chose as his entrée into motion pictures a film in which he both starred and directed. It was Z. Libin's *Tsebrokhene Hertser* (Broken Hearts), a starkly realistic portrait of Jewish life in New York's Lower East Side. The story is about Benjamin Rezanov, a young immigrant writer who has just fled Russia. With little money and no understanding of English, the youth seeks employment while laboring at the study of the language. He marries Ruth, the daughter of a cantor who is opposed to the match. Benjamin proves himself worthy, but then learns that his first wife is still alive in Russia. He returns to see her, only to find that she has just died during his voyage.

Writer David Denk, who was at the New York City studio on 163rd Street and Third Avenue where the film was being made, was witness at the set.[16] Though Schwartz seemed to be in charge, the shooting overwhelmed him. Not yet completely comfortable behind the camera, he had trouble setting the pace and angles for his technicians. Schwartz also found differences between the direction he was used to giving his actors on the stage and that required for the camera. To even further complicate matters, Schwartz played the lead of Rezanov, hindering his ability to take full control. Though his actors were supportive, many of them players from his Yiddish Art Theatre, they could not save the film.

> With Maurice Schwartz, it was not just a question of one issue, but rather many which are related to theater, where he not only wanted to be great, but rather the greatest, and to a certain point he accomplishes this. In this case, everything seemed to fall apart....[17]

Mordaunt Hall of the *New York Times* put the blame squarely on Schwartz when he wrote: "The chief failing in this production is due to Mr. Schwartz's inexperience as a director."[18]

This was the last attempt at American Yiddish silent pictures. Within a year, sound captured the hearts of the American viewer, bringing to a close another chapter of Yiddish filmmaking. No longer would it be a question of what you saw on the screen; of great concern now was what you heard and whether you understood the language spoken — Yiddish talking pictures were not far away.

3

The Soviet Yiddish Film, 1925–1933

The Revolution of 1917 brought classic liberties to Russian Jews who had suffered through years of persecution. Anti-Jewish legislation was lifted and an era of good will and Yiddish cultural development was ushered in.

Recognized now as a national minority, though they lacked autonomous territory, Jews were free to set their own way of life within the Soviet umbrella. Unable to become involved in politics, Soviet Jews sought expression through the arts, and the first decade of the new regime was witness to a Russian Jewish cultural renaissance. Jewish artists and writers now found an atmosphere in which they could create; within the first few years, nearly 1,000 Yiddish books were published, journals of artistic and literary merit appeared, and Jewish theater was established.

The Communist Party was most supportive of the development of national culture as it saw it as a way to bring about the sovietization of its people. Yiddish creative expression fit well within those guidelines, and with Soviet support, a quantity of unparalleled innovative Yiddish art soon emerged. The publications and productions of the period proved that with freedom of expression, a vital Yiddish culture could be created that was consentient with the new regime.

In drama, two groups, the Hebrew "Habima" and the "Yiddish Art Theater" created a new theatrical medium, drawing on Jewish tradition and folklore. Habima began as an amateur troupe whose raison d'être was producing Hebrew theater. It evolved in the post-Revolution period, under the genius of Yevgeni Vakhtangov, as one of the more innovative of Soviet theaters, effectively setting new trends in stylized drama. The Yiddish Art Theater, under the tutelage of Alexander Granovsky, stood out among Soviet national theaters in its creativeness. It produced such great artists as Solomon Mikhoels and Vinyamin Zuskin. In 1925, players from Habima went to Leningrad to act in *Der Mabul* and artists of the Yiddish Art Theater prepared *Yidishe Glikn* in the Ukraine.

The Soviet Film Industry was still in its infancy in 1925. Its growth had been hampered by a paucity of film stock, equipment, and materials in the years following the Revolution. It was only in the previous year that Soviet cinema began to take its place as a major artistic force in world cinema. Yiddish pictures were conceived of as an important part of this growing force.

Habima and *Der Mabul* (The Deluge)

Der Mabul (The Deluge) was the first Soviet effort to attempt a transfer of Sholom Aleichem from book to screen. Set in St. Petersburg during the 1905 Revolution, the film is about solidarity between Jewish and Russian workers. It tells of Masha Foreman who joins the Social Democratic Party and takes an active role in the Revolution. At a factory meeting, she shoots a policeman in self-defense, and she and her cohorts are taken and sentenced to death. When word reaches her home, members of the anti-Semitic "Black Hundreds" use the opportunity to stage a pogrom, but fellow workers come to the Jewish community's aid.

Der Mabul was an attempt to show the unity of the Russian people, in their common historical quest for change and revolution. The picture showed how Jews suffered under Czarist rule, intimating that under the Soviet regime no such horror could befall them.

Although the Habima troupe was invited to play a vital role in the creation and development of *Der Mabul*, only a very few of the actors ventured to Leningrad for the filming.[1] Many of the actors were suffering from a prevailing sickness, and the few that did come had little say about production. They played small, insignificant acting parts, much to their disappointment.

The director of the picture, Yevgeni Ivanov-Barkov, took great care to convey in the picture the tragedy yet humor for which Sholom Aleichem was known. In order to best simulate conditions, he took the cast and crew to small villages where he hired townspeople to serve as extras. He even hired real Cossacks for a massacre scene. One of the actors, Raikin Ben-Ari, described in his memoirs what happened when these Cossacks were called upon to effect a pogrom.

> And now came the pogrom. Bearded actors, in prayer shawls and phylacteries, stood swaying in prayer. The police, hooligans, and Cossacks poised in readiness. The cameramen stood waiting. A whistle from our gentile director and the attack started. The Cossacks and the policemen threw themselves into the part enthusiastically and began to beat the extras whose pure Slavic faces were masked with long beards and earlocks. Too enthusiastically, it seemed, for not all the director's whistling and shouting could stop them. This was "realism" with a vegeance. As it turned out, there were quite a few among the "pogromists" for whom rehearsals were unnecessary.[2]

As the first Soviet picture dealing with a Jewish theme, the film was carefully scrutinized by the government. One official, who was responsible for supervision of the political complexion of the picture, was dissatisfied for apparent ideological reasons and had director Ivanov-Barkov replaced. Since the end of 1924, considerable control had been exercised over Yiddish literature and drama and the Party took care to see that "petty bourgeois psychology" was eliminated from Jewish creative expression. When the second director also proved unsatisfactory, a new director, Boris Vershilov was hired. Vershilov, who had staged the Habima's "Golem" a few months earlier, tied up the loose ends. The film was not released until 1927.

Vershilov may have been able to complete *Der Mabul,* but he could effect no such magic for Habima. As a theater in 1925, Habima had a precarious place in the Soviet arts, for its very goal was to present productions in Hebrew, a language and culture which came to be identified with "reactionary clericalism" and "Zionism." Authorities believed that only through Yiddish, a language of the "people," could the sovietization of the masses be brought about; Yiddish phrases rooted in Hebrew or dealing with religious ceremony were slowly sifted out. As the Habima cast pondered its future, a number of lucrative offers came from European countries. The company left on tour in January of 1926; it was little surprise that they did not return. The Hebrew language was no longer an acceptable means of expression in the Soviet Union.

The Moscow Yiddish State Art Theater (GosET) and *Yidishe Glikn* (Jewish Luck)

In contrast to Habima, the Yiddish Art Theater was experiencing growth and acceptance. Alexander Granovsky had created a Yiddish theater that gained acceptance as veritable theater. Granovsky, whose real name was Abraham Azarkh, was born in Moscow in 1890 of assimilated Jewish parents. Educated in St. Petersburg and Munich, he left for Sweden in 1917 to study film directing after a stint in the Russian army. In 1918, Granovsky returned to Petrograd where he became involved with the Yiddish theater, took charge of its acting studio, and created a repertory theater. After two years, the ensemble came to Moscow where it was stimulated by other national theaters and blossomed.

Ever since Granovsky had studied film in Sweden, he looked forward to the time when he might work in the medium. After five successful theater seasons he got his chance, when in 1925 his theater group was performing in the Ukraine. After a tour to the United States was cancelled, the idea of producing a film was conceived of as a wonderful way of affording American audiences the opportunity to see the troupe.³ However Granovsky, rather than prepare a brief film recording of one of the group's plays, chose to develop a full length motion picture.⁴ This was done with the able help of his assistant, Grigori Gricher-Cherikover. Isaac Babel wrote the inter-titles. All the actors were from Granovsky's company.

Solomon Mikhoels was cast in the lead role of Menakhem Mendl in the projected film *Yidishe Glikn* (Jewish Luck).⁵ Mikhoels had studied with Granovsky in Petrograd and came with him when the Yiddish State Art Theater moved to Moscow. Almost immediately, with his warmth, talent and ability at pantomime, Mikhoels ingratiated himself with audiences and became the premiere star of the troupe. Making the transition from the stage to film came easy for Mikhoels. His character study of Menakhem Mendl, a Chaplinesque figure who succeeds in leaving the shtetl yet is still confined by it, ranks as one of the finest in cinema. In that role, Mikhoels is at once both repulsive and lovable, tragic and comic. Soviet critic G. Riklin wrote of Mikhoels:

> He puts out words as if each one were a ruble.... There is, in his smile, a certain meaning every time. Mikhoels is a wonderful Menakhem Mendl—he felt him, understood him like Sholom Aleichem and was very warm to him. His laughter is mixed with grief.⁶

Yidishe Glikn was based on Sholom Aleichem's "Menakhem Mendl Letters." Each of these letters followed the basic outline of the hero leaving his home and family in search of some promising business deal which may make him rich. No sooner does he succeed than he loses his "millions" through some unforeseen tragedy. In *Yidishe Glikn,* Menakhem Mendl first fails as a corset salesman. He then finds a thick book which contains a list of brides from an area town and tries his luck as a shadkhn (matchmaker). Content, he falls asleep and dreams that he is outside Odessa's Grand Palace with Baron de Hirsch, preparing to export these brides to America. The dream ends and after a matchmaking calamity, Menakhem Mendl leaves in search of better "luck."

The picture moves extremely well and is nicely structured to evoke the necessary tears. One of the more interesting segments is a dream sequence shot on the steps of the Odessa harbor. Filmed from a variety of angles, the scene shows a woman walking up the steps inter-cut with reaction shots of Menakhem Mendl watching her. Edward Tisse, who was chief cameraman on the picture, worked a year later with Soviet filmmaker Sergei Eisenstein on his mammoth film *Battleship Potemkin*. There is little doubt that the famous "Odessa Steps" sequence from that picture was influenced by this film.

Yidishe Glikn was well received by the Jewish population, while its critics gave it mixed reviews. Many would have preferred treatment of the modern Soviet Jew, instead of the shtetl Jew, but their reaction was not so much a criticism of the film as it was of the subject. Mikhoels' portrayal of this "luft-mentsh" (a merchant of air and dreams) who is in a constant state of movement, surviving as he can, from one undertaking to another, is magnificent and over-powering.

The VUFKU Ukrainian Films

The art of Isaac Babel as a writer is undisputed, but his accomplishment as a film artist and film creator has long been obscured. Isaac Babel had always shown a strong interest in the cinema, as well as a great affection for Jewish life, but a fusion of the two did not take shape until the mid-Twenties. His early stories, filled with Jewish protagonists, are infused with a striking cinematic style with highly visual descriptions. Working with Granovsky and Gricher-Cherikover, Babel was finally given the opportunity to take part in Jewish film in 1925, when he worked on *Yidishe Glikn*. Shortly afterward, he began planning *First Cavalry Army* with Sergei Eisenstein, however, the film never materialized. Unrelenting, Babel developed a screenplay, *Benye Krik* (Bennie the Howl) from his *Odessa Stories* in 1927 and brought it to VUFKU, the Ukrainian film studio, for production.

Benye Krik—1927

Vladimir Vilner directed *Benye Krik* with Yu. Shumski as Benye and M. Leorov as his father Mendl. The picture however was not as well received as writer Isaac Babel had hoped. The film is about a "legendary" Jewish gangster who is the terror of Odessa, and his friends who were Jewish robbers, prostitutes, beggars, and speculators. The Jewish public was not exactly ready to watch these types of Jewish characters on the screen, and one irate viewer wrote that "the picture has spread bitterness and hatred [of Jews].''[7] It is also questionable as to how pleased the Party censor was with the film, for although the picture was seen in the Ukraine, I found no evidence of its having been shown elsewhere. Film historian Jay Leyda, arriving in the Soviet Union only seven years later could not find anyone who could recall having seen the film.[8]

The picture is the only original screenplay that Babel wrote. Though no print of the picture is known to exist, a reading of the screenplay provides a good sense of how remarkable this work really was. Interest-

Photo: YIVO Institute for Jewish Research.

Photo: YIVO Institute for Jewish Research.

Left: Solomon Mikhoels as Menakhem Mendl, a shadkhn (matchmaker), here negotiating the export of brides to America in *Yidishe Glikn* (Jewish Luck) (1925). In the background are the Odessa Steps, where cinematographer Edward Tisse filmed the dream sequence. A year later, Tisse returned with Soviet film genius Sergei Eisenstein to film *The Battleship Potemkim* here. Above: Menakhem Mendl's cargo of brides from Berdichev, ready to be loaded onto ships in *Yidishe Glikn* (Jewish Luck) (1925). Each train carries a different "kind of merchandise." The car on the right reads "With Dowry." The one in the middle is labeled "Fat Ones."

ingly enough, of all the Soviet scripts written at the time, this one was one of a very few chosen for translation into English.[9]

Blondzhende Shtern (Wandering Stars) — 1927

Sholom Aleichem's work, with its tragic but humorous Jewish characters had become a great favorite not only with Jewish readers but with Russian viewers as well. Isaac Babel chose *Blondzhende Shtern*, the story of two artists who must choose separate careers, as the basis for his next screenplay. In Babel's adaptation, a violinist unable to marry the woman he loves seeks fame outside of Czarist Russia. After achieving success, he returns to find that she is about to be sent away for revolutionary activity. Joining her in exile, they are finally able to live together in peace. In the Sholom Aleichem original, the girl, Reyzl, is not an activist, but rather a singer; Babel changed this in order to make the picture more politically attractive.

G. Gricher-Cherikover who had been co-scenarist and assistant director with Granovsky on *Yidishe Glikn* directed the picture. Both he and Babel were well aware that the further removed in time the picture was from the present, the less ideological and political problems they would have. However, the critics, particularly Jewish critics, wanted greater emphasis on the present-day Soviet worker. Critic Y. Lubomirsky spoke for others when in a biting attack on *Blondzhende Shtern* he tore down the picture for being "ideologically deficient, over-involved with the Jewish past and 'small-townish.'"[10] Yiddish film producers were beginning to feel the Soviet political tightrope. No matter what subject they would choose, they would "be damned if they did, and damned if they did not."

Babel temporarily left film work in 1928 to give greater attention to his short story writing. In the late thirties, he resumed active film writing, maintaining close relationships with filmmakers Eisenstein, Alexandrov, and Dovzhenko. His letters written between 1937 and 1939 indicate just how much of a force film had become in his life. Even in the last letter his relatives received from him, he wrote of the near completion of yet another film script, this about Maxim Gorky's life. In 1939, he was arrested and disappeared.

Durkh Trern (Through Tears) — 1928

In 1928, Gricher-Cherikover began work on VUFKU Studio's third Jewish film, *Durkh Trern* (Through Tears). A bit fearful to venture on too politically explosive a topic, he, with assistance from scenarist I. Skvirski, turned again to Sholom Aleichem's writing. They chose three stories from the collection *A Bletl Geshikhte* (Pages of History): "Motl Peyse dem

Khazns" (Motl, Son of Peyse the Cantor), "Der Farkishefter Shnayder" (The Enchanted Tailor) and "Dos Meserl" (The Pocket Knife). The "Motl Peyse" stories worked within a set framework, each about the child's involvement in mischief, his success, and the misfortune that befalls him. In *Durkh Trern* the scenarists used Motl's scheme with Shimen-Elye in making money selling punch as the central story. With it, they interwove several stories, including the tale of a tailor who goes out to purchase a milk-producing nanny goat only to receive a billy goat.

The film provides for a delightful picture of shtetl life, in all its barest elements. Gricher-Cherikover focuses in with a marvelously satirical touch on the kheyder system of education where the "melamed" (teacher) tries (and fails) to hold the attention of his students. His treatment of the "Bezdn" (religious court as the rabbis do "pilpl" (talmudic debate) over whether a goat is female is poignantly farcical. Even the family's expulsion from their home, which has become a major theme in Jewish tragedy, is handled with delicacy and good taste. Although the three parallel stories do not work particularly well together, *Durkh Trern* succeeds in bringing across the irony of the tragi-comic shtetl Jew and his/her way of life.

The shtetl, a recurring setting in many of the Yiddish films is used in *Durkh Trern* as metaphor for Judaism. This market town, isolated from the outside world, provides a certain security, where life is bound to custom and tradition. There is no assimilation or intermarriage in the shtetl, as long as it remains insulated from extrinsic intrusion.

In *Durkh Trern*, contact with the rest of the world is through the postman. He, symbolic of external forces, is kept under close scrutiny while visiting the town. All the children meet him on the edge of the shtetl and escort him to the town center where everyone is gathered. As he gives out the mail, he provides a great deal of excitement, yet he is watched closely for fear that something which he is bringing in might upset the state of the shtetl; this very fear is realized in the picture.

When the heroes are asked to leave the shtetl, it is as if they leave the womb; there is fear of what lies outside. The shtetl, like Judaism, has provided a framework of life for so many years that it is difficult to perceive another existence. Some will find communism; others America and assimilation. In *Durkh Trern,* the shtetl is a symbol of the past. The filmmakers, while providing a nostalgic glimpse are really calling for a spiritual return to it and to Judaism. Only in an atmosphere, resistant to external change and bound to tradition could Judaism, like the shtetl, survive.

Soviet critics' response to the picture was mixed. M. Makotinski praised the film for pointing out how "Czarist Russia was responsible for anti-Semitism" and for providing a lesson for youth in the post-Revolution period who "do not understand the nightmare of Jewish pogrom, and...

Photo: YIVO Institute for Jewish Research.

Photo: YIVO Institute for Jewish Research.

Two of the Sholom Aleichem stories used in *Durkh Trern* (Through Tears) (1928). Left: Motl, son of Peyse the Cantor, carries a jug full of punch, part of a scheme to make a fortune. S. J. Silberman plays Motl. Above: The tailor is bewildered, for each time he goes out to buy a nanny goat, he somehow returns to his town of Zladeyevke with a billy goat. A narration was later added in America and the picture was re-released as *Laughter Through Tears* (1933).

poverty."[11] In contrast, Yiddish poet and activist Itzik Fefer castigated the "screenwriters" for missing the irony of Sholom Aleichem, while praising the "director" for showing good knowledge of Jewish life and artistic taste in relating it.[12] Fefer pointed out that Sholom Aleichem is not sentimental, "his work shows more than tears—it also contains laughter—'laughter through tears.'" Still, the picture was extremely well received, both in the Soviet Union and America.

In 1933, American producer Joseph Burstyn had actor Michael Rosenberg add a Yiddish narrative and released the picture in the United States as *Gelekhter Durkh Trern* (Laughter Through Tears).

Motele Shpindler (Motele the Weaver) — 1928

VUFKU released one more Yiddish picture in 1928, *Motele Shpindler* (Motele the Weaver), directed by Vladimir Vilner. Based on the short stories "Motele the Tailor," "Motele the Idealist," and "The Simple Tailor," the story is of Jewish poverty and persecution in the years immediately preceding the Revolution. Although the film starred M. Leorov and A. D. Goricheva, each having appeared in all four VUFKU Yiddish films, the picture was not nearly as well received as the previous films.

The picture is not known to have ever been shown theatrically. Strangely enough, both of the pictures directed by Vilner, *Benye Krik* and *Motele Shpindler,* have disappeared.

By 1928, a Jewish writer could not be sure of what might be deemed as acceptable Soviet writing. With greater harrassment from the Soviet state, contemporary writers were most careful about what they wrote. Taking greater care at a time when Yiddish authors were being called to task on a number of issues, filmmakers stopped making "shtetl" films. They feared either being accused of too much "connection" with the Jewish past, Jewish nationalism, or failure to sufficiently apply "the methodology of class struggle" to their work. Even Sholom Aleichem's work had become problematic. Itzik Fefer was one of the more vocal critics.

> One field is terribly backward in the realm of Jewish cultural creativity. That is cinema.
> It's true, that among all cinema organizations, the one that pays closest attention to this question is "VUFKU." Yet, even here, we have achieved little.
> Of three completed films, *Blondzhende Shtern* (Wandering Stars), *Durkh Trern* (Through Tears) and *Benye Krik* (if we can even consider this to be a *Jewish* film,) two are dramatized according to works by Sholom Aleichem, and are somewhat representative of the pre-revolutionary lifestyle. The third film gives the audience a short account of the great "activity" of the famous Odessa "King of the Moldavanke."
> The life of the Jewish working man and woman, their struggle against the rich and the "benefactors," their struggle against the Jewish Bourgeoisie, and the great part they played in the overall revolutionary movement both before and after "October" [1917] have not as yet been embodied through film.

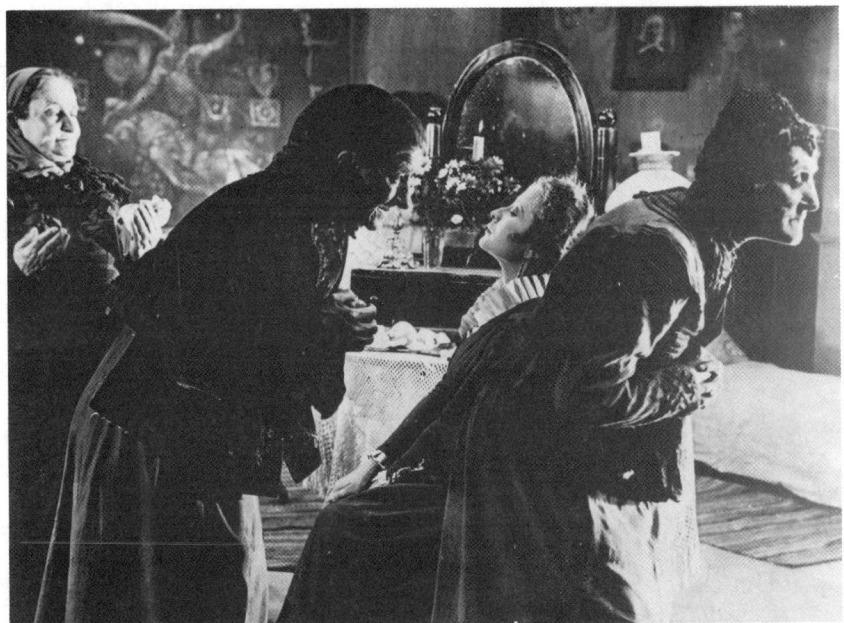

Photo: Jay Leyda.

Motele Shpindler (Motele the Weaver) (1928), one of two films directed by Vladimir Vilner for the VUFKU studio. The film is not known to exist.

We know that more than one Jewish man or woman has laid down his or her life in the struggle against all kinds of gangs. They are still not portrayed in film.

The workers ask: "...Why do you only write about *Jewish Luck*? About *Benye Krik* and *Wandering Stars*? Why don't you write about us?" They ask: "Is Benye Krik more interesting than we?" The working class wants to see itself, its struggle and life in the new art. The working class is right.

"VUFKU" must therefore, as soon as possible, involve itself with the Jewish literary community, and with its help, create the film for which the Jewish laborer has waited so long, and which he has earned.[13]

No one seemed able to come up with a solution. Unable to resolve all the contradictions, VUFKU, the Ukranian film studio finally closed down all Jewish film production, thereby ending one of the richest periods of Jewish cultural development of all time.

Grigori Roshal

In 1927, Grigori Lvovich Roshal took upon himself the task of producing a film dealing with revolutionary motifs. As a Jew, growing up with strong

Jewish attachments, it was only natural that he would draw on elements from his past. Roshal, whose name is an acronym, *R*abbi *Sh*lomo *L*uria, was born in 1899 and began working in theater as a stage manager. From 1922 to 1925 he directed a number of plays for the Theater of [the] Youth and Habima while lecturing on methodology of art study. Roshal's first film was *The Skotinins,* based on Denis Fonvizin's eighteenth century comedy "The Adolescent," which he directed in 1926. Having proved that he could be trusted with a modern subject, Roshal immediately made preparations for his first "Jewish" film, *Zayn Ekstselents* (His Excellency).

Zayn Ekstselents (His Excellency) — 1928

Based on a true incident the film, set in the 1905 Revolution period, is about the malevolent Russian governor Von Wahl who breaks up a workers' demonstration, killing a large number of participants, many of whom are Jews. The Rabbi, non-violent in ideology, comes to the leader to plead for leniency, only to watch the ruler taking personal pleasure in flogging his captives. Hirsh Lekert, a rebel frustrated by the events, takes it upon himself to rectify the situation and assassinates the governor.

According to Roshal, his motive in making the picture was to show "how individual action is not a course which can bring positive results"[14] The Rabbi's "peaceful" practices, although he is portrayed as a righteous and pious man, do not work. Lekert's single actions are also meaningless, but it is his fervor that stirs the people to rise up. The only true results, accordingly then would be through revolution by the masses.

Roshal made *Zayn Ekstselents* for Belgoskino in Leningrad with little money and primitive conditions. Shot almost entirely in studios, it took about six months to complete. The script was prepared by Roshal's sister, Sofya, and his wife, Vera Stroeva, from three novelettes: "Hirsh Lekert," "The Governor and the Shoemaker," and "The Jew." In the lead, playing the dual role of governor and rabbi was Leonid Leonidov of the Moscow State Art Theater. The picture was so closely scrutinized for conflict with Soviet ideology that the Commissar of Education personally supervised production. It was well received by both party and people.

A Mentsh fun Shtetl (A Man from the Shtetl) — 1930

After making *Two Women* in 1929, Roshal returned to a Jewish story, prepared by his sister and wife. They adapted the script from the novelettes, "David Gorelik," "The Dreamer," and "Break of the Period." In addition, a synchronized musical score was composed to accompany the film. *A Mentsh fun Shtetl* (A Man from the Shtetl) — 1930 starred Vinya-

Photo: Eric Goldman.

Grigori Roshal with the author in 1977 outside the Lenin Filmmakers' Club in Moscow.

min Zuskin, whose brilliant characterizations made him, along with Mikhoels, a central figure of the Moscow State Yiddish Art Theatre. Shot in and around Odessa, the film focuses on David Gorelik, a poor youth who fights in the Czar's army. On the front, he battles with a German soldier who turns out to be his old friend, Brandt, from Galicia. The two join forces and fight in the Revolution. When Brandt is convicted of stealing money in his role as commissar, it becomes David's responsibility to execute his friend. The Revolution is what is of "utmost" importance and David serves the cause by doing his duty.

The theme of the film is clearly that of the Jew seeking acceptance into the new Gentile/Revolutionary world. Whether David can kill his friend is a major question, for there is a struggle with his Jewish conscience that shuns murder. David is not the stereotyped frail Jew, but rather a man of valor who must uphold the principles of the Revolution at the expense of friendship. This choice is not easily made, but he stands committed first to the Revolution.

Roshal uses a motif in the two films with which Babel was very much concerned; that of being a Jew seeking acceptance into a Gentile/Revolutionary world. Killing is a question that haunts many of Babel's protagonists. One begs God to allow him "the simplest of all proficiencies, the ability to kill fellow men." There is a constant struggle with the Jewish conscience that shuns murder. But just as Babel's heroes bear little resemblance to the stereotyped frail Jew, Roshal's Jews are revolutionaries and men of valor. For Roshal, the Rabbi could not hope to grapple with the problems of his people, since the Rabbi's passive ways are old and ineffective. It is left to the hot-headed Lekert in *Zayn Ekstselents* to strike a blow for his fellow man. Such is also the case for *A Mentsh fun Shtetl*'s Gorelik who upholds his principles at the expense of a friendship. The Jewish person Roshal is portraying is the Jew of the "new" era, the revolutionary.

In his two Jewish pictures, Roshal used Jewish subjects to deal with two important questions of his time. He drew on Yiddish sources to raise the questions of individual action vs. group action and responsiblitiy to Party vs. responsibility to coreligionist and friend. In this way, Roshal succeeded in working within a Soviet ideological framework while still dealing exclusively with Jewish subjects. However, in contrast to the sensitivity portrayed by Sholom Aleichem's Old World shtetl character, Roshal's Jewish hero is a New World-revolutionary committed first to Soviet doctrine. Where Isaac Babel had begun to develop this theme in *Blondzhende Shtern,* Roshal gives it shape in *A Mentsh fun Shtetl.*

Roshal made only one more picture on a Jewish subject, the Russian-language film, *The Oppenheim Family,* in 1939. Based on the Lion Feuchtwanger novel, the picture was one of three powerful anti-Nazi pictures made in the Soviet Union just prior to World War II. It was greatly enhanced by an exceptional performance by actor Solomon Mikhoels.

The Soviet Yiddish Sound Picture

Stalin's Five Year Plan, introduced in 1928, set into motion the industrialization of the Soviet cinema, bringing with it new demands. The cinema was to be forged as a propaganda tool and political art form. New technology was to be used for the development of the medium and new subject material corresponding to Stalin's definition of Soviet art was to be introduced.

Soviet filmmakers were aware in 1928 of the development and use of sound in the United States. Sergei Eisenstein, joined by filmmakers Pudovkin and Alexandrov, warned against incorrect use of the new form before it could be fully integrated with the aesthetics of Soviet cinema. Despite the cautions, most Soviet pictures by 1931 were either being made with sound or were provided with soundtracks in post-production.

The coming of sound brought with it the creation of Yiddish sound pictures in America; no such effort had yet taken place in the Soviet Union. With Stalin's new policies, Yiddish artists were reluctant to express themselves artistically for fear of creating something unacceptable within the shifting limits of the prevailing ideological policy. Preoccupation with the Jewish past, which had been the mainstay of Soviet Yiddish cinema was now considered as bourgeois and nationalist. No longer could scenarists turn to Sholom Aleichem's pre-Revolution shtetl life without fear of contradiction with policy. Roshal had provided a new form by introducing the post-Revolution Jew, but even that positive depiction became "negative" with a change in doctrine. There had even been criticism of story-lines that dealt exclusively with Jewish life as being "restricted to a nationalist point of view."

In this period of change, it is quite understandable that a new Yiddish film form had to be created, different from the VUFKU works of the Twenties. Roshal had developed the Jewish revolutionary, corresponding to Stalin's doctrine of being national in form and socialist in content, but even this formula no longer worked. Now, the Yiddish cinema had to serve more as a means of party propaganda.

There was a great demand for socialist realism, and Peretz Markish developed a screenplay that would follow that line, be acceptable to the Party, focus on Jewish life, and be made in Yiddish. Markish, a poet and author, first drew attention to himself as a member of the distinguished "Kiev group" of Yiddish writers. He later left Russia in 1921 for Poland

and France where he was most involved in Yiddish literary circles but returned to the Soviet Union in 1926. Committed to Communism, Markish wrote a great deal about collectivization and industrialization, yet always centered his works around Jewish heroes. Criticized, because he wrote only about Jews, Markish rejected creation of non-Jewish heroes and continued his writing as before — for Jews and in a Jewish language. In this very way, he prepared the screenplay for *Noson Beker Fort Aheym* (Nathan Becker is Going Home).

Making a sound picture had its own complications, but Markish wanted his film to be made in Yiddish. Since his story dealt with industrialization in support of the Five Year Plan, as well as the return home of a Jewish native from America, permission was granted to make the picture. Two versions were made: one in Yiddish, the other in Russian. The story revolves around Nathan, who returns to his village after being away in America for twenty-eight years. He is then given a construction job and loses in a contest meant to test his American way of doing things. Although his methods are different, Nathan is accepted by his fellow workers.

The picture was intended to give a clear message of how much better Jewish life is when committed to a Soviet way of life. Nathan, who has been in America, has no meaning in life until he returns home. In contrast, his father, a committed Soviet citizen, is enthusiastic about life and contributes to society as a construction foreman for a new steel plant. Filmed by Boris Shpis and Mark Milman in a most realistic manner, the picture was well received in all parts of the world. The difference between the Americanized Yiddish speech of David Gutman as Nathan and the native "clean" Yiddish of Solomon Mikhoels as the father, provided a further indictment of America's corruptive effect on Jewish life as represented here by language.

That same year, Lev Kuleshov made a film with a similar story, *Horizon, the Wandering Jew*. However, Kuleshov's film was more of an indictment of Jewish life than praise for it. It dwells on Jewish unhappiness and disillusionment. The film is far from a Yiddish film not only because it was released only in Russian, but also in concept and content.

Noson Beker Fort Aheym was the only Soviet sound film made in Yiddish. By 1933, Yiddish intellectuals were under close scrutiny and options were few. In the mid-thirties, purges began, so there could be no return to Yiddish cinema. There were other pictures with Jewish themes, but all of them were made in Russian. Korsh-Sablin's 1936 *Seekers of Happiness* (also released as *Greater Happiness*) which starred Vinyamin Zuskin, dealt exclusively with life in the Jewish territory of Birobidjan and was filmed there. Other pictures with Jewish stories were Roshal's *Oppenheim Family* and Herbert Rappoport and Adolf Minkin's *Professor Mamlock*, both made in 1939 as anti-Nazi films.

Photo: Jay Leyda.

The filmmakers so much wanted to create realism in *Noson Beker Fort Aheym* (Nathan Becker is Going Home/The Return of Nathan Becker) (1932), that they shot extensively on location in Russian Jewish villages. This was difficult as they were making a sound picture (the first and last to be made in the USSR in Yiddish), and the microphones were not easily moveable. The film was written by Peretz Markish and directed by Boris Shpis and Mark Milman.

The Yiddish film experiment in the Soviet Union was a brief one. It had been cut short by ideological change and a growing reign of terror. Yiddish, which once was acceptable as a minority language, had for Stalin become an instrument of Jewish nationalism. This came in conflict with an ever-changing Soviet doctrine forcing a curtailment of Yiddish culture.

The great enthusiasm for Yiddish cinema in the Soviet union had resulted in a number of fine film productions. Involved in this work were many of the artistic giants in Soviet-Jewish cultural life. They worked with great expectations toward the creation of a high caliber film form, set within the mainstream of Soviet cinema. However, their hopes were not fulfilled as national ideology changed. Many of them were forced to pay the supreme price for their involvement—Solomon Mikhoels was found dead in 1948, killed by secret police; Vinyamin Zuskin was taken from his hospital bed in 1952, never again to be seen; Isaac Babel was arrested and disappeared in 1939; Itzik Fefer was imprisoned in 1948, and, together with Peretz Markish, was executed on August 12, 1952. Much had been accomplished; so much more could have been done....

Photos: Jay Leyda.

Photo: Jay Leyda.

Master of Soviet Yiddish stage and cinema Solomon Mikhoels (1890–1948). Mikhoels "put out words as if each one were a ruble." With his warmth, talent and unique presence he quickly ingratiated himself with a generation. He was not only an actor of unusual range, but a spokesperson for his people. Left: Mikhoels as Nathan's father in *Noson Beker Fort Aheym* (Nathan Becker is Going Home/The Return of Nathan Becker) (1932). Above: Mikhoels in *The Oppenheim Family* (1938), adapted from Lion Feuchtwanger's novel, directed by Grigori Roshal.

4

The American Yiddish Sound Picture, 1929–1937

Talking pictures had been a technical possibility since the turn of the century, but the requirements for production as well as projection made it at first an undesirable medium. Motion picture companies experimented with it, but Warner Brothers, in search of a novelty to turn around its financial woes, was the first studio to exploit it. Whether one points to *The Jazz Singer* (1927) or another picture as being the force which brought sound to the industry is not central for our purpose. What is important is that once theaters became equipped with sound systems, people began to queue up outside the "talkies," no matter what the quality of the picture.

As the Depression hit America in 1929, the motion picture industry was experiencing growth and great profit in contrast to the economic disaster which the rest of the country was encountering. In 1930, theater attendance was better than the year before. However, motion pictures were failing to respond to the ethnic urban populations who thronged in great numbers to witness the miracle of sound on film. These New Americans found themselves watching films unaware of what was happening on the screen; English was still a foreign tongue. Now that motion pictures were so dependent on audible language to carry their message across, the New Americans were frustrated. Unable to comprehend, they stopped going to the cinema.

Jewish immigrant film-goers faced the same problem as their fellow New Americans. For many of them, English was a mystery and Yiddish a way of life. A number of Jewish filmmakers sensitive to this sought to meet this need by producing sound pictures in Yiddish. Author and playwright Abraham Schomer first announced in 1928 that he would be filming his play "The Green Millionaire" in Yiddish, but the project never was realized. Then producer Max Cohen at New York's Metropolitan Studios began preparations in 1929 for a Yiddish sound film. He enlisted the aid of Sidney Goldin, who made two Yiddish silents in Austria in addition to many Jewish subject pictures of the teens. Goldin had the distinction of being acquainted with the material, the language, and many of the actors. Having just completed *East Side Sadie* for Worldart Film, a picture which included talking segments, he had experience, albeit limited, with "talking" pictures. For this picture, Goldin pulled together many of the well-known talents of the Yiddish stage like Lucy Levine, Lazar Freed, Anna Appel, and Mark Schweid. He also used Samuel Kelemer, a youth known as "Shmulikel, the boy khazn (cantor)" to chant Jewish tunes and prayers. Sound discs were used for the recording.

The film *Ad Mosay* (Until When), released as *The Eternal Prayer,* is about a youth who finds out that his father has been killed in Palestine during the Hebron riots of 1929. I was fortunate to locate a short segment of this 36-minute film. In it, a fixed camera records a choir, led by Shmulikel, chanting the memorial prayer, "El Mole Rakhmim." For the entire sequence, we watch the actors, some of whom are clearly uneasy about being in front of a camera, turn often to the side, seeking direction. According to Kelemer, the film was shot with little rehearsal time and no second takes.[1] The picture, a succession of acts, had little content and no transition from scene to scene except a brief blank interval. Critic Harry Potamkin, seeing the picture in New York was rather contemptuous of it, calling it "about the worst film ever made, indicating absolutely no knowledge of the cinema, even the most elementary, on the part of the makers."[2]

Judea Pictures, Incorporated

The first Yiddish language production was feeble, but it was well received and proved that Yiddish sound pictures had a potential market. In late 1929 Joseph Seiden, owner of a motion picture sound equipment rental outfit (the first of its kind in New York City), brought together a few movie house owners and created Judea Pictures. Seiden produced the pictures, and his associates Sam Berliner and Moe Goldman guaranteed exhibition. Goldin, who had established himself as the "dean" of Yiddish language cinema and the only person immediately capable of directing in the medium, was hired as director. Judea's immediate goal was to make two short films, "two-reelers," of about 20 minutes, which could be exhibited between live stage performances in Jewish neighborhood theaters. If the films were successful, then further production would ensue, including feature-length films. *Variety* publicized that the premier pictures were budgeted at $15,000 apiece.[3] In truth, the pictures were made for less than $3,000 each, as actors worked largely on a deferred percentage basis and little cost was incurred for equipment rental.[4]

In February, 1929, production was begun on the first of the Judea pictures, *Style and Class*. It was a filmed recording of a musical revue featuring Marty Baratz and Goldie Eisman which was being presented at Gabel's Public Theater in New York. The following week, *Shuster Libe* (alternately titled Shoemaker's Romance or Cobbler Love), a comical story of Jewish life in Eastern Europe was produced. Written by Louis Kadison, the 21-minute film featured members of the Vilna Troupe—Joseph Buloff, Liuba Kadison, Leah Noemi, and Kadison himself. The pictures were made at the old Talmadge studios on First Avenue in Manhattan, and released the following month in theaters in Brooklyn and the Bronx.

Response to the two short films was most favorable and almost immediately, plans were readied for the next production. Judea signed Jennie Goldstein, noted for her "tear-jerking" portrayals on the Yiddish stage, to star in a series of projected pictures. However, Goldstein, after a series of disagreements with the company, backed out of her contract and was not seen on the Yiddish screen until she made *Tsvey Shvester* (Two Sisters) in 1938. This setback not withstanding, Judea quickly went to work on its first feature picture, *Mayne Yidishe Mame* (My Jewish Mother) with Mae Simon. Simon, enthusiastic about the new technology she witnessed at the RCA Sound Studios on East 38th Street where production was taking place, described her experience:

> The thrill of grinding cameras, glaring batteries of lights, cameramen inside soundproof booths, sound engineers and many other workers standing around during our performance was surely most novel and I am looking forward to seeing and hearing myself on the screen.[5]

With *Mayne Yidishe Mame* ready for release, Judea explored expanding its distribution by creating a national chain of theaters devoted to exhibiting Yiddish talking pictures. By late May, three New York theaters, one in Brooklyn's Brighton Beach, another in the Bronx, and a third on the Lower East Side of Manhattan had contracted to serve as the nucleus for this national chain. According to several accounts in the Jewish press, there was tremendous response in New York's Jewish neighborhoods. Judea reasoned that they could successfully take the pictures to other Jewish enclaves around the country.

As soon as distribution plans were readied, Seiden directed Judea to produce a number of one and two reel pictures for national consumption. A major source for these early pictures were plays and skits being presented on the Yiddish stage at that time. In this manner, short films like *The Broken Doll* with Sadie Banks and Celia Person, *The Jewish Gypsy* with Hymie Jacobson and Miriam Kressyn, *Oy Doctor* with Menashe Skulnick, and Abraham Reisen's *Mai-Ko-Mashma-Lon* (What Does It Mean) with Harry Peld were all produced in June 1930; all but the Skulnick short

Photo: Harold Seiden.

One of the cantorial short films produced by Joseph Seiden for Judea Pictures. *Kol Nidre* (1930) with Shmulikel.

have apparently disappeared. Upon screening a surviving piece of *Oy Doctor* I watched a playful and talented Skulnick acting for a static camera that was recording his Yiddish vaudeville act which was soon to be sent around the country. There was only one "take" with segments limited to a maximum of 10 minutes, the amount of time the 16-inch sound disk was capable of recording. When Skulnick made a mistake, it was captured on sound film for posterity.

Judea also filmed some of the great cantors of the day. Two separate renditions of the moving Yom Kippur plea for the annulment of vows, *Kol Nidre,* were filmed of Cantors Shmulikel and Leibele Waldman. Waldman was also filmed in the 10-minute picture, *Yidishe Nigun* (Jewish Melody) in which he sang liturgical music composed by Sholom Secunda.

Judea's films were being shown and were making money, so the company expanded production. In mid-June, it was announced that twenty-six Yiddish sound films, twelve feature-length and twenty-four short films would be completed by the end of 1930. The Yiddish daily, *Der Tog*

Yiddish pictures were not only comedy or melodrama, as testified by Marty Baratz and Goldie Eisman in *Style and Class*. The film was one of a number of short features produced by Joseph Seiden and directed by Sidney Goldin in 1929-1930.

Mayne Yidishe Mame (My Jewish Mother) (1930) was the first Yiddish feature-length picture with sound. It was well received everywhere, except in Israel where riots broke out protesting the showing of a Jewish picture in a language other than Hebrew. Seated on each side of the cake are Mae Simon and Sidney Goldin. To the right of Simon is her daughter Bernice and Seymour Rechtzeit. To the right of Goldin is David Denk, Helen Blay, associate producer Moe Goldman and cameraman Don Malcames (left of camera on right). On the far left (seated) is producer Joseph Seiden.

Photo: Harold Seiden.

reported in 1930 that Judea was planning to film classics, like Ansky's "Dybbuk," Leivick's "Golem," and Sackler's "Ashmidai."[6] However, production ground to a halt when on June 25, the Yiddish Actors' Union adopted a resolution prohibiting members of the union from appearing in Yiddish "talkies." It was feared that the reputation of Yiddish theater was being "injured" by the caliber of films being produced by Judea Pictures. Further claims were levelled that "the Jewish public was being misled into believing that actors would personally appear in the theaters where the films were being shown."[7] The crux of the problem was that although Judea was using only union technicians and cameramen, they were hiring non-union actors. The Yiddish Actors' Union was a very powerful body at the time and production was shut down for nearly two months. An agreement was finally reached between Seiden and Yiddish Actors' Union manager Reuben Guskin requiring compensation when non-union actors were used; production began anew in late August.

Joseph Seiden, president of Judea Pictures and producer of all their pictures, began work in Yiddish pictures as a cameraman and sound equipment dealer. Beginning in 1907 as a fifteen-year-old "picture machine" operator in his father's nickelodeon in Greenpoint, Long Island, he soon became as assistant cameraman for the N.Y. Motion Picture Company. Later, Seiden did camerawork for World Film, Equitable, and Fox. In 1918, he opened his own business, Seiden Films, specializing in industrial and educational pictures. Two years later, he went to Europe with Herbert Hoover, filming relief administration work. Over the next decade, Seiden filmed many boxing bouts, including the Tunney-Dempsey fight. With the advent of sound, he opened New York's first sound equipment rental facility. Feeling competent as a producer, Seiden called upon Goldin to direct and on friends like Don Malcames, and J. Burgi-Contner to do cinamatography.

In September of 1930, Seiden produced a number of short subjects: Seymour Rechtzeit's *Land of Freedom; Sailor's Sweetheart* with Hymie Jacobson and Miriam Kressyn; *Natasha* with Pinchus Lavenda and Mildred Block; *An Evening in a Jewish Camp*, with music by Sholom Secunda; *Ets Khaim* (Tree of Life); Z. Rubinstein's *Jewish Day Hour;* and Cantor Leibele Waldman chanting the Yom Kippur prayer *Unsane-Toykef.* Seiden had a number of pictures available and he turned to the international market for distribution. Palestine seemed a suitable location to try and Seiden made arrangements with Rivlin & Company of Tel Aviv for the exhibition of *Mayne Yidishe Mame* at the Mograbi Theater. However, the Saturday night premier of this, the first Yiddish talkie to be presented in Tel Aviv set off a minor riot as members of the audience threw ink at the screen and set off foul smelling bombs.[8] They were protesting the use of Yiddish, a language seen as the idiom of the Diaspora, particu-

One of the storefront "nickelodeons" where Yiddish pictures were exhibited.

Photo: Harold Seiden.

Theaters were clamoring for more Yiddish short features and Joseph Seiden's Judea Films was most happy to oblige. *Sailor's Sweetheart* was one of these shorts. In the center (with sailor's hat) is Sidney Goldin. On his lap is Miriam Kressyn; to the right is Hymie Jacobson receiving a five dollar bill from Joseph Seiden. Below the dollar-bill is cameraman Don Malcames. In front of Goldin is composer Sholom Secunda.

Photo: Harold Seiden.

larly Eastern European Jewry. Hebrew was their language and though many residents of Tel Aviv knew Yiddish from their places of birth, it was not considered by most as an acceptable means of expression in the new land. Outside the theater large crowds gathered to protest the use of Yiddish; British police had to be called to control the crowds. The following day, the picture was barred from being shown by the vice-mayor of the city until some kind of arrangement could be made. The "decision" was that the talking and singing parts in Yiddish were removed and the film was shown without sound. *Davar,* the Hebrew labor newspaper called what happened "futile fanaticism."[9] A Yiddish picture was not to be shown again in Palestine or Israel, in its original language, until the sixties. Interestingly enough, a Yiddish film was finally produced in Israel in 1983, *Az Men Git, Nemt Men* (When They Give, Take) was well received.

In late August, Goldin directed Judea's second feature film, *Eybike Naronim* (Eternal Fools), based on a story by H. Kalmonowitz; the picture starred Yudel Dubinsky, Yehuda Bleich, and Seymour Rechtzeit. It was the first "all-talking" (using sound on film, rather than discs) Yiddish film; its story centered on the tragedy of a traditional Jewish family trying to cope with contemporary society. *Eybike Naronim* was representative of the type of picture which became Seiden's trademark—a quickly made, overly-sentimental, melodramatic film.

In 1931, Seiden produced a few more low-budget short films, *Eli Eli* (My God, My God) and Goldfaden's *Shulamis,* but the novelty of Yiddish sound film was wearing off, and theaters were less inclined to exhibit this product. Audiences wanted a quality film, and were no longer prepared to spend their money just to hear Yiddish on the screen. Judea released one more picture in 1931, *The Voice of Israel.*[16] It was a film recording of cantorial renditions by great cantors like Rovner, Roitman, Katchko, Waldman, and Rosenblatt. Record companies have turned to this film as one of the few remaining recordings of many of the great cantors of the day.

One-time Independent Companies

Jacob Berkowitz, an independent producer, lured Sidney Goldin away from Judea in early 1931 in order to direct two cantorial shorts, *A Cantor on Trial* and *The Feast of Passover.* Nathan Hirsh and Morris Kleinerman then formed High Arts Pictures Corporation with Goldin and set about making *Zayn Vaybs Lubovnik* (His Wife's Lover). The play written by Sheyne Rokhl Semkoff and loosely based on Molnar's "The Guardsman" had played Second Avenue successfully the previous two seasons. In large part, the play succeeded because of the fine performance of comedian/actor Ludwig Satz; it was around him that the film was built.

Photo: Harold Seiden.

Joseph Seiden's audience wanted to see and hear the cantors of the day. Sound pictures were still very much a novelty. Seiden gave them what they wanted—a series of renderings by the greats—Shaile Engelhardt, Mordechai Herschman, Adolph Katchko, David Roitman, Yossele Rosenblatt, Seidel Rovner, Josef Schlisky, Joseph Shapiro, Leibele Waldman. Cantor Schlisky sings in this segment of *The Voice of Israel* (1931). On the left is Joseph Seiden; choir director Machtenberg is third from the right, leaning on the bannister.

Zayn Vaybs Lubovnik (His Wife's Lover) (1931) was developed as a vehicle to showcase the many talents of actor/comedian Ludwig Satz, "the man with a thousand faces." Satz stands in the middle with cane in hand. Far right is Isidore Cashier. At the piano is composer Abraham Ellstein. Far left is Michael Rosenberg.

Photo: Yiddish Theater Collection, Museum of the City of New York.

Zayn Vaybs Lubovnik was the largest Yiddish film production to date. The film adaptation, however, failed to remove itself from the stage original. Better camerawork might have covered up overtheatrical acting, but long sequences with *one* static shot make these "stagey" performances all the more glaring. The real problem of this and many of the Yiddish pictures that followed was low budget. Had more production money been made available, covering shots and a variety of camera set-ups would have been possible. Extensive rehearsals and second takes were other "luxuries" infrequently available to Yiddish cinema of this period. With time and money at a premium, the Yiddish film viewer was forced to watch long, static sequences filmed in long-shot. Occasionally, as in *Zayn Vaybs Lubovnik,* there is some distinguished acting which helps "save" the picture. In *Zayn Vaybs Lubovnik,* the great talent of Satz is apparent in this unrealistic comedy of an actor who disguised himself as an old man, wins the hand of a young girl, then tries to prove her unfaithful by switching back to his own identity.

In 1932, Goldin could take credit for having directed every Yiddish narrative talking picture to date. Another production company, Yiddish Talking Pictures, set up by Louis Weiss and Rubin Goldberg undertook to make Sholom Asch's *Uncle Moses;* Goldin was asked to direct. Co-directing with Goldin was Aubrey Scotto, an established director who had just completed the English language *Divorce Racket* a few months earlier. Speaking with two members of the cast, Zvee Scooler and Judith Abarbanel,[10] it appears that Scotto was brought in primarily to enhance film technique.

Uncle Moses opens with a camera pan across Orchard Street on New York's Lower East Side, with the camera jerking as it moves from person to person. The rest of the picture is shot indoors, in a two room studio. The film is highly theatrical in style, with mediocre camerawork and editing that is often crude. Only during the "sweatshop scenes" does the picture pick up momentum. *Uncle Moses* is the story of a community of Jews from Poland who now work together in a Bowery sweatshop. One of their fellow townsmen rules the shop with a tight grip, and it takes love to open his eyes. Maurice Schwartz is at his best as the "despot," the same role he played on Second Avenue. He is supported by Judith Abarbanel, Mark Schweid, Zvee Scooler, and producer Rubin Goldberg who plays Alter. The picture was the first Yiddish sound picture to deal with a contemporary social theme.

Attempts to Transform Silent Films For the Current Market

Director/editor George Roland created a new form of Yiddish cinema in 1932, the Yiddish compilation film. Taking old silent films from a number

Hollywood was tackling difficult contemporary issues in the early 1930's. Sholom Asch's *Uncle Moses* (1932), too, brought to the screen an issue of concern to its audience—working conditions and labor-employer relations. Below: Uncle Moses (Maurice Schwartz) takes a "tight grip" on a worker (Michel Gibson) in a New York sweatshop. Opposite page: "Love conquers all"—especially in Yiddish pictures. Uncle Moses' wedding. His bride Masha is played by Judith Abarbanel.

Photo: David Matis.

Photo: Harold Seiden.

of sources, Roland filmed a prologue, narration, and/or epilogue in Yiddish and pieced it together, releasing it as a new picture. For his first effort, *Joseph in the Land of Egypt,* Roland used segments from a 1914 Italian picture, *Joseph in Egypt.* He added his own opening and closing, using Yiddish actors Ben Adler, Joseph Greenberg,[11] and Wolf Goldfaden. Roland repeated this procedure in 1933 with *Yidishe Tokhter* (Jewish Daughter), also called *A Daughter of Her People.* He had actors Chaim Shneier, Greenberg, Michael Rosenberg, and Ben Besenko tell the story of Judith Trachtenberg using silent footage taken primarily from the 1921 German picture, *Judith Trachtenberg.* After beginning with the actors sitting around a table, the action would shift to the silent picture as the Yiddish narration continued. This was repeated a third time with *Avrom Ovinu* (Abraham Our Patriarch), alternately called *The Eternal Jew* and *The Wandering Jew.* Here Roland used clips from various Bible story silent films; Jacob Mestel wrote the script for this and the Trachtenberg film. That same year Roland took the Polish-made 1924 silent *Tkies Kaf,* added prologue and epilogue[12] and released it alternately as *Dem Rebins Koyekh* (The Rabbi's Strength) and *A Vilna Legend;* Roland took credit as director of the picture and neglected to credit half the original cast. The director of the original film, Zygmund Turkow, then in Brazil was certainly surprised when he received an information sheet from New York publicizing the film.

> Between the said sheets, on both sides of the page is a large picture of (Joseph) Buloff with the inscription: "The eminent Yiddish star-actor in the great Yiddish talkie *Dem Rebins Koyekh.*" On the right side of the page is written "Text—Jacob Mestel, Film Direction—George Roland." On the left in small letters is written "An Outstanding Cast...."[13]

The picture had literally been stolen and recast in new form. Furthermore, Turkow was astounded by the fact that it not only listed a strange director, but of the six cast members mentioned, four were Americans who only provided the prologue, the other two being himself and Ida Kaminska. No mention was made of the other great actors who participated in the original picture, like Esther Rokhl Kaminska and Moyshe Lipman. "It would have been interesting had [Joseph] Buloff or [Jacob] Mestel guessed that the director of the picture was by chance still alive and living in Brazil."[14]

Joseph Burstyn's Worldkino showed a little more discretion when they took advantage of the new market by adding Yiddish sound narration to silent Yiddish films from the Soviet Union. Michael Rosenberg narrated at least two films, *Durkh Trern* (Through Tears), released as *Laughter Through Tears* and *Yidishe Glikn* (Jewish Luck), released as *The Matchmaker.* Each had a score by Sholom Secunda; each was very well received. The cast and directors were all given proper credits.

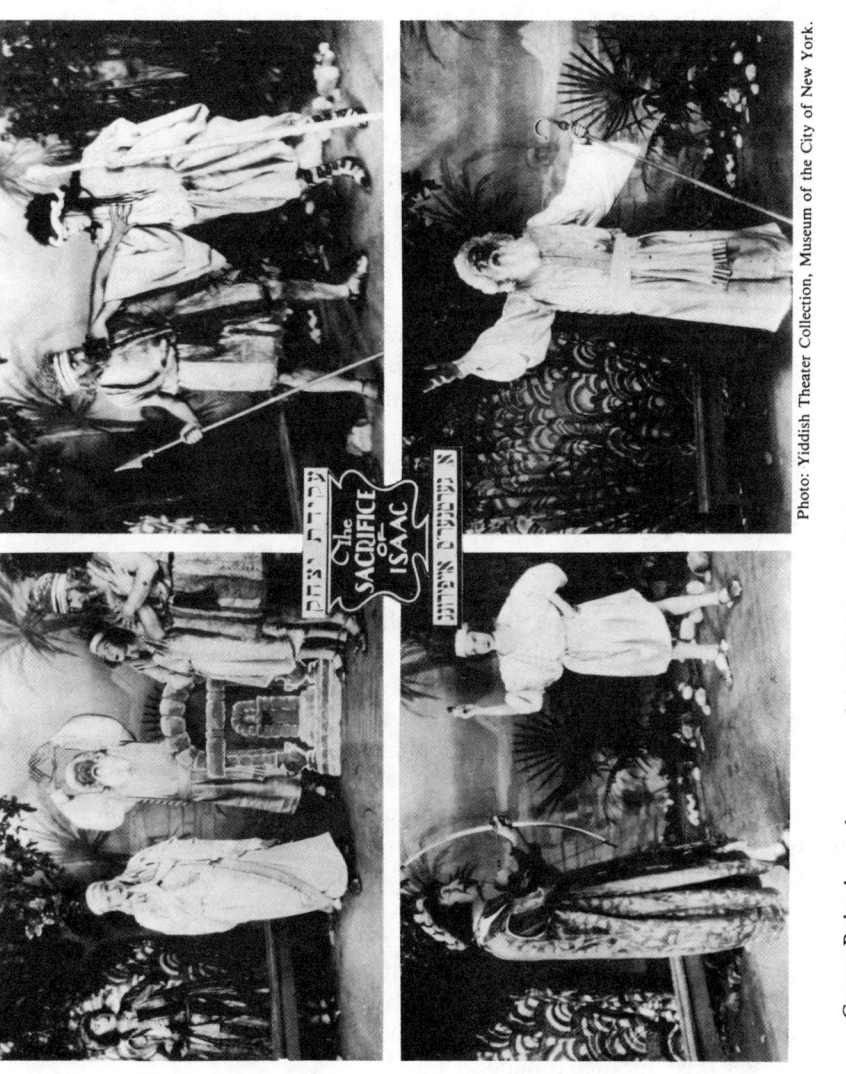

Photo: Yiddish Theater Collection, Museum of the City of New York.

George Roland was the master of the Yiddish compilation film. He would take a silent picture, usually produced in Europe, and release it as a new picture. Here is the "akedah—sacrifice" scene from his *Avrom Ovinu* (Abraham Our Patriarch) (1933).

Henry Lynn

In 1934, Henry Lynn, an independent businessman and writer became interested in Yiddish filmmaking, and formed Sov-Am Productions. Very little is known about Lynn, except that he was an avid writer and theater patron, especially of the Yiddish theater. He was involved in many enterprises, and in the Forties he owned a plant that manufactured fiberglass and plastic products. Over the next year and a half he monopolized Yiddish picture production.

Lynn wrote and directed his first film, *Yidishe Foter* (Jewish Father), also known as *A Youth of Russia,* in 1934. Set in pre- and post-Revolution Russia, it is about a lumber dealer who attempts to become a shoemaker under the new Soviet regime. The poor man is having problems adjusting to the new government. He cannot understand the new laws, especially the marriage laws which allow his winsome daughter to constantly find new partners. The cobbler, like his fellow Jew, is questioning his existence in the Communist state. In one of the more telling scenes, a group of old Jews are seated at a clandestine feast discussing the merits and evils of the new system. The film is clearly an attack on the Soviet Union. Lynn is challenging not only a few new laws or Soviet morality, but the entire Soviet system.

The following year, Yiddish theater matinee idol Boris Thomashefsky contracted with Lynn to star in *Bar Mitsve,* which Thomashefsky wrote. Regina Zuckerberg plays his wife, believed to be dead ten years, who returns just before their son's Bar Mitzvah, set in Europe. Israel (Thomashefsky) has already made plans to marry a woman who is plotting with her lover to take Israel's money. The film predictably comes to a climax at the boy's Bar Mitzvah, when the wife appears. Filmed in what seems to be a two room studio, *Bar Mitsve* is static, has poor sound, out of focus shots and incongruent scene transition.

One of the key issues raised in the film for the American audience is to what extent someone should remain a Jew while becoming American. The father points out to his son, just before the Bar Mitzvah, that one is not exclusive of the other. "Study the World's literature—don't be *just* a Jew.... Learn new languages—but *don't forget* your own!" Contrasted with the father's admonition is the visiting Jewish youth from America who speaks only English. For the Yiddish-speaking audience, this American lad very clearly represented their children who would also most probably forget their mother tongue.

Despite its poor technical quality, *Bar Mitsve* did well financially; it was one of the first American Yiddish pictures to reach Europe. Lynn, hoping to capitalize on the interest in his pictures, made *Shir Hashirim*

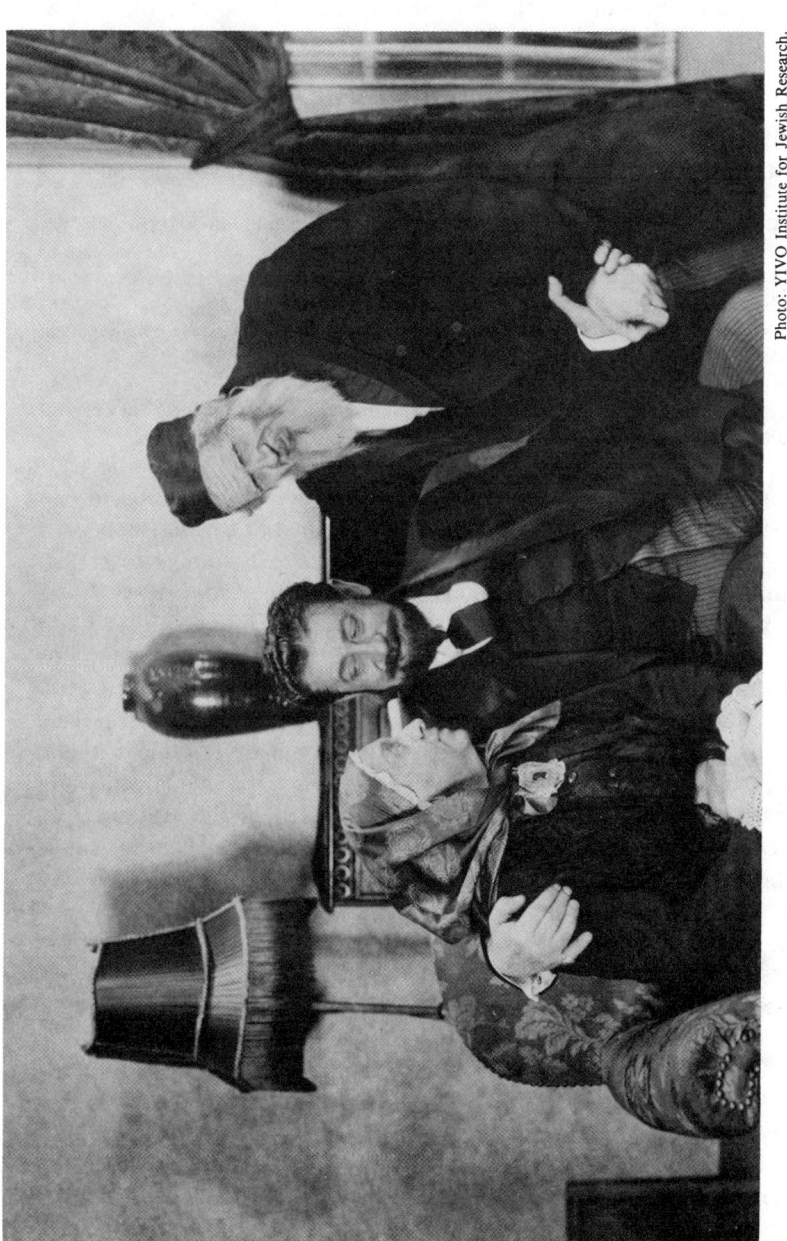

Yiddish theater legend Boris Thomashefsky (center) appeared in only one Yiddish film, *Bar Mitsve* (1935). The film was overly theatrical, but the opportunity to watch Thomashefsky on screen still wooed viewers to the theaters both in America and Europe. Here, Thomashefsky sits with Leah Noemi and Morris Strassberg.

Photo: YIVO Institute for Jewish Research.

(Song of Songs) that same year. Based on a story by Anshel Schorr, with music by Joseph Rumshinsky, the story revolves around an incestuous relationship between niece and uncle that breaks a family apart. Similar to *Bar Mitsva* in its poor technical quality, *Shir Hashirim* was not only an artistic disaster but a financial one as well; what it lacked was a big name like Thomashefsky to save it. In taking apart the film, Critic Wolfe Kaufman of *Variety* used the opportunity to make a plea for better Yiddish pictures.

> Had the producers spent just a bit more in an honest attempt to do a worthwhile job, had they found a director who knows his job, had they dug up a cameraman who knows where the crank is, had they bought not only a story but a scenarist, they would have had a film which they could peddle all over the world with ease.
>
> Today, with films as a medium, this basically splendid theatre art can go much further in globe girdling. If only attempts are made to turn out a product that's worthy of the name and that's not necesarily great art but good average entertainment. Yiddish films have a corner which is enviable and exceptional. They can go places. They can get not only glory but coin. But they can't do it with junk like *Shir Hashirim*.[15]

Interestingly enough, this plea appeared in both Yiddish and English.

After a hiatus of nearly two years, Lynn formed Menorah Pictures in 1937, with Abe Leff; Leff had worked with Seiden in a number of capacities on many of the early Judea pictures. Together, they co-directed *Vu Iz Mayn Kind?* (Where is My Child), based on a Louis Freiman story. Lynn wrote the screenplay of a widowed mother who turns over her child for adoption and then is committed to an asylum for a number of years. There, twenty years later, she is reunited with him. Though primitively shot, the picture raises the important issue of inhumane treatment of the mentally ill, the only Yiddish film to take on such a difficult subject. Lynn wisely cast the highly respected actress, Celia Adler, in the lead so as to guarantee immediate box office returns. George Roland's editing stands out in this picture as a masterful attempt to cover faulty direction and camerawork.

Lynn reemerged in 1938 with a film based on a story by Isidore Zolatarefsky, *Di Kraft fun Lebn* (The Power of Life). Starring Michel Michalesco, the film is about how a father's sacrifice for his children goes unappreciated. The following year, Lynn made *Mothers of Today* on a five-day shooting schedule. While other Yiddish productions were being "lavished" with money, Lynn was left working with a tighter budget than he had ever had. Using Esther Field, who played the mother in *Mayne Yidishe Mame* (1930), Max Rosenblatt as the cantor, and author of the play Simon Wolf, Lynn built a film around the collapse of a Jewish family. This melodramatic story is about a cantor's son who steals, runs off with a woman of "questionable morality," and takes the deed of his mother's store. The daughter elopes with a gangster and is charged as an accomplice

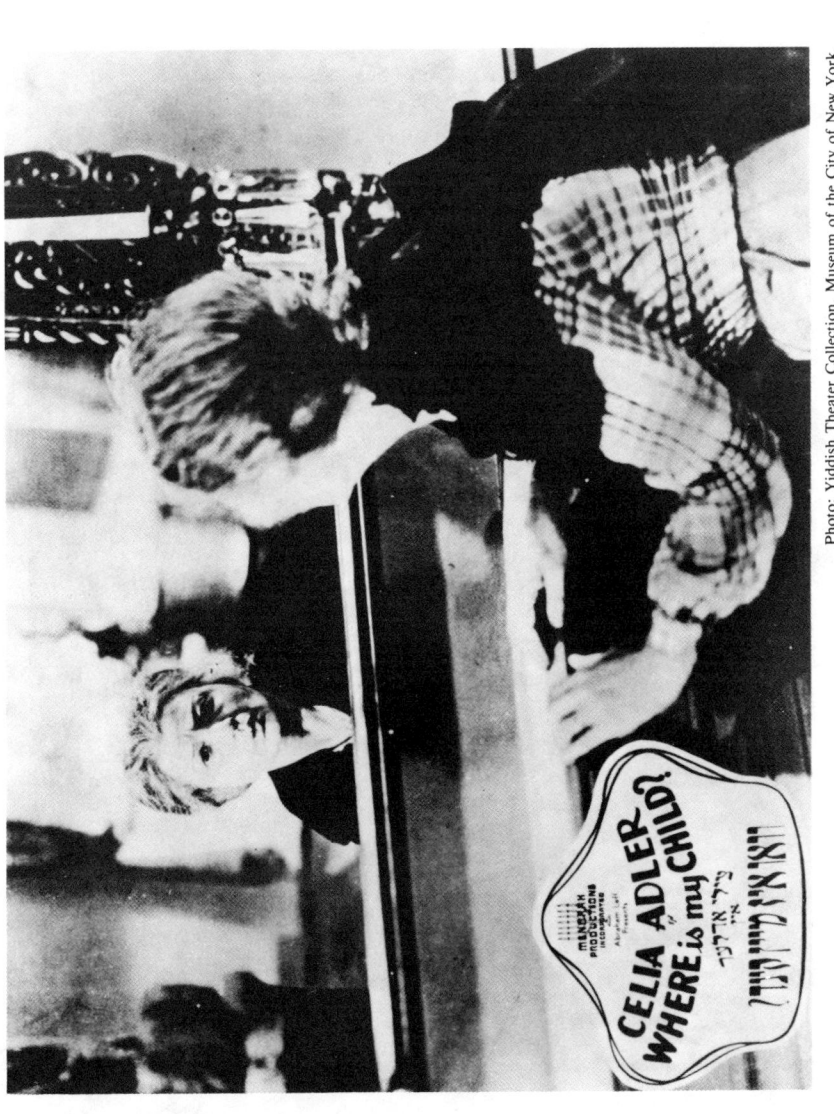

Sometimes, Yiddish pictures presented important issues for its viewers. Treatment of the mentally ill was a topic dealt with in Henry Lynn and Abraham Leff's *Vu iz Mayn Kind* (Where is My Child) (1937), starring Celia Adler.

Photo: Yiddish Theater Collection, Museum of the City of New York.

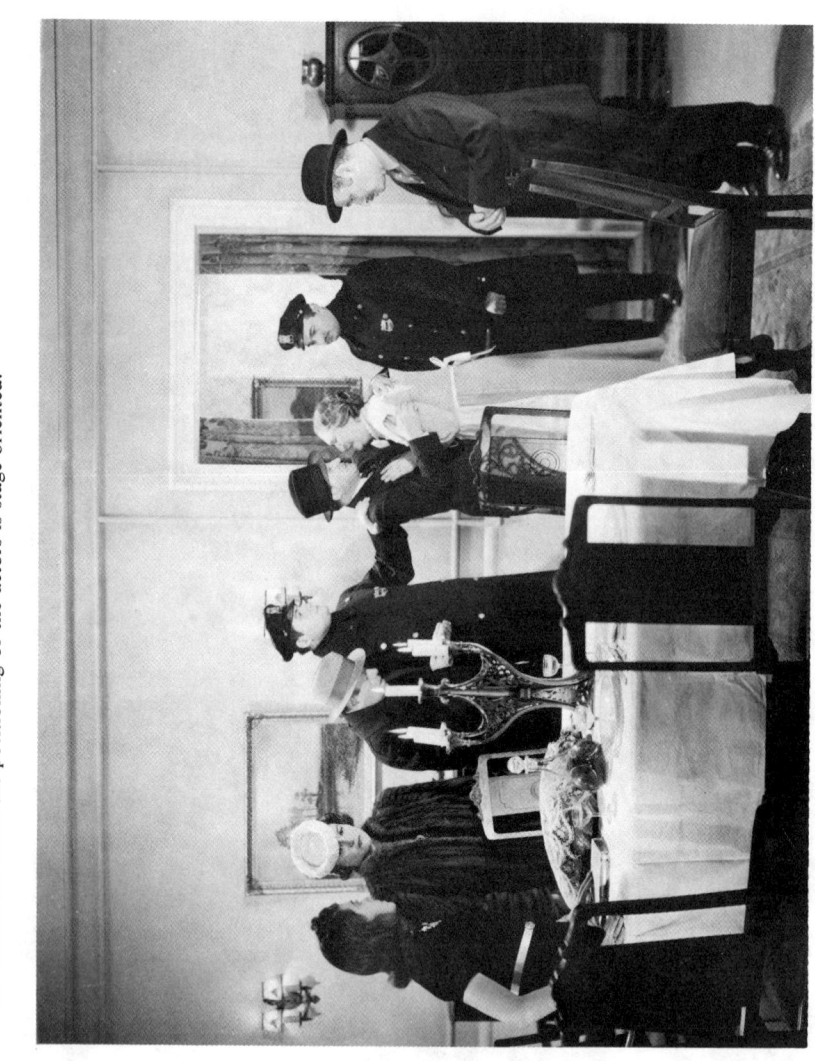

Melodrama was a popular form in Yiddish theater and cinema. Here, in *Mothers of Today* (1939), calamity seems to be the catchword. Embracing are Max Rosenblatt and Esther Field. Looking on are (left to right) Gertie Krause, and Vera Lebedoff. Far right is Simon Wolf. The picture was too theatrical. Notice that even the positioning of the actors is stage-oriented.

Photo: Yiddish Theater Collection, Museum of the City of New York.

in a murder. As if that is not enough, the mother goes blind. Lynn failed to take into account the growing sophistication of his audience. Melodrama had become an acceptable vehicle in Yiddish cinema, but for all these "calamities" to happen to one family was a bit too much for anyone to accept. The financial failure of *Mothers of Today* all but ended Lynn's filmmaking career.

Ben K. Blake felt that by using a well-known star he could generate a commercial success. To this end, he cast Jennie Goldstein, known in Yiddish circles for her vaudeville and theater work. His film, *Tsvey Shvester* (Two Sisters) written by Sam Cohen, is one of rivalry and passion. It is the story of one sister's love and the other's greed. This 1938 attempt at portraying suffering and disruption of traditional Jewish mores in a changing society is overly melodramatic, to the point of being comical. It, like Lynn's *Mothers of Today,* failed to speak to its intended audience. Blake, who planned a series of Yiddish films, was not heard from again.

Henry Lynn made one last attempt at Yiddish film production by releasing *A People that Shall Not Die* in 1939. He used segments of Lothar Mendes' 1934 British-made *Jew Süss,* adding new scenes which he shot, plus footage from other sound and silent films. Using Roland's compilation techniques of the early thirties, he attempted to pass off the picture as "an extravaganza made with a cast of 10,000." The picture was billed in the *New York Post* as "the first million dollar Yiddish film spectacle ever made," and re-released as *A People Eternal*.[16] This method of moviemaking and unusual marketing strategy may have succeeded in 1933, but by 1939 it could attract little interest, and a debt-ridden Henry Lynn was forced to stop making pictures.

Production, 1935-1937

Joseph Seiden took over complete control of Judea Pictures in 1931. Rather than continue to knock out twelve to fifteen pictures a year, he chose to produce *The Voice of Israel* and a few short subject films like Max Wilner's *Gelebt un Gelakht* (Live and Laugh) with Menashe Skulnick over the next three years. In 1935, Seiden formed a new company, Jewish Talking Pictures. He negotiated with Harry Thomashefsky and two financial backers to make Jacob Gordin's classic, *Yidishe Kinig Lir* (Jewish King Lear). Seiden was to give only technical assistance and supervision while Thomashefsky, whose background was in theater, handled direction. Slow paced, with one camera set-ups, the picture, based on Shakespeare's "King Lear," is about an aging father in 1892 Vilna who divides his fortune among his three daughters as he takes leave for Palestine. Because of greed, two of the daughters are cut off from the inheritance and the father,

Ben K. Blake wanted to give a more realistic look to Yiddish cinema, recreating settings from normal everyday Jewish life. Here: the kosher butcher shop. Blake's attempt may have been a valiant one, but *Tsvey Shvester* (Two Sisters) (1938) was his only Yiddish picture. Rebecca Weintraub is behind the counter.

Photo: Yiddish Theater Collection, Museum of the City of New York.

for want of money, is forced to return from the Holy Land as a beggar and wanderer going blind. To the modern day viewer, it is dull and "overstaged."

In 1936, Seiden, ready to begin full production moved into a West 60th Street office/studio and hired George Roland to direct. Roland was not only director but a master editor, responsible for a large amount of editing work on foreign versions of Warner Brothers pictures. In addition, he had the experience of directing Yiddish segments which he edited into his compilation pictures of 1932–1933. Roland was a multi-talented actor, painter, musician, lyricist, scenarist, and filmmaker. Seiden, who felt as yet unprepared to direct, trusted Roland to handle the job. Their first production was *Libe un Laydnshaft* (Love and Passion), also released as *Love and Sacrifice.* It is a "tear-jerker" about a woman falsely accused of a crime who must suffer years of agony. Seiden, trying to have a picture ready for release on Passover was desperate:

> On March 9, I didn't have the faintest idea for a story. And the Passover, three weeks away—our best season. Then, that Saturday, in a bookstore on Allen Street, I found this dog-eared little booklet. It was out-of-date, had been printed in Poland and was called "Love and Passion."
>
> I bought "Love and Passion" for 20 cents, spent Saturday afternoon rewriting it—oh yes, I do my own scenario—and on Monday started casting. I get my casts very easily. I hang around the beaneries on Second Avenue, there's always an actor who wants to get in the movies. I don't pay him nothing. Over a cup of coffee, I give him a smile, a promise and he's willing.[17]

The film was indeed ready for Passover and did well enough financially so as to allow Seiden to begin preparations for yet another picture.

The following year, Seiden hired Leo Fuchs and Yetta Zwerling to act in a short comedy, *Ikh Vil Zayn A Pansyoner* (I Want to be a Boarder) and was so pleased with the results that he designed his next feature, *Ikh Vil Zayn a Mame* (I Want to be a Mother) around the two actors. In contrast to the short, the feature was a melodrama about an unwed mother who is forced to give her daughter away. Years later, at the child's wedding, the mother reveals herself, resulting in a series of complications that finally end happily. Roland again handled direction with a cast of Seiden regulars like Rose Greenfield, Esta Salzman, and Cantor Leibele Waldman; Fuchs and Zwerling provided comic relief. The film was shot at night and on weekends, as were all the Seiden pictures of this period, the reason being that Seiden's studio was not certified by the Fire Department as combustible nitrate film was being used. Filming had to be done when the building was vacated.

Completing films was difficult under those conditions, but Seiden

In 1936, Sidney Goldin saw a potential for greater and better Yiddish pictures. He felt that with greater interest in Europe, larger budget pictures could be undertaken, resulting in better production values. He now need not be confined to an indoor set. Goldin (in director's chair) is coordinating production of Dem Khazns Zundl (The Cantor's Son) (1937). Standing center, looking down at Goldin is Moishe Oyster. Between them is Judith Abarbanel. Goldin did not live to see the realization of his dream. Below: In one of the opening scenes in the Old country (in Belz), Shloymele is about to be disciplined by his father. He wants to act and sing—pursuits condemned by his parents. From left to right: Vicki Marcus, Yehuda Bleich, Lorraine Abarbanal, Bertha Guttenberg.

Photos: Harold Seiden.

managed. Harold Seiden, son of the producer described production on West 60th Street.

> At that time the film was so slow—about 25 ASA—that the backlight was 2000 (candles) and on a hot day they used to use a cake of ice. Everybody in the crew used to be stripped to the waist and they used to have a towel on the cake of ice. When they got full of sweat they used to take that cold towel to keep themselves cool.[18]

Sidney Goldin's Last Picture

While Seiden was completing *Ikh Vil Zayn a Mame,* during the summer of 1936, his former director-in-residence Sidney Goldin, was preparing his first Yiddish picture since *Uncle Moses* (1932). Just a few months earlier, Joseph Green's Polish-made *Yidl mitn Fidl* had proved that a well-budgeted Yiddish picture could turn a nice profit. Able to point to this success, Goldin was able to raise sufficient funds to allow him, for the first time, to make a picture as he wished. *Dem Khazns Zundl* (The Cantor's Son), written by Louis Freiman, was based on singer/cantor Moishe Oysher's life story; how he left his home in Eastern Europe to attain success as one of America's finest voices. Goldin was working for the first time with a good budget, so that he was able to take his crew and actors for "on-location" shooting near Easton, Pennsylvania. The Oysher character, once having achieved success, forsakes his new world "girl friend" and returns home to his village sweetheart. Florence Weiss, Oysher's real-life wife, played the American woman, with Judith Abarbanel as the childhood sweetheart. In reality, Weiss was the Eastern European girl for whom he returns home. When asked about the divergence of story by one reporter, Oysher replied, "Well, poets are allowed a little license in telling a tale, why not a Cantor's Son?"[19]

Sidney Goldin died before *Dem Khazns Zundl* was half completed, and independent director Ilya Moteleff was brought in to finish production of the picture. Goldin's passing marked the end of an era of filmmaking. He was one of Yiddish cinema's pioneers. He had developed it in Europe and was one of the key persons responsible for its emergence as a talking medium. Goldin had brought the art of Yiddish cinema from its beginnings to its "Golden Age," a four-year period when quality fair-budget classic Yiddish pictures were made. Like Moses, who saw the promised land only from a distance, Goldin did not live to witness this feat. Less than one month after Goldin's death in September 1937, Edgar G. Ulmer and Jacob Ben-Ami's *Grine Felder,* the first picture of the American "Golden Age," opened in New York City.

5

The Golden Age of Yiddish Cinema
Part I: Poland, 1936–1939

Since the advent of sound in the late 1920s, European Jewry exported Yiddish sound pictures from the United States. Although a few films were being made on Jewish subjects in European sound studios,[1] no Yiddish language pictures (except the Soviet-made *Noson Beker Fort Aheym*) were being produced outside of the United States. There was tremendous interest in Yiddish culture. Yiddish was not just a spoken language in Poland, it was a way of life. Its use was limited not only to the home, but Yiddish could be heard in the streets, on tramways and in market places.

Resourceful entrepreneurs brought over silent pictures from the United States dubbed with Yiddish dialogue. Most of the pictures contained "inserted" prologue and epilogue; films like *A Vilna Legend* (Tkies Kaf), *Mazel Tov* (Mizrekh un Mayrev), and *Joseph in the Land of Egypt*. There were over three million Jews in Poland, and there was no lack of interest in motion pictures in Yiddish.

As the supply of Yiddish film product waned, American exporters began sending Yiddish "talking pictures," starring actors with whom Polish Jewish audiences were acquainted, like *Uncle Moses* (1932) with Maurice Schwartz and *Bar Mitsve* (1935) with Boris Thomashefsky. Yiddish journalists in Poland criticized the pictures as "merchandise" being brought over strictly for financial gain rather than as creative forms of expression which embodied certain artistic values. Journalist M. Kitai of the Yiddish Journal *Literarishe Bleter,* painted a morose graphic picture of the Polish-Jewish consumer/spectator, who cares little about what goes on around him, except that he be spoonfed these makeshift Yiddish pictures which he digests much like the cholent[2] which he is accustomed to eating on Sabbath.

> On the Sabbath table, there must be cholent. Whether you eat it with joy, or God forbid, with tears in your eyes, or with a sigh or without thirst — what's important is that

you get a little fatter. Anyhow, cholent is eaten. America (I'm now talking only of their Yiddish films) has served up the cholent, which is drooling from your mouth! It is both sweet and fatty, also a bit sour having stood too long, and it stinks. But still, it is cholent! Something special! So good as to be licked off your fingers.[3]

Depite the tremendous interest in "cholent" on the part of the Polish Jewish audience, no one seemed interested in capitalizing on what clearly seemed to be a good financial risk, a Polish-made Yiddish sound picture. Some feared making an investment in an unknown medium, despite the proven success of the Yiddish imports. Others feared that the production of a Yiddish sound film might stir up anti-Semitism in a country with already strong anti-Jewish sentiment. Many of those most fearful were themselves Jews who controlled Poland's film industry. Finally, in 1935, a group calling themselves "The Initiative of Jewish Actors and Artists" formed a film cooperative called "Kinor." Their interest was not just a financial one; they saw Yiddish cinema as a means of fostering Jewish culture and counteracting assimilation.

At the core of the cooperative were actors Shimen Dzigan and Yisroel Schumacher and entrepreneur Shaul Goskind. Dzigan and Schumacher were a comedy team well known throughout Poland for their political satires and zany skits. Shaul Goskind was, along with his brother Yitskhok, the owner of the Sektor film laboratory and studio, which handled film work for MGM, Fox, and Warner Brothers in Poland. Their common dream was the production of a well-made Yiddish sound narrative picture in Poland.

Mir Kumen On (We Are on Our Way) — 1935

Before production on this most exciting first picture was started, preparations were begun for the making of a documentary film about the Medem Sanatorium at Miedzeszyn, just outside of Warsaw. This was to be the first, certainly the most significant feature-length documentary-style film to be made in Yiddish. The film *Mir Kumen On,* was the idea of Shlomo Gilinski who had been trying to enlist support from the Sanatorium's directors. Once accepted by the Board, Aleksander Ford, one of the bright talented young Polish Jewish directors of the period, a member of the avant-garde film group "Start" and a friend of the Goskinds, came on as director. The previous year, Ford had completed the Hebrew language film *Chalutzim* (*Pioneers*) or *Sabra*. Ford, along with a group of writers led by Polish author Wanda Wasilevka began preparing the scenario. Ford had spent a number of weeks at the youth village trying to get a better understanding of what was taking place. The budget was

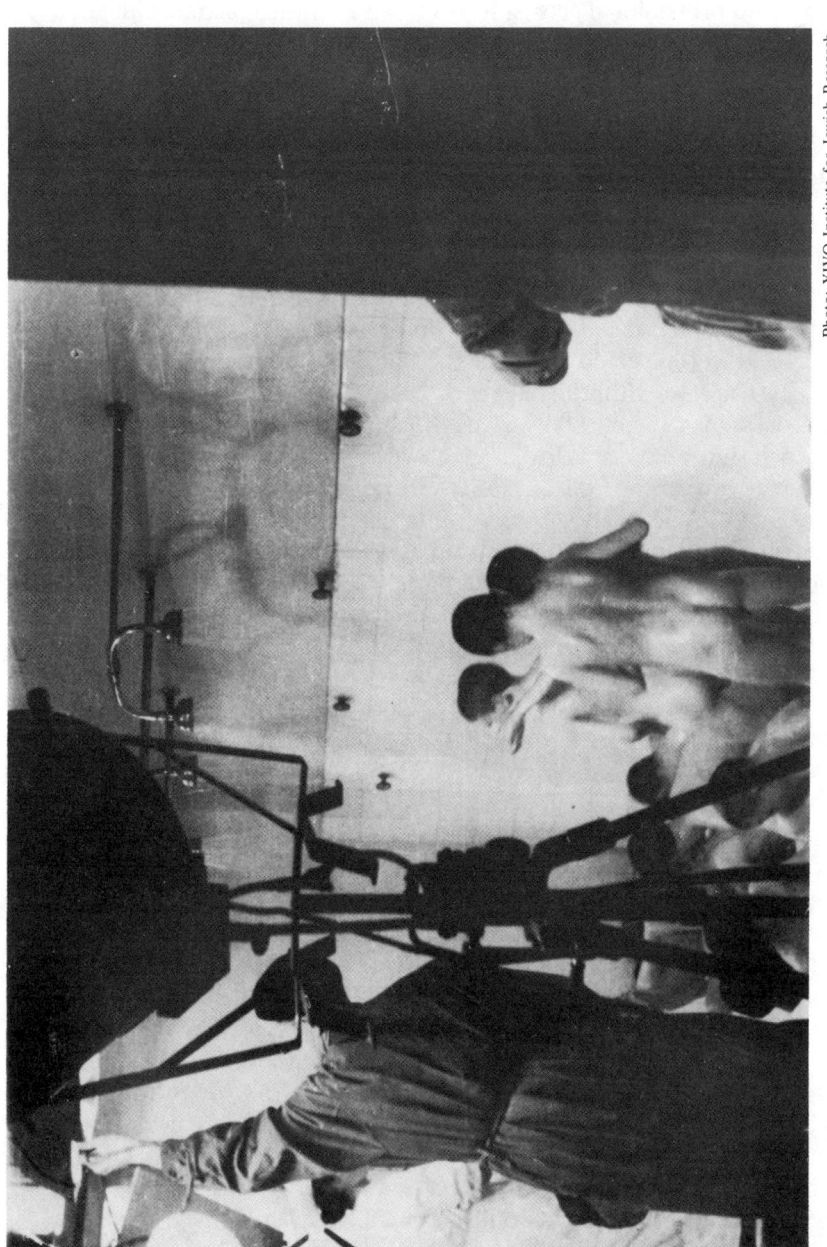

Preparing to shoot a scene at the Medem Sanatorium for *Mir Kumen On* (We Are On Our Way) (1935). The picture was directed by Aleksander Ford.

Photo: YIVO Institute for Jewish Research.

very limited, so a great deal of care was taken in pre-production. There were to be no professional actors; it was to be a scripted picture with "non-actors" playing the parts.

The film begins by documenting the awful living and working conditions in the Polish-Jewish ghetto. Ford then contrasts this with a picture of fresh air and open spaces at the Sanatorium. Happy, healthy children involved in all aspects of the running of the institution, from self-government to broadcasting, are the focus of the film. True, the picture was made to raise additional funds for the Sanatorium, but it is the children themselves who make the plea for assistance; in one instance, a pretty young girl announces over the radio that there are "an estimated 75,000 Jewish children still suffering from infected lungs," who need help.

Before the film could be released, it had to be brought before the Polish censor, who withheld release of the picture. Exactly why the film was not passed is still not totally clear, though some believed it was because of the inclusion of a "socialist" scene, where a group of 190 youngsters offer to make room for Polish children whose fathers are on strike.[4] However, despite the fact that *Mir Kumen On* could not be shown in theaters commercially, there were "underground" screenings of the picture in Poland. Prints of the film reached all parts of Western Europe, and a special gala was arranged for the New York premiere of the picture, sponsored by David Dubinsky of the International Ladies Garment Workers' Union and New York councilman Barney Vladek.

The First Yiddish Narrative Sound Film in Poland—*Al Khet* (For the Sin/Confession)—1936

No Yiddish film had been made in Poland since Jonas Turkow's 1928 *In Poylishe Velder* (In the Polish Woods). Although indications pointed to the fact that a well-made Yiddish picture would enjoy a sizable following, investors were hesitant to put money into such a venture. For the Goskind brothers, who would play no small role in both the production and financing of the film, there was also the risk of loss of business to their laboratory. There was the real fear that unsympathetic companies would withdraw work from a business connected with Jewish film production. As if in spite, Goskind and his fellow cooperative members vowed to make a film that would be twice as good as any Polish picture. To achieve this, writer J.M. Neuman of the Warsaw Yiddish paper, *Haynt,* was hired to prepare an original screenplay making sure to write in comedy for Dzigan and Schumacher. The picture would be titled *Al Khet*.

Neuman first became interested in film when he took a small acting part in *Tkies Kaf* (1924). Since that time, he had written a number of screenplays on Jewish subjects; they ranged from "Far Unzer Gloyben" (For Our Faith), written together with Sholom Asch, to biographies of leading Polish Jews like Ludwig Zamenhoff. Despite the fact that none of his previous work had been realized on the screen, Neuman took on his new task with great enthusiasm.

Born near Warsaw in 1893, Neuman received traditional schooling and later studied electro-mechanics, while flirting with drawing and writing. At age twenty, his writing talent landed him a position on the Lodz morning paper. Six years later, he moved to Warsaw and joined the staff of *Haynt*, where he was appointed theater editor in 1933. In his new position, Neuman quickly became a leading figure on the Jewish theater scene as one of the leading advocates for Yiddish language film. Between 1936 and 1938, Neuman would become one of the central figures in Yiddish cinema.

Al Khet, the first Yiddish sound picture to be made in Poland, is quite melodramatic. This is reflected even in its title *Al Khet,* a prayer for repentance recited on Yom Kippur, the Day of Atonement. However, in this film, the writer, director, and producer were attempting to go beyond the melodrama which had up to that time been synonymous with Yiddish film. They endeavored to add a realistic, documentary element and succeeded, if somewhat unevenly, in picturing the squalor and congestion of Ghetto life as well as the limited upward mobility of the Polish Jew. This clearly was a new kind of Yiddish picture, and in fact *Al Khet* would usher in a Golden Age of Yiddish Cinema in Poland. The seeding had been done and we would see the first fruits, but, unfortunately there would be no great harvest.

To insure the quality of the production, Goskind asked Polish cameraman Stanislaw Lipinski to take charge of cinematography and composer Henikh Kahn, (both worked on *Mir Kumen On*) to write the music. Also recruited were three recent refugees from Nazi Germany: painter Yankl Adler, actor Kurt Katch and director Aleksander Marten. Adler had been painting in Dusseldorf where he gained world recognition; Katch had already established himself on the German stage (later in American cinema); Marten, a Lodz Jew who studied acting and directing with Reinhardt, had apprenticed and had been assistant director on a few German theater productions. The latter had changed his name from Marek Tennenbaum by taking the first three letters of each name, Mar-Ten.

Al Khet is about Esther, the daughter of a Rabbi who falls in love, against her father's wishes, with a German-Jewish lieutenant stationed in her town during the First World War. Just before they are to be married,

Rokhl Holzer and Khevel Buzgan in *Al-Khet* (Confession) (1936). The story is unleashed by the love of a Polish Rabbi's daughter for a German-Jewish lieutenant.

Photo: YIVO Institute for Jewish Research.

the soldier is sent to the front where he is killed. Esther has a baby but is forced to put the child up for adoption, and goes off to America. It is only years later, after she has prospered, that she returns to seek out the child.

After the picture was completed, no company was interested in distributing it. It was not just a question of the picture being in Yiddish or of Jewish content, there simply was no distributor who felt that there was a chance for financial return. Shaul Goskind finally decided to distribute the picture himself. He rented a theater of 500 seats in a Jewish section of Warsaw, and the picture did so well that it played for over six months. *Al Khet* was distributed throughout Poland and Western Europe, and reached New York the following year.

Producer-Director Joseph Green

Joseph Green spent half of his year in Poland, his country of origin, and the other half in New York City, his home for over a decade. He was one of those who brought over Yiddish language pictures from the United States. He even was one of the actors who recorded the prologue and epilogue to some of the earlier "dubbed" films.

Born in Lodz, Green, whose name was originally Greenberg, studied drama in Berlin and toured Europe with the Vilna Troupe. Arriving with the troupe in New York in 1924, he acted with the Unzer Teater; later with the Schildkraut Theater, and with Maurice Schwartz' Yiddish Art Theater. In 1925, he followed the Schildkrauts to Hollywood where he played small parts in a series of pictures. Although Green enjoyed acting, he spent a great deal of his time in Hollywood watching films being made; a growing affection for the medium developed. According to Green, it was during the filming of *The Jazz Singer* that he began dreaming of Yiddish talking pictures. On the set, Green remembered hearing more Yiddish than English. It was clear to him that a picture like *The Jazz Singer,* with some modification, could easily be made in Yiddish for a Yiddish-speaking audience.[5]

The year and a half in Hollywood served as a period of indoctrination and study, and although Green returned to the New York stage the following year to be with the Schildkraut Theater, the world of cinema had become a part of him. Leaving acting in the early 1930s to go into business, Green purchased rights for Yiddish pictures made in the United States and brought them to Poland. His American imports had done fairly well, but poor technical quality and static performances restricted their potential market. As a Polish-born Jew, Green felt that he knew what kind of Yiddish picture would do well in Poland; he also wanted a picture he could release in America. In a 1936 interview in the Yiddish journal *Literarishe Bleter,* Green laid out his four aims:

1) to take all technical opportunities to make films on a suitable technical level.
2) the subject of the film will be Jewish, yet universal, avoiding past stereotypes, but still pulling a certain amount from folklore and ethnography.
3) the film should have cultural value and purity of Yiddish language, while at the same time maintaining humor. A great deal of effort will also be made with music.
4) quality acting to bring the film to a given artistic level.[6]

Green first negotiated with Maurice Schwartz who was touring in Poland that year to star in an adaptation of Goldfaden's "Di Kishefmakhern" (The Sorceress). However, the project never reached the filming stage, for Schwartz's interest waned. Schwartz wanted to make Sholom Aleichem's "Tevye" for the screen, but Green felt it had too many anticlerical elements for it to be filmed in Poland. Green refused to change the project and the agreement was broken.

Green did go on to make four Yiddish films in Poland between 1936 and 1938. The first two, *Yidl mitn Fidl* and *Der Purimshpiler* were codirected with talented young Polish director, Jan Nowina-Przybylski. After Przybylski's sudden death in 1937, Green co-directed *Mamele* with Konrad Tom and *A Brivele der Mamen* with Leon Trystan.

Joseph Green had a flair for business, but unlike others in the field of Yiddish filmmaking, he was interested not only in a finished product but also in quality production. Green searched for authenticity. He attempted to produce as realistic a picture of Jewish life in Eastern Europe as was possible and felt that only in Poland could he do this. If he could not film "on-location" in a shtetl, he had a shtetl built. If he needed a circus, he hired a real one. Green also availed himself of outstanding artists like Manger, Ellstein, and Brodsky to assist him in his work. He hired leading performers from the Warsaw and New York Yiddish stage. He had high standards. True, it was less expensive to make pictures overseas than in America, but Poland of the 1930s was rich with Jewish theater, art and culture; Green turned this to his advantage. At the opening of the First New York Yiddish Film Festival, in October 1977, he was presented with a special citation for excellence in Yiddish filmmaking. His contribution had finally been recognized.

Yidl mitn Fidl (Yidl with a Fiddle) — 1936

Joseph Green knew that he needed a big star for his first Yiddish picture, so with a basic outline in his hands, he left Warsaw for Paris where Molly Picon and her husband Jacob (Yankl) Kalich were doing theater. Offering her close to $10,000, the highest salary paid at that time to an artist in a

Photo: Joseph Green.

The cast and crew of *Yidl Mitn Fidl* (Yidl with His Fiddle) (1936). This picture was taken after 28 consecutive hours of filming of the "wedding" scene. In the center with hands clasped (and eyes closed) is a tired director, Joseph Green. To his right is Molly Picon, Jan Nowina-Przybylski, Jacob Kalich and director of photography Jacob Janilowicz. Behind Green is Max Bozyk. Behind Picon and Nowina-Przybylski is Simche Fostel. Behind Janilowicz is Leon Liebgold. On the left of Joseph Green is his wife, Annette.

Yiddish picture, Green was able to sign Ms. Picon, with Kalich contracted to supervise art direction. Molly would play a woman fiddler disguised as a boy, *Yidl mitn Fidl* (Yidl with a Fiddle), who roams the countryside with a quartet of klezmorim (musicians) until she falls in love with one of them and reveals that she is a woman. American composer Abe Ellstein was hired to write the music and owing to its folk manner, the master folk-writer, Itzik Manger, was asked to write the lyrics. Talented Polish film director Jan Nowina-Przybylski handled most of the technical direction.

Green wanted to film shtetl life, as had been done in the Soviet-made pictures of the twenties and early thirties. The shtetl stood as a symbol of a strong unified Jewish community where Judaism was a way of life and not just a religion. Green wanted to shoot "on-location" and charged designer Jacek Weinreich to search for appropriate locations; preparations were made for filming in Kazimierz nad Wisla, where Jonas Turkow had made *Der Lamedvovnik* in 1925. The opening sequences are set in the marketplace of the town. From there the action moves to the countryside and eventually to the city. Despite all the poverty, the village was a cinematographer's paradise; a Middle Age town that once served as home for King Casimir and his Jewish bride. To recruit extras, an announcement was made that anyone showing up in the marketplace would get 2 zlotys; they would also get another 2 zlotys for each animal they brought.

> When a call was sent out for a hundred extras at two zlotys a day, all the nearby villagers turned out and it began to look as though we were in for a super-super production, a la Hollywood. Business in the town came to a standstill, as two zlotys a day was much more than what they customarily earned by the daily toil.[7]

Filming continued in Kazimierz for ten days and the rest of the picture was completed in a studio in Warsaw in five weeks. The total cost of *Yidl mitn Fidl* was $50,000. The picture did so well in Poland, that it brought back a profit from domestic distribution alone. Polish film historian Jerzy Toeplitz called it one of the three most successful Polish pictures of 1936. Within a year the picture was being screened in all parts of the world. *Yidl mitn Fidl* has proved to be the most commercially successful Yiddish musical film of all time.

The "Golden Age of Yiddish Cinema" was launched with the unmitigated success of both *Al Khet* and *Yidl mitn Fidl*. Polish picture companies of 1937 were showing a great deal of interest in Yiddish language productions. Leo-Film, a film conglomerate that grew out of Leo Forbert's production company of the twenties set out to remake *Tkies Kaf*. Phoenix Film, a Warsaw-based company subsidized in part with American money, was making preparations to film S. Anski's classic, *Der Dibuk*. At the same time, Joseph Green was constructing a shtetl on the outskirts of Warsaw for the filming of his next picture, *Der Purimshpiler* and the Kinor group, with original script in hand by Yiddish writer Moshe Broderson, was planning *Freylekhe Kabtsonim*.

Tkies Kaf (The Vow) — 1937

Tkies Kaf had been one of the most exquisite Yiddish film productions of the silent period and seemed a natural for a sound remake. Leo-Film, a film conglomerate that evolved from Leo Forbert's production company of the twenties, still owned the rights. Zygmund Turkow, who directed and starred in the silent version was asked by the company to serve as codirector, with his primary responsibility that of coordinating acting. He also took the same role of Elijah the Prophet that he had played fourteen years earlier. Turkow had by this time gained a reputation as one of the foremost directors and leading actors on the World Yiddish stage. Henryk

The four klezmorim, traveling "male" musicians, in *Yidl Mitn Fidl* (Yidl with His Fiddle) (1936). Max Bozyk, Leon Liebgold, Molly Picon and Simche Fostel. *Yidl Mitn Fidl* will always remain both a classic and favorite.

Photo: David Matis.

Photo: Yiddish Theater Collection, Museum of the City of New York.

Itskhok Grudberg (Turkow) as a "yeshive bokhr" (student) in *Tkies Kaf* (The Vow) (1937). The youngest of the multi-talented Turkow brothers (Grudberg was his pen name) followed his brothers Zygmund and Jonas into acting. Both Itskhok and Zygmund had major roles in the film. The film was a remake of the 1923 picture.

Szaro, who had directed *Der Lamedvovnik* (1925), supervised the technical aspects of production.

Tkies Kaf is a story of love with an admonition against the breaking of vows, and a denunciation of careless pledges. Two friends have pledged that their as yet unborn children would marry. The families lose contact with each other, and although the children meet and fall in love, their love is overlooked as the father of the boy makes other marriage plans for his son. The prophet Elijah intervenes and after a series of mishaps, the son marries the girl to whom he was pledged.

Turkow's participation is visually quite apparent as there are many scenes quite similar in structure to the original *Tkies Kaf* (1924). One of the more striking segments is the wedding scene. Rokhl is about to marry a man other than her "basherter" (fated one). The Prophet Elijah intervenes and reminds the girl's father that a vow was made years before, providing for her marriage to another. Camerawork in both versions is striking in contrasting the joy of a wedding ceremony with the impending doom associated with broken vows. Both versions of *Tkies Kaf* present the forthcoming events with parallel precision. However, where the 1924 film presented the climax in long shot, the 1937 version used a montage of shots, climaxing with a closeup of the wedding couple's hands.

Der Dibuk (The Dybbuk) — 1937

So similar was the plot of *Der Dibuk* to that of the previously-produced *Tkies Kaf,* that the Phoenix producers took special care to banish any similarities between the two. For example, Dina Halpern who played young Rokhl, the fated bride in *Tkies Kaf,* was given the role of the elder aunt, Freyde, in *Der Dibuk,* although she might have been a possible choice for the lead role of young Leah. Other actors who appeared in the earlier film, like Moyshe Lipman, Max Bozyk, and Shmuel Landau had very different roles in *Der Dibuk.*

Der Dibuk was like no other Yiddish film made in Poland. It was based on a play which in its short history had become one of the great classics in theater. Originally written by S. Anski (Solomon Zeynwil Rapaport) in Russian at the insistence of Stanislavsky, the play was banned by Czarist censors and translated into Yiddish by the author. Anski approached the Vilna Troupe to produce the play and though they almost agreed, it was finally turned down. In the meantime, Hebrew poet-laureate Chaim Nachman Bialik translated it into Hebrew for the Habima Theater, but again the play was not produced. It was only after Anski's death in 1920, that the Vilna Troupe decided to produce the play. It was a retranslation into Yiddish of Bialik's Hebrew version that was finally produced in Warsaw.

Writer Alter Kacyzna, who was left the rights to Anski's work was approached by Ludwig Prywes, to adapt the play for the screen. Prywes was the nephew of Naftal Prywes, the man who financed the original Vilna Troupe production. Kacyzna, who was very knowledgeable about the cinema (having written film reviews for the Yiddish journal *Literarishe Bleter*), immediately accepted and with the assistance of Yiddish writer and stage director Mark Arnstein prepared the screenplay. Professor Meyer Balaban of Warsaw University oversaw historical accuracy and Henikh Kahn, who had established himself as a leading composer for Yiddish pictures, wrote the music.

The producers wanted someone to direct who was well versed in film technique, yet who would feel comfortable with a Jewish subject; It was rumored that Hollywood director Ernst Lubitsch might direct, but Michal Waszyński, who had developed a reputation as an efficient, quick, and meticulous director, was finally selected. He completed all the pictures he made for less than their projected budgets and would usually finish filming earlier than scheduled. Waszynski, a Polish Jew whose name was originally Waksz (Wax), knew some Yiddish, but more important, he had a strong list of film credits to his name. He began his career as an assistant director with Henryk Szaro, and by the early 1930s had established himself as a respectable filmmaker. *Der Dibuk* is considered by many to be his finest effort.

Der Dibuk is a story of unfulfilled love. Parents make a pledge to have their children marry (as they had in *Tkies Kaf*). The destined couple, Khonen and Leah, meet and fall in love, but the girl's father, forgetting his vow, keeps them apart. Elijah does not intervene, as he had in *Tkies Kaf*. Khonen, despondent, tries to find answers through mystical kabbalah and perishes. Just as the girl is about to marry another, Khonen's persona enters her body and possesses her. She is brought before the Rabbi who finally succeeds in exorcising the spirit, the "dybbuk," from her body, but as it leaves, so does she to join him in death. The story pits good against evil; traditional Judaism against Kabbalistic (mystical) practice.

Avrom Marevsky, a respected and distinguished actor, was cast as the Rabbi of Miropol, the same part he played seventeen years earlier as a member of the original stage cast. His interpretation remains one of the great portrayals in Yiddish cinema. Lili Liliana, veteran of a few Polish pictures, won the lead part over thirty-five other actresses. She is the perfect Leah, plain and beautiful. Her real-life husband, Leon Liebgold as Khonen, the one pledged to her, is both mysterious and spiritual.

The design by Rotmil and Norris is highly influenced by past theater productions of *Der Dibuk* rather than clear cinematic considerations. The set design attempts to provide a grotesquely expressionistic setting without relying heavily on lighting. Judith Berg's choreographies are some of the best of the day, particularly her "Dance of Death" and "Dance of the Beggars."

Exterior shooting, lasting two weeks, was done in Kazimierz, by now a favorite Yiddish film location.

> This still, dreamy, romantic, elevated shtetl Kuzmir (Kazimierz), with its narrow, old alleys and with its specific archaic wood architecture is truly a beautiful location for Anski's dramatic legend, in which is woven, as in a mystical web, Jewish folklore and dream-like romance of longing. Only here, in the shadow of genuine folk primitiveness, can the wonderful legend blossom and grow.[8]

Studio filming in Warsaw was completed in five weeks.

Der Dibuk did extremely well at the box office and received exceptional reviews. B. Tsavion of the *Jewish Daily Forward* called it "a true treasure."[9] Parker Tyler called it "a beautiful anachronism,...one of the most solemn attestations to the mystic powers of the spirit the imagination has ever purveyed to the film reel.[10] Another critic, Nazi Joseph Goebbels, had quite a different impression of the picture when he saw the film in February, 1942,

> In the evening I had a look at the Polish-Yiddish motion picture, *The Dybbuk*. This film is intended to be a Jewish propaganda picture. Its effect, however, is so anti-Semitic that one can only be surprised to note how little the Jews know about themselves and how little they realize what is repulsive to a non-Jewish person and what is not.[11]

Der Dibuk was extremely well received by "most." Prints of the film are in many of the major film archives of the world. A new Hebrew version was made in Israel in 1970 by Ilan Eldad, in terms of quality, it does not begin to bear resemblance to the Yiddish version. Later, a film recording in color, of the E.R. Kaminska Jewish State Theater of Poland's Yiddish stage production of *The Dybbuk* was made. It was shown in New York during the summer of 1982.

Der Purimshpiler (The Jester) — 1937

After the tremendous success of *Yidl mitn Fidl,* Joseph Green wasted little time in making preparations for a new Yiddish musical comedy. Working in New York with writer/playwright Chaver-Pahver, he came up with the story for *Der Purimshpiler.* It was a story involving a shoemaker's daughter, a vaudeville circus player, and a jester. The young woman falls

Photo: Yiddish Theater Collection, Museum of the City of New York.

Photo: YIVO Institute for Jewish Research.

Photo: Amatsia Hiuni/Addi Cohen.

"The dance of death," one of the brilliant choreographies in *Der Dibuk* (The Dybbuk) (1937), by Judith Berg. Lili Liliana is Leah, a woman possessed by the spirit of her "intended"; Judith Berg dances the part of death. Lower left: The forces of good do battle with evil as the Rabbi of Miropol (Moyshe Lipman) attempts to exorcise the "dybbuk" from Leah's soul. Above: David Opatoshu as the Rabbi of Miropol in the 1970 Israeli remake of the Dybbuk.

in love with the circus player, ignoring Getsl, the third member of the love triangle. The circus is used as a web in which all the intrigue is spun, climaxing with Purim and traditional Purim jesting.

The part of Getsl was created for American Yiddish actor Joseph Buloff, who initially agreed to come to Poland to play the part. Fellow actors from the New York Yiddish stage, Miriam Kressyn and Hymie Jacobson were to play the other leads. However, just before the three stars were to leave for Poland, Buloff was offered a Broadway part. Green then turned to Zygmund Turkow, who had just finished work on *Tkies Kaf* to take Buloff's place. Also playing in the picture were Isaac Samberg, Shmuel Landau, and Max Bozyk who had become regulars in Polish Yiddish films.

Most of the scenes were set to take place in a shtetl, so Green had contractors erect a "shtetl set" on the outskirts of Warsaw. One observer at the time described the surroundings:

> ...A Jewish "shtetl" with a street and alley way, with a row of houses and shops, where part of the action in the new film takes place. A shtetl in Warsaw...a lively shtetl: An entrance with a wide gate, all kinds of Jewish workers with specific signs, half Polish and half Yiddish, a comfortable home with a garden in front, where the wealthy man of the shtetl is likely to live and further on, one and two story small shtetl houses, which all together create an "illusion" of a true Yiddish shtetl in great detail.[12]

Additional shots were filmed in Cracow.

Green again asked Jan Nowina-Przybylski to co-direct; Przybylski did most of the film work, while Green handled some acting direction and the financial side of the picture. Nicholas Brodsky was brought to Warsaw from Vienna to write the music; shortly afterward Brodsky left for the United States to work for MGM. Itzik Manger wrote both lyrics and dialogue for the picture, and Seweryn Steinwurcel, considered at the time to be one of the best cameramen in Poland, served as director of photography. Filming was completed in seven weeks.

Di Freylekhe Kabtsonim (Jolly Paupers) — 1937

The busiest person in Yiddish film in 1937 was Zygmund Turkow. He co-directed and played a lead in *Tkies Kaf,* starred in *Der Purimshpiler,* and soon after became involved with *Di Freylekhe Kabtsonim,* a Kinor production. Kinor had succeeded in beginning the "Golden Age" with the success of its first feature, *Al Khet,* but it was slow to come up with a new offering. In late 1937, Kinor was presented with a muscial comedy written by Moshe Broderson with music by Henikh Kahn. For Broderson, who was a poet and writer of short plays, this would be his first and only film

Esther (Miriam Kressyn) is oblivious to the advances of Getsel (Zygmund Turkow) in *Der Purimshpiler* (The Jester) (1937). Isaac Samberg, Ms. Kressyn, Mr. Turkow, Berta Litwina, Jacob Rajnglas and Max Bozyk. Below: Joseph Green's "shtetl — Hollywood style," complete with stores and alley way. In the center is Turkow.

Photos: Joseph Green.

script. Broderson knew not only the audience he was writing for but the actors as well; it was he who years before had discovered both Shimen Dzigan and Yisroel Schumacher, two well known comedians who had contracted with Kinor. The proposed comedy, *Freylekhe Kabtsonim* was about a promoter who tricks a local tailor by "planting" oil on a farm. Investigators are brought in and this results in comic situations until the real source of the oil is finally discovered.

With Aleksander Marten, who had directed the first Kinor picture, away in Germany, Turkow was hired to direct by producer Shaul Goskind. One of the all-time great inprovisators of the Yiddish stage, Turkow was very much at home with theater. Though he had directed the silent *Tkies Kaf* in 1924 and co-directed the sound version earlier that year, Turkow was still not totally at ease with cinema technique. Great pains were taken to make the picture as commercially attractive as possible, including extensive outdoor shooting near the shtetl of Brzeziny; however, in comparison with the other Yiddish films made that year, the Kinor picture was received very poorly. Little screened outside of Poland, the film failed to regain its initial investment and Kinor was forced to cease producing Yiddish pictures.

A Brivele der Mamen (A Letter to Mother) — 1938

Joseph Green, despite only the fair commercial acceptance of *Der Purimshpiler*, returned to Poland in 1938 for another round of Yiddish filmmaking. In addition to the Polish Jewish viewer, Green knew he had an audience for his pictures — an America hungry for quality Yiddish films.

Shortly after *Der Purimshpiler* was completed, Joseph Green began to work with Mendel Osherowitz on the screenplay for his next film. Osherowitz, a journalist for the *Jewish Daily Forward*, was the author of several volumes, including works on the lives of actors Paul Muni and David Kessler. Although he had never worked on a film script before, he and Green toiled for two months in Green's New York apartment and came up with *A Brivele der Mamen* (A Letter to Mother), from S. Shmulewitz's song of the same title. It is an historical narrative of an Eastern European Jewish family broken up by custom, war and jealousy.

The story of *A Brivele der Mamen* revolves around the melody of a prayer used in the Passover feast, the "seder." The father of the family, a dreamer and part-time composer composes the melody to the joy of his friends. However, tunes do not make money and it is only through the toil of the mother that the family eats. The children do not accept their father's "laziness" and he, out of shame, leaves for America to earn money. However, the father is only able to raise enough money to bring his

Shooting the film *Di Freylekhe Kabtsonim* (Jolly Paupers) (1937), the second Kinor production by Shaul Goskind. The picture starred Zygmund Turkow, his daughter Ruth Turkow, Shimen Dzigan, and Yisroel Schumacher. The "helmeted warrior" in the center is Menashe Oppenheim.

Photo: YIVO Institute for Jewish Research.

youngest child to join him in America. As the war breaks out the family loses contact with each other.

Many issues are tackled in the picture, the clearest one being the breakdown of family life. The father leaves, the daughter runs off with a married man, one son goes to war, and the other goes to America. Before, the family was together for traditional gatherings, a most important one being the "seder." Where once custom and tradition kept the family together, it no longer has that power. Still, despite war, separation and tragedy, there must be hope. It is no coincidence that it is the father's liturgical melody that finally reunites the remaining family. The melody carries with it a chain of tradition, glimpses of the shtetl where families remain together, as well as a sense of connection to Judaism.

Maintaining one's connection with Judaism and one's ties to custom and tradition is the message of the film. Even in times of despair, there is hope that tradition will keep families together. It is no mistake that each of the Green pictures has at least one major Jewish custom in it. There is the wedding in *Yidl mitn Fidl,* the "seder" in *A Brivele der Mamen,* a sukkah (booth) celebration in *Mamele,* and the "purimshpil" (Purim play) in *Der Purimshpiler.* A connection with the Jewish people is the major thrust of *A Brivele Der Mamen* and all the Green films; in fact it is the governing force of all Yiddish cinema.

Mamele (Little Mother) — 1938

As the filming of *A Brivele der Mamen* was being readied in Poland, Joseph Green was contacted by Molly Picon's husband and agent, Jacob Kalich, about the possibility of making another picture together. *Yidl mitn Fidl* had been such a success — why not follow it up? They chose one of Picon's favorite plays, *Mamele* (Little Mother) written by Meyer Schwartz, and Green agreed to hold up production on *A Brivele der Mamen* long enough to work in the filming of *Mamele.* There was a feeling that if the picture was not made then, there would be no opportunity to make it the following year; a premonition which proved correct.

Konrad Tom, who had worked on *Yidl mitn Fidl* was engaged as co-director of *Mamele.* With the help of scenarist J. M. Neuman, Tom adapted the play, localizing it from an American to a Polish setting. Both Seweryn Steinwurcel who was to do camera and Abe Ellstein who came from America to prepare the music on *A Brivele Der Mamen* agreed to work on *Mamele.* Actors Max Bozyk, Simche Fostel, Gertrude Bullman, Edmund Zayenda, and Adam Domb also agreed to take part in both films.

Mamele was shot in six weeks beginning in late summer in a Warsaw studio and backlot; some exteriors were filmed at the resort town of

Photo: Joseph Green.

Every one of Joseph Green's films includes some sort of holiday scene. The family sits around the Passover Seder Table in *A Brivele der Mamen* (A Letter to Mother) (1938). Yet, joy is absent from their faces as the oldest, Meyer, recites the festival kiddish (sanctification over wine). He has taken his father's place who has gone off to America to earn enough to bring his family over. The empty chair on the far side is for the father; on the near side it is left for Elijah the prophet. The actors are (left to right) Itskhok Grudberg (Turkow), Lucy Gehrman, Irving Bruner and Gertrude Bullman.

For Khavtshi, the "Mamele," even her wedding must wait until she is sure everything is okay in *Mamele* (Little Mother) (1938). Molly Picon is Khavtshi. On the far left is Simche Fostel. Directly over Molly is Max Bozyk. Gertrude Bullman has the bouquet, she is surrounded by Edmund Zayenda (left) and Max Perlman.

Photo: Joseph Green.

Ciechocinek. The picture is about Khavtshi, the daughter of a widower, who is left with the responsibility of tending house for a helpless and indifferent family of seven. As such, she becomes the "mamele," their "little mother." It was a perfect film for Picon, showered with that special brand of humor and song that made her famous. One of the highlights occurs when she dons the guises of various ages, and dances as one would if she were a teenager or an octogenarian.

Shkheynim (Neighbors) — 1938

Leon Trystan who had co-directed *A Brivele der Mamen* saw the far-reaching commercial possibilities of Yiddish cinema in America. Yiddish films were very well received in American theaters and by the American press; such was not the case with Trystan's Polish-language pictures shown in America. Therefore, he took one of his Polish pictures, *Pietro Wyzej* (The Apartment Above), and rereleased it in New York in a dubbed Yiddish version as *Shkheynim* (Neighbors). It was a light comedy by Polish writers about two families who live in the same apartment building and their inability to get along with each other. The picture featured Polish actors Eugene Bodo and Helen Gross (Grossowna). Whereas the Polish release failed to attract any attention in New York a few months earlier, the Yiddish version did extremely well. No one repeated this tactic.

On A Heym (Without A Home) — 1939

Aleksander Marten had just finished a Polish film when producer Adolph Mann approached him to make another Yiddish film. Marten, who had to leave Nazi Germany the year before because of restrictions on Jews, liked the idea of making another Jewish picture. In a 1938 interview, Marten commented that he hoped that he would be able to touch on contemporary questions and problems.[13] However, fear during that time was so great in Poland that no filmmaker, let alone a Jewish filmmaker, dared to openly make an anti-Nazi film.

Mann and Marten instead chose a Jacob Gordin classic, *On a Heym,* which writer Alter Kacyzna adapted for the screen with one eye on the potential American audience. The Gordin story is a nostalgic look at Jewish life in Eastern Europe at the turn of the century. The story, filled with tragedy, begins with the drowning of the oldest Rivkin son. Disgusted with life in Eastern Europe, the father sails for America where he can only find a job as a cafe dishwasher. Still, with financial assistance from an attractive cabaret singer, he sends for his remaining son, wife, and elderly father. No one finds happiness in America; everything goes wrong from apparent adultery to poverty and suicide. *On a Heym* is a story of Jewish grief and

Shimen Dzigan (center) and Yisroel Schumacher were a comedy team well-known throughout Poland for their political satire and zany skits. They made three Yiddish films during the "Golden Age of Yiddish Cinema in Poland (1936–1939)"; and a fourth after the War. Here they are with Muriel Gruber in *On a Heym* (Without a Home) (1939). Schumacher died in 1961; Dzigan in 1980.

Photo: YIVO Institute for Jewish Research.

hardship, at a time of foreshadowed tragedy. The film does end on an optimistic note, although in 1939 Poland there was little to hope for. How unfortunately apropos the title—*On a Heym* (Without a Home) was! Only six months later, the Jews of Eastern Europe would be non-citizens.

Unlike Yiddish efforts of previous years, the cast of *On a Heym* was limited. Director Marten played the part of Avreyml, the father. Dzigan and Schumacher as Motl and Fishl are present to give zany comic relief as they had done in *Al Khet* and *Di Freylekhe Kabtsonim*. In addition, Ida Kaminska, by now a leading actress and director on the Warsaw Yiddish stage, was hired as the female lead. Kaminska took the part on the condition that she be paid daily, apprehensive of the financial stability of the enterprise. When money did run out before production was completed, Kaminska quit, and the film had to be completed using a standby's side and back. That the film was even released is credit to Marten's unyielding determination. Despite all these efforts the picture was not received well by audiences.

Ten quality pictures were to be made in Poland between 1936 and 1939. Involved in this cultural phenomenon were to be writers like Manger, Broderson, and Kacyzna, composers like Kahn, Ellstein and Brodsky, artists like Adler and Weinreich and actors like Picon, Turkow, Kaminska, Halpern, Dzigan, Marevsky, and Schumacher. They left us a legacy for centuries to come and a record of a life that would be ro more.

The last picture of this period, Aleksander Marten's *On a Heym* was released in March of 1939, seven months before the Nazis marched into Warsaw. Joseph Green had plans for a new film musical set for production the summer of 1939 and Marten discussed the future of a "pure Yiddish cinema." With the war, Green would never again return to Poland and Marten would disappear in the Holocaust. Despite some efforts after the war, Poland ceased to be one of the great centers of Yiddish life and culture; instead, it became its burial ground.

6

The Golden Age of Yiddish Cinema Part II: United States, 1937–1940

In 1934, the American film industry shifted gears as a new set of production codes changed the type of product being made in Hollywood. As American film historian Robert Sklar points out in *Movie-Made America,* this was brought about by a change in national mood caused in part by Roosevelt's "New Deal" as well as the growing influence of the Catholic Legion of Decency, which moved moviemakers toward greater support of a more traditional Anglo-American culture.[1] One of the immediate results was a rash of "respectable" pictures drawn from the past and adapted from classic literature.[2]

Three years later, a similar film form ushered in the American "Golden Age" of Yiddish cinema. More time and money was invested in these films and a superior group of artists, writers, and technicians participated in production. There was a clear effort to give Yiddish cinema a fine artistic foundation as well as better technical quality.

As producers sought to make "quality" Yiddish films, they too drew from the classics of Yiddish theater and literature. The subjects usually dealt nostalgically with Jewish life in Eastern Europe which many Yiddish-speaking Jews still considered "home." There, in the shtetl, Jewish values and culture seemed more clearly defined. In the West, assimilation and acculturation had changed the mores of Jewish existence; the shtetl represented a pure Jewish spirit, lost in Americanization. Over the next four years these classics served as the foundation of Yiddish cinema in America. This is what the Yiddish-speaking film audience wanted to see and this is what they were given.

The first Yiddish film producer to adapt a literary classic for the screen during this period was Roman Rebush. Rebush saw that there was an excellent market for "good" Yiddish pictures, when Joseph Green, in early 1937, successfully exhibited his Polish-made *Yidl mitn Fidl* in New

York. Rebush defined "good" pictures as films which were well-budgeted and professionally produced. In a 1939 interview he said:

> Money is not as freely available for "minority" films as it is for more general productions. That is why the earlier Jewish films were so inadequate. It takes a lot of money to turn out a product that is professionally up to standard, and I have always gone on the theory that it is better to make one good picture than half a dozen poor ones.[3]

Other producers followed Rebush's lead, with six pictures, drawn from classic sources, being completed within a two and a half year period. Producers were also aware that the choice of a "big name star" made their picture all the more attractive. Henry Lynn first used this to his advantage when he lured actors Boris Thomashefsky and Celia Adler to the screen. Ben K. Blake later filmed theater star Jennie Goldstein in *Tsvey Shvester* (Two Sisters). However, both Blake's film and Lynn's pictures were overly melodramatic and of mediocre technical quality. With the advent of the "Golden Age of Yiddish Cinema," film productions were finally prepared on a high technical plane and actors no longer feared that their participation in Yiddish pictures would leave them open to ridicule. In Poland, fine leading actors like Molly Picon, Zygmund Turkow, and Avrom Marevsky participated in Yiddish films. In America, the list included Moishe Oysher, Maurice Schwartz, and Berta Gersten. A "star system" had begun to evolve in Yiddish cinema.

Grine Felder (Green Fields) — 1937

Peretz Hirschbein's play *Grine Felder*, had become a classic of Yiddish drama and it seemed natural to choose it as the first large-budget classic from Yiddish literature to be adapted for Yiddish screen. In 1918, the Folksbine presented the world premiere of the play at the Neighborhood Playhouse, an event which Yiddish theater critic Jacob Fishman claimed "marked the birth of the Yiddish art theater."[4] The film's producer, Roman Rebush, felt that *Grine Felder* would do the same for Yiddish films; that is, raise the artistic level and draw new audiences who had spurned previous efforts. He was correct. This "well-budgeted" classic would usher in the Golden Age of Yiddish Cinema in America.

Roman Rebush had a dream. He wanted to produce a Jewish motion picture that was good enough to draw both Christian and Jewish audiences to the theater. This required a film budget far larger than previous ethnic film efforts, as well as a fine writer, a good director and well-known actors. At a time when Jewish film producers were making picture after picture on the lowest of budgets, Rebush courageously chose to upgrade the product considerably. Choosing material from the Yiddish classics,

Rebush first made Peretz Hirschbein's *Grine Felder* in 1937, then *Der Zingendiker Shmid* (1938), based on a David Pinski play, and Jacob Gordin's *Mirele Efros*, made in 1939.

The story of *Grine Felder* is a pastoral one, about a young student who leaves the Yeshiva in search of common people and the outside world. He is looking for a meaningful existence more closely connected with the soil. In his travels, the lad meets a farmer who convinces him to stay on his farm and tutor his son. Much of the action takes place outside on the farm. In the past, Yiddish filmmakers in America filmed few exterior shots with most of the picture being made in the studio where costs were lower. This time, a greater quantity of shooting was done outside, in an attempt to remove a theatricality that had plagued previous efforts.

When playwright Peretz Hirschbein was asked for permission to adapt his play for the screen, he consented on the condition that actor/director Jacob Ben-Ami would be involved with the production. Ben-Ami, a fine actor and director of theater, was one of the original members of Hirschbein's Theater Troupe in Odessa. In New York, Ben-Ami's name, along with that of Maurice Schwartz had become synonomous with quality Yiddish art theater. If Hirschbein's work was to be considered as an integral part of Yiddish art theater, Ben-Ami played a large part in effecting that.

It was therefore no great surprise to producer Rebush that Hirschbein not only wanted Ben-Ami to direct the film, but envisioned Ben-Ami in the lead role as well. It was Ben-Ami, who a decade earlier, made the part of Leyvi-Yitskhok famous. Yet, Leyvi-Yitskhok was a yeshive-bokher, a young student, and Ben-Ami, already forty-five, could not hope to fool the camera. Hirschbein compromised and agreed to allow the film to be made if Ben-Ami were on the set establishing the necessary mise-en-scene; in a sense making sure that the film had the proper interpretation.

Rebush also wanted to ensure that his film would be technically well made, so he hired film director Edgar G. Ulmer to take charge of production. Ulmer and Rebush first met when Ulmer was in New York making a Ukrainian picture, *Natalka Poltavka*. At that time, the two shared a hope and desire to create a new kind of quality Yiddish picture. Ulmer was the kind of person that Rebush was looking for; he was Jewish, had extensive experience in filmmaking, and was searching for work.

Edgar George Ulmer began his career in Vienna as an actor, later moving to Berlin as a set designer for theater giant Max Reinhardt. He also assisted film director F.W. Murnau, accompanying him in the mid-twenties to Hollywood. After returning to Germany in 1929 to collaborate with Robert Siodmak, Billy Wilder, and Fred Zinnemann on the picture *Menschen am Sonntag* (People on Sunday), Ulmer returned to Hollywood. There, he made but a few pictures, the most notable being *The Black Cat*,

The importance of education is one of the themes in Jacob Ben-Ami and Edgar G. Ulmer's *Grine Felder* (Green Fields) (1937). Leyvi-Yitskhok has been engaged to teach young Avrum-Yankev. The neighbor Alkune would rather that he teach his children. Helen Beverly, Herschel Bernardi as Avrum-Yankev, Michael Goldstein as Leyvi-Yitskhok, Max Vodnoy. Below: Beautiful Helen Beverly as Tsine in *Grine Felder* (Green Fields). Beverly, who later became Mrs. Lee J. Cobb, graced three Yiddish Pictures.

Photo: Shirley Ulmer.

Photo: Harold Sieden.

released in 1934 with Boris Karloff and Bela Lugosi and still considered a horror film masterpiece. With filmmaking opportunities dwindling by the mid-thirties, Ulmer went east to New York. Knowing nothing of Yiddish theater, he visited the Jewish Art Theater and was stunned by the enthusiasm it seemed to generate in New York. The idea of taking material from the rich Yiddish theater and adapting it for the screen excited him.

When Edgar G. Ulmer was introduced to Jacob Ben-Ami, it became clear that the two were not in the least compatible. Both men were strong-willed and neither was prepared to have the other oversee his work. Ben-Ami was on the set to see that the film was consonant with Hirshbein's intentions, while Ulmer's primary interest was to make sure that the film was technically sound, well acted, and well produced. Each saw the other's role as peripheral, and a clearer division of labor had to be worked out. In an interview with Jacob Ben-Ami, he said:

> When I saw the circumstances under which it was done, I refused to take part in it. But then Hirschbein, who was a dear friend of mine (we had worked together) asked me to direct. If I don't want to play [Leyvi-Yitskhok] then [I should] find somebody to work with him [Ulmer]. That's what I did.[5]

As it turned out, Ben-Ami directed the actors and gave the film his interpretation. Herschel Bernardi, who played young Avrum-Yankev in the film, told me: "He [Ben-Ami] was the dramatic person. He was the person that tried to get the essence of Hirschbein, and the beauty of that period.[6] Ben-Ami chose actors from the New York Yiddish theater who he felt would fit Hirschbein's intended spirit. Many of the actors had worked with Ben-Ami before, some having played with him in past theater productions of *Grine Felder*. Ulmer, on the other hand, worked with the technicians, choosing shots and locations. He showed the actors, few of whom had ever acted before in front of a camera, how to react with film and how to move.

Producers' Service Studio in Ridgefield, New Jersey was contracted for technical services, with owner, J. Burgi-Contner, hired as cameraman. Burgi-Contner agreed to provide free services in exchange for a percentage of the picture. Interiors were shot at the studio, with exteriors filmed on a nearby Jersey farm, the same place where Ulmer had shot his Ukrainian picture, *Natalka Poltavka*. Shooting of the film lasted eight days.

The picture was released in October 1937, at New York's Squire Theater, near Broadway. It was well received not only by Yiddish-speaking persons, but by the public at large; it played twenty weeks downtown. For many Yiddish-speaking Jews it was a celebration, a chance to return home to the old world, to the shtetl, to their roots.

Rebush's dream for a quality Yiddish picture had come true. He had proved that the Hollywood formula of quality adaptation of a classic could be brought to Jewish films. *Grine Felder* was a milestone. It had opened a Golden Age of Yiddish cinema in America. At a special screening of the picture in 1938, Peretz Hirschbein told the audience: "Twenty years ago, the play, 'Grine Felder,' was the beginning of a better Yiddish theater in America — Let's hope that the film, *Grine Felder*, is a beginning of better Yiddish cinema."[7] It was!

Martin Panzer of the *American Hebrew* in an article on Jewish movies related the impact the picture made on him:

> I had seen one or two Jewish movies before, and if the truth must be told, I was rather ashamed that they had been produced. It was my opinion that if it were not practical to produce a Jewish motion picture that would compare favorably with other types of films, it might be a good idea to let the whole matter go by default. Now at last, however I feasted on a film that a Jew might be proud of — one that he might urge his Christian friends to see without fearing any misunderstanding beyond that of language. The name of the picture was, of course, *Green Fields*.[8]

Der Zingendiker Shmid (The Singing Blacksmith) — 1938

Grine Felder was so successful that Roman Rebush's Collective Films Producers, Inc. set out immediately to make a second picture. Rebush chose to adapt another successful play that drew on the Eastern European Jewish experience, David Pinski's "Yankl der Shmid" (Yankl the Blacksmith).

"Yankl" is the story of a blacksmith who sees too many women and drinks too much liquor. However, after meeting Tamare, he promises to change his ways. Later despite a happy marriage and a child, he finds it difficult to "resist temptation." The story, set in a shtetl, deals with important issues like alcoholism and fidelity. Though these were not necessarily the most pressing questions in Jewish life, they were still pertinent issues. The film raised important social subjects, while still offering the film-goer a dreamlike withdrawal from American life.

Rebush tried to make the picture more attractive by choosing Moishe Oysher, a leading singer/actor on the Yiddish stage, known for his rich cantorial voice, to play the blacksmith. Born in Bessarabia, Oysher went to Canada in 1921. After performing in a number of Canadian troupes, he came to New York in 1928 and became the protegé of Boris Thomashefsky. Within a few years Moishe Oysher gained a reputation not only for his acting but for his voice. Like his father and grandfather, he became a cantor. Oysher led services in New York where he became known for his Hasidic interpretations of traditional prayers. Oysher's film debut came in 1936 with *Dem Khazns Zundl* (The Cantor's Son), fashioned after his life. After *Der Zingendiker Shmid* (The Singing Blacksmith), followed *Der Vilner Shtot Khazn* (The Vilna Cantor) in 1940. In 1956, shortly before his

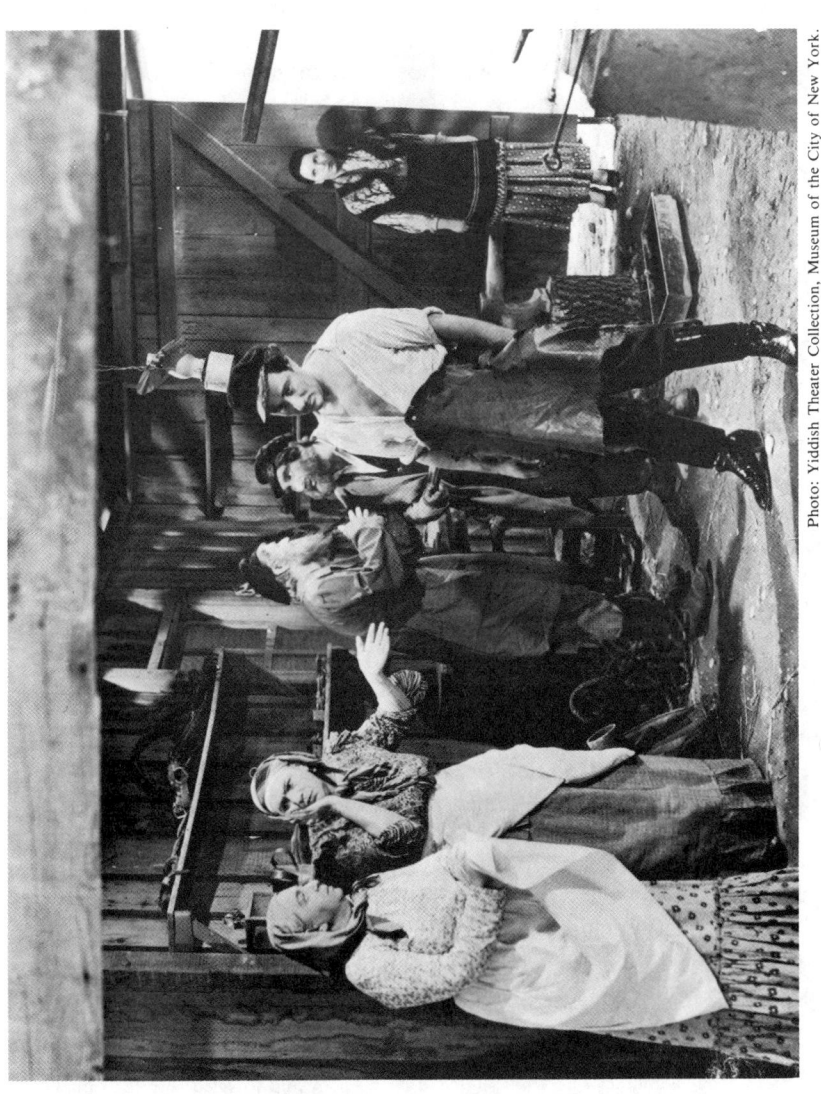

Melodrama often found its way into Yiddish pictures. Married Yankl (second from right) has been found cavorting with the "temptress" Rivke (right). Leah Noemi, Anna Appel, Max Vodnoy, Ruben Wendroff, Moishe Oysher, Florence Weiss in *Der Zingendiker Shmid* (The Singing Blacksmith) (1938).

Photo: Yiddish Theater Collection, Museum of the City of New York.

death, he made the English language film *Singing in the Dark,* directed by Max Nosseck. In supporting roles Rebush enlisted Miriam Riselle and Oysher's wife Florence Weiss, as well as fifteen-year-old Herschel Bernardi to play a young Oysher.

Rebush asked Yiddish writer/playwright Ossip Dymow to write the screenplay for the picture. Dymow, whose real name was Joseph Pearlman, began his career as a Russian language playwright, dealing with Jewish life and suffering. Only late in his life, following his arrival in America in 1913, did he begin to write in Yiddish. Dymow's work has a unique visual quality to it and it is not surprising that he would be approached to write screenplays. After "Yankl," Dymow adapted Jacob Gordin's "Mirele Efros". In 1940, he wrote a screenplay for "Der Vilner Shtot Khazn" (The Vilna Cantor), taken from a play by Mark Arnstein; Dymow had a cameo part in the film. Working with Dymow on the adaptation was Ben-Zvi Baratoff, a physician by training, who had earned a reputation as an exceptional actor; Baratoff played the part of Bendl in the picture. Playwright Pinski, in this, his first time writing for film, also collaborated with Dymow and Baratoff.

Ulmer, with the experience of directing a Yiddish picture under his belt, undertook to direct this picture alone. His experience working with Ben-Ami had been a difficult one and he sought free artistic control over *Der Zingendiker Shmid.* Ulmer who felt completely at ease with the camera and film technique, was, unfortunately, still not comfortable working with a cast with whom he could not fully communicate. As a result, actors were left to draw on their own talents with little direction. Baratoff, who was the elder on the set, did help wherever he could.

Ulmer realized that extensive use of outdoor shots was essential to making this a better picture. The story of *Der Zingendiker Shmid* is set in a shtetl, and Ulmer convinced Rebush that a reconstructed shtetl was a necessity of production. The budget for this picture was much less than that for *Grine Felder,* so certain luxuries like an electricity generator were not possible. What this did, in effect, was limit the placement of the makeshift shtetl to a location close to electric high lines where a "pig" connection could be made, enabling cheaper electricity. They found the perfect spot near Newton, New Jersey. Ulmer, in an interview with Peter Bogdanovich, recalled searching for the location:

> I finally made a contact with City Service in New Jersey and traveled with their plans along the high lines to find the place. My big staff consisted of two boys and four old Jews, in a station wagon we had bought for $110.... After driving for about half an hour, we came to a monastery [Shrine of the Little Flower] — so you can imagine how we felt! ... This was Friday, I was up to the main door in the building — the Jews kept sitting in the station wagon frightened....

> Of course, my Jews outside were dying! They saw me come out with this monk and get in his car.[9]

The monks were most cooperative and allowed Ulmer to film at the monastery. They even offered to let their bearded "brothers" serve as extras. Everything seemed perfect, except the location.

> We found out when we came back with the plans that next to this ground was Camp Ziegfried, the camp of the (Nazi) Bund. And on the left side was a nudist camp! So that nothing should happen to the sets as we built them, the academicians and their pupils stood at night with guns, so the Bund couldn't do anything to our construction.[10]

Quite the combination—Nudists, Bundists, and a Yiddish film crew and cast. The *New York Daily Mirror* found the story to be of great interest and dispatched photographers and reporters to the site. They even carried a full page human-interest story with color photographs, "There's freedom in 'them thar hills!"[11]

The film was released in November 1938 and was fairly well received by the Yiddish-speaking public. The film is almost completely carried by Oysher's voice, with each musical interlude another highlight of the film. Particularly delightful is a "dudele" that Oysher sings with Ms. Weiss, where a superb rapport is visible. The film is also complimented by the comical stammering of character actor Benjamin Fishbein.

Di Klyatshe (The Dobbin, also released as The Light Ahead) — 1939

After Rebush and Ulmer made *Der Zingendiker Shmid*, they went their separate ways; Rebush to make *Mirele Efros*, and Ulmer to direct another Ukrainian picture, *Zaporosh sa Dunayem* (Cossacks Across the River). Once production was completed on the Ukrainian film, Ulmer began making preparations for a third Yiddish picture. He was attracted to a stage adaptation of *Fishke der Krumer* (Fishke the Lame), written between 1869 and 1888 by the grandfather of modern Yiddish literature, Mendele Mokher Seforim.[12] The play was written by Chaver-Pahver, a journalist for the Yiddish newspaper, *Freiheit*, and author of several plays and children's books. Chaver-Pahver had entered the work in a 1938 contest for original Yiddish play writing and won first prize. Ulmer was enamored with the idea of making a film from a new and as yet unproduced play, and he approached Chaver-Pahver to adapt it for film. Chaver-Pahver already had film-writing experience, having worked with Joseph Green in 1938 on the screenplay of *Der Purimshpiler*. He, Ulmer and Ulmer's wife, Shirley, set about to readapt the play.

With each successive Yiddish film, Ulmer grew more comfortable with

Yiddish language and culture and the Eastern European setting of his stories. Each film focused on the bittersweet realities of life in the shtetl, the Eastern European hamlet where rich or poor, learned or ignorant, a Jew remained a Jew. It was no accident that in 1939, Ulmer was drawn to the story of *Fishke der Krumer* (Fishke the Lame). It is but another story of "Dos Klayne Mentshele", the little man, a figure which dominates Yiddish literature. This "anti-hero," with crippled body, is caught in a whirlwind of events beyond his control, much like the European Jew of that day, about to be trapped in Nazi Europe.

The Ulmers and Chaver-Pahver chose to call the film in Yiddish *Di Klyatshe* (The Dobbin), alluding to Mendele's 1873 allegorical satire of Jewry as the world's scapegoat; in English, the film was called *The Light Ahead*. In this work, the narrator looks out his window only to see a poor, undernourished Jew lashing out at a weakened emaciated horse unable to pull his heavy burden. The narrator perceives the dobbin turning to his master saying, "You fool, you too are a beast of burden serving a master, who abuses you and fills you with fear" So too is Fishke, a lame man who is ward of the community, abused. He is kept from marrying Hodl, a blind woman because of their extreme poverty and handicaps. Only when an epidemic strikes, do the rich, fearing a supernatural force, present the couple with wealth, enabling them to marry and achieve a better life.

Ulmer turned to twenty-year-old actor David Opatoshu to play the lead of Fishke. Opatoshu, the son of noted Yiddish writer Joseph Opatoshu, had some Yiddish stage experience but had never before acted in a film. Opatoshu won the role because in his own words, "I was scrawny, thin, emaciated; therefore, perfect for the part."[13] Helen Beverly, later married to actor Lee J. Cobb, played Hodl.

With the screenplay readied for production, Ulmer again enlisted the services of cameraman J. Burgi-Contner and leased his New Jersey studios. Actor Isidore Cashier who had played the father in *Grine Felder* was engaged to play Mendele, as well as supervise acting. Cashier took on the responsibility of staging the performance, much as Baratoff and Ben-Ami had done on the two previous Ulmer pictures. Ulmer knew his limitations. Although he knew some Yiddish by now (he understood but could not speak) he still felt uncomfortable with the language. Cashier was close to the literature and stage, so he could create the necessary nuance. This arrangement satisfied Ulmer. Actor David Opatoshu related his experience.

> Actually the man who directed it was Izzy Cashier — who staged my thing for him (Ulmer). He directed — he staged it actually. Filmically, Ulmer staged it, but the acting, Izzy did.
>
> The only way he [Ulmer] worked with actors from my point of view was to teach me the difference — because Izzy (Cashier) couldn't do it — between the theater performance and performance for film. I was playing for the second balcony. On the second day of

Photo: Herman Axelbank.

The lame Fishke and blind Hodel are well looked after by Mendele Mokher Seforim (right) in Edgar G. Ulmer's *Di Klyatshe* (The Dobbin) (1939), taken from stories written by Mendele. Helen Beverly, David Opatoshu, Isidore Cashier. The film was also released as *The Light Ahead*.

shooting, I felt as if I were encased in cement. I couldn't raise a hand; I couldn't do this because I'd move out of frame....

He (Ulmer) said, "Now come on slower." He was the one who told me, "Now, a camera lens is stronger than an X-Ray. You just flick your eyebrow [and] you say more than if you make four of your faces play to the second balcony."[14]

Visually, *The Light Ahead* is Ulmer's most interesting Yiddish picture. He contrasts light and darkness in much the way that he does natural with supernatural. The sets and most of the picture have an expressionist aura reminiscent of his earlier *Black Cat* (1934) which is not present in his other Yiddish films. He also seems to be freer in his use of cinematic punctuation with a variety of dolly shots that work nicely.

Shortly after *The Light Ahead* was released in 1939, all traces of the film disappeared. With the outbreak of the war, limited copies were made for showing in Europe. In New York, the film opened for short periods in neighborhood theaters, with the few prints of the film being circulated. The negative of the picture was destroyed a few years later in a fire at the warehouse where it had been stored. Unlike other Yiddish films, where prints of pictures found their way into the hands of private collectors and distributors, as early as 1950, no copy of *The Light Ahead* could be found.

Although the film was apparently lost, film collector Herman Axelbank, who had seen the film at its premiere showing in 1939 was sufficiently moved years later to have traveled five continents spending thousands of dollars to trace it. "This film is for me the essence of Jewish life and culture," Axelbank told me in 1976. "It was the first and only time that I was moved to tears watching a Jewish picture." Axelbank finally located the film in a suburb of Amsterdam. It is his print of the picture that I eventually saw in 1975.

In 1981, shortly after Axelbank's death, the National Center for Jewish Film, a film archive in Boston, in association with the American Jewish Historical Society acquired the picture from Axelbank's children. A restored print with new English sub-titles prepared by the Center was shown as part of a special retrospective at the 1982 New York Film Festival. Several months later, the film "opened" at a New York City theater.

Mirele Efros — 1939

As soon as work was completed on Roman Rebush's second picture, *Der Zingendiker Shmid*, he quickly selected Jacob Gordin's *Mirele Efros* and began developing it. Gordin's play already enjoyed widespread popularity as a staple of the Yiddish stage; it was a natural choice. Ossip Dymow who worked with Rebush on *Der Zingendiker Shmid* was engaged to adapt the play for the screen together with Josef Berne, a writer/director who was hired to direct the picture. Berne was co-writer and director of the 1933 independent film, *Dawn to Dawn*, and had just finished directing another independent ethnic film, *La Vida Bohemia*, a few months earlier. Berne knew cinema and film writing and Dymow knew the literature; they made a perfect combination.

Rebush cast Berta Gersten as Mirele, a self-sacrificing matriarch, a sort of "Jewish Queen Lear," who triumphs over rapacious son and daughter-in-law. Gersten knew the play well, having earlier played the part of the daughter-in-law, Sheyndl, on the stage. She succeeded a long line of Mireles, going back to tragediennes Kenni Liptzen, Jennie Goldstein, and Esther Rokhl Kaminska who appeared in the first filmed version made in Warsaw in 1912. Mirele was a role with which many mothers, Jewish and non-Jewish, could identify — that of a woman pushed aside when her usefulness no longer serves the purposes of her children.

Despite good acting and direction, *Mirele Efros* failed from a technical standpoint. The picture has an overabundance of extended long shots, faulty editing, and too few "cut-aways." In effect, the film is visually stifled. The entire picture was shot inside a studio with little change of scenery. In Rebush's previous two films, Ulmer had insisted on filming a great deal of the action outdoors; this greatly enhanced these pictures.

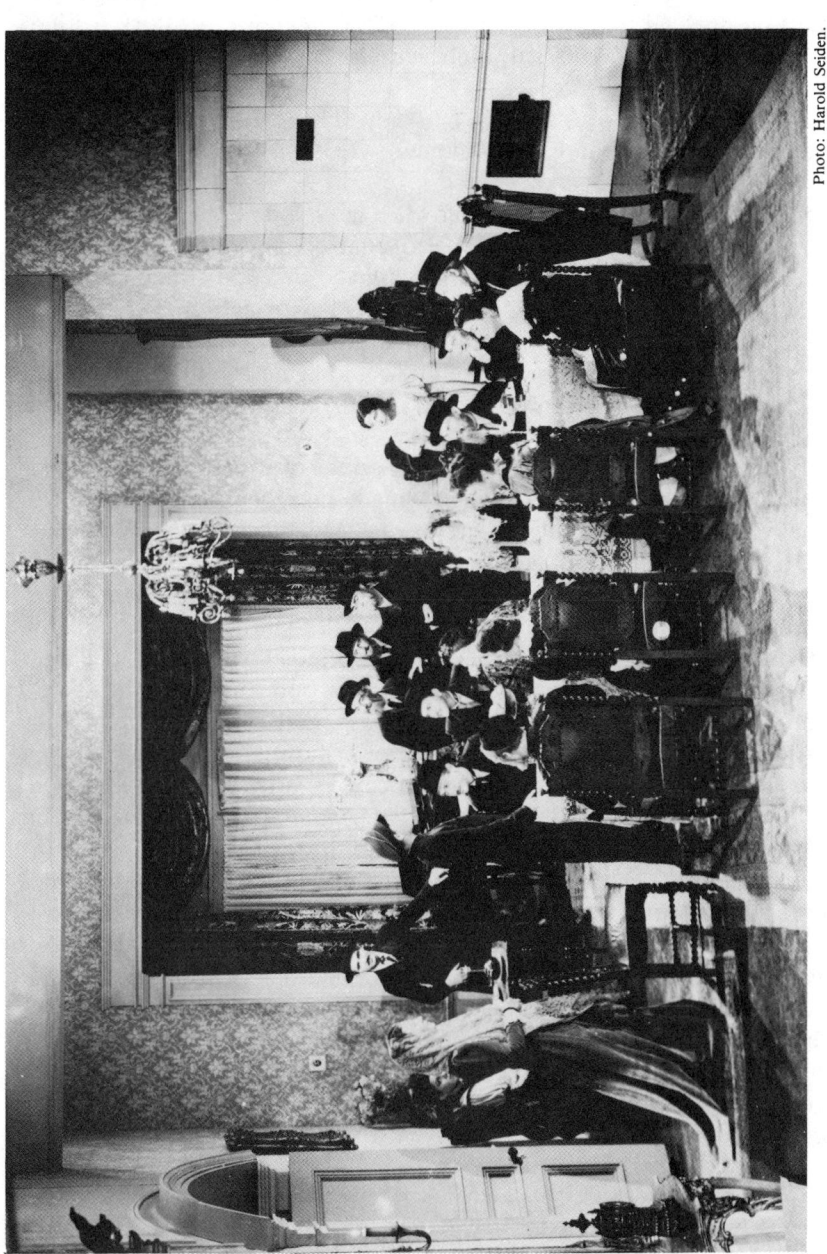

The climactic Bar Mitzvah scene in *Mirele Efros* (1939) when Mirele arrives to be with her grandson. Berta Gersten is Mirele.

Photo: Harold Seiden.

Here, no such choice was made and as a result, *Mirele Efros* is little more than a well directed recording of the stage play. A powerful story, with a great deal of emotion, it is still quite hard-hitting, never failing to draw some tears from its audience.

Tevye der Milkhiker (Tevye the Milkman) – 1939

Although scarred thirteen years earlier when he first directed film (the 1926 silent picture *Tsebrokhene Hertser* [Broken Hearts]), Maurice Schwartz believed that he was ready to mount a film production by himself. He knew stage direction and acting, but he had had extreme trouble in the earlier film translating his understanding of theater to the screen. He waited cautiously for the right moment when he could again try his hand at film direction. Schwartz put it off, as he said in a 1939 interview, until he could answer for what he did.[15]

In the summer of 1939, Schwartz, conscious of widespread interest in the classics and quality Yiddish cinema, made that long awaited return to filmmaking. Sholom Aleichem's "Tevye der Milkhiker (Tevye the Milkman)" had been one of his favorite stage roles and he had been anxious to film it. Schwartz had wanted Joseph Green to make *Tevye* in Poland three years earlier but Green was not ready. Green felt that there were too many anti-Clerical and anti-Church elements in the original play and he believed that Schwartz' adaptation did not break away from that enough. Undeterred, Schwartz secured the film rights to this and two other plays by Sholom Aleichem and undertook production on his own.[16]

Along with a group of friends, Maurice Schwartz set up the Maymon Film Company. They hoped that *Tevye der Milkhiker* would be the first in a series of films made by the new company; this never materialized. For location shooting, Schwartz chose the Underhill Farm just east of Jericho, Long Island. Schwartz felt that the topography of the region was almost identical to that of the countryside which Sholom Aleichem depicted. There, Schwartz attempted to recreate a Ukrainian shtetl. Using thatch and plaster, contractors converted the exterior of a wheat barn into a "church-like home" for the Greek Orthodox priest of the village and changed a cowshed into Tevye's simple dwelling; a wagon load of straw made the conversion complete. Thomas M. Pryor of the *New York Times* visited the location:

> Mr. Schwartz, who was born in the Ukraine fifty years ago and therefore can be quoted as an authority, claims the setting could pass for the real thing any day. It certainly seemed like something out of the Old West at that — what with the men folk masquerading behind luxurious growths of beards and the women garbed in picturesque costumes which went clear down to the ankles.[17]

Photo: YIVO Institute for Jewish Research.

Maurice Schwartz's dream was to adapt Sholom Aleichem's "Tevye" for the screen, just as he had done for the stage. Schwartz (1890–1960) brought his considerable theater talents as producer, director and actor to the Yiddish screen. He had plans for many more pictures, but the War broke out. Maurice Schwartz as Tevye teaching psalms to his grandson (Vicki Marcus), as his granddaughter (Betty Marcus) looks on in *Tevye Der Milkhiker* (Tevye the Milkman) (1939). Miriam Riselle (in lower left corner) plays Khave.

Maurice Schwartz' *Tevye Der Milkhiker* is adapted from Sholom Aleichem's "Tevye" stories written between 1895 and 1916. Set during the last decades of Czarist rule in Russia, attention is centered around Tevye, a man of warmth and piety, and his daughter Khave. Khave is in a constant state of inner struggle regarding her relationship to Fedye, her Gentile boyfriend, knowing full well the impact their union would have on her parents. She tells Fedye, "When I'm not with you I can't wait to see you, but when I see you I wish to run away." She is warned by Tevye that any bond between her and Fedye would be unacceptable; she responds by promising him that she plans no such thing. Despite this, Tevye learns that Khave has finally married Fedye and is left only one recourse — he declares her dead. This is portrayed in a moving scene in which Tevye rips his clothes (as a sign of mourning) and pulls out a small stool (used during the period of mourning) to sit on. The camera, in an extended sequence, focuses on Tevye's eyes in order to capture the ache that Tevye is experiencing. One of the two candles on the table bends over in a distorted way symbolically illustrating the lost daughter, while the other candle stands upright as the older daughter, Tsaytl, firmly holds her father's arm to support him in his loss. "Khave is no more," cries out Tevye. "She is dead." Later Tevye meets her on the road but he will not stop to listen to her. Her fate, as far as he is concerned, is sealed. Khave's intermarriage is depicted as a tragedy not only for the hero Tevye, but for the Jewish people at large.

Schwartz and his audience were troubled by the problem of intermarriage. To them, it posed the single greatest threat to the continuation of Jewish life. Intermarriage had become synonymous with a renunciation of Judaism, and Schwartz centered his 1939 film on Khave's story to emphasize the point that intermarriage is unacceptable to the Jewish community. In the film, Tevye tells a priest who intimates that Jewish children are joining the church through intermarriage, "I would rather see them perish than see them betray our faith." No such comment appears in the Sholom Aleichem original, and one can only wonder whether Schwartz is asking his audience to agree with it.

The actors for the film were chosen from Maurice Schwartz's Yiddish Art Theater. Schwartz also picked his niece, Miriam Riselle, who had played Tamare so well in *Der Zingendiker Shmid*, to be Khave. Leon Liebgold who had a lead role in *Yidl mitn Fidl* and *Der Dibuk* played Fedye. The filming began after six weeks of rehearsal on stage; it lasted twenty-two days. Exteriors were shot in Jericho and interiors were filmed at the Biograph studios in the Bronx.

Schwartz was not only behind the camera as director, he also played the leading role of Tevye. A great deal of energy was invested by Schwartz to see that the picture was not only theatrically perfect, but made with a high degree of technical quality. Schwartz told one interviewer:

> You can't hope to pass off a cheap, inferior picture, even if it's in Yiddish on audiences today.... Patrons of Yiddish films are just as particular about their entertainment as other audiences.[18]

Tevye der Milkhiker received good reviews in the press and did very well commercially. Schwartz had finally demonstrated that he could successfully work with film. Unfortunately, he never had another opportunity.

Two other feature-length film adaptations were made of Sholom Aleichem's "Tevye" stories. In 1968, Israeli producer Menachem Golan made the Hebrew language *Tuvya V'Shiva B'notav* (Tevye and his Seven Daughters), which he and Haim Hefer adapted. Three years later, Norman Jewison filmed Joseph Stein's Broadway success, *Fiddler on the Roof*. Aspects of the original "Tevye" stories are chosen and adapted to suit each audience. In the Israeli version, pursuit of economic wealth is the overriding theme; the Jewison film focuses on the generational differences in values. Interesting to contrast is the conclusion of each film. At the close of Schwartz's film, Khave deserts her Gentile family and returns to the comfort of her Jewish home. The Israeli, Golan, focusing on the Jewish calamity, shows a disgruntled Khave who, realizing that she has no place in a Gentile world, prepares to leave for Palestine (Israel). In *Fiddler*, Khave and her Gentile husband, choose to leave behind a community where bigotry is condoned; as they leave, Tevye mumbles under his breath his belated blessing, "Peace be with you," as if to finally accept their marriage. Whether seen by Greek, Italian, or Japanese audiences, Tevye symbolizes an ethical and moral human being who refuses to ignore his roots and traditions.

Amerikaner Shadkhn (American Matchmaker) — 1940

Edgar G. Ulmer made one more Yiddish film, a comedy, *Amerikaner Shadkhn* (American Matchmaker) in 1940. Hastily made and filmed completely in a studio, it was Ulmer's lowest-budget Yiddish film. With the world changing around him, Ulmer chose to make a "light" picture, a film set in modern times with a Yiddish flavor.

Unlike his previous three Yiddish films, this was not taken from a classic of Yiddish literature. As such, Ulmer felt that he could, with his wife Shirley's help, produce a simple, entertaining film for his new audience. Actor Leo Fuchs, who starred in the film recalled:

> It was a difficult task to perform — it was a light story. If one thinks about a play like "Green Fields" or "The Singing Blacksmith," most of the characters have more depth than the film we made, because they were of higher value.... We didn't think it was going to shake up the world; we just thought of it as pleasant, nice entertainment, which I suppose certain people wanted.[19]

Two other film adaptations of Sholom Aleichem's "Tevye" stories. Tevye (Shmuel Rodensky) is surrounded by his daughters in *Tuvya V'Shiva D'notav* (Tevye and his Seven Daughters) (1968). Below: Motl Kamzoyl asks Tevye for his daughter Tsaytl's hand in marriage Topol (right) is Tevye. With him is Leonard Frey and Rosalind Harris.

Photo: Cannon Films.

Photo: From the United Artists release "Fiddler on the Roof" © 1971 Mirisch Productions, Inc. and Carter Productions, Inc.

Photo: Harold Seiden.

Nat Silver (Leo Fuchs) becomes a matchmaker in order to bring happiness into the lives of others, for he has none. He interviews a potential client (Judith Abarbanel), whom he realizes, too late, is most suited for him in *Amerikaner Shadkhn* (American Matchmaker) (1940).

The story revolves around a wealthy man, unhappily married several times, who decides that if he cannot have happiness he can at least bring joy to the life of others by becoming a modern day "matchmaker." As if to tie this film with his others, Ulmer inserts a flashback of the uncle in the Old Country who also served as a matchmaker. *Amerikaner Shadkhn*, despite good performances by Fuchs and Judith Abarbanel, was not well received, either at the box office or by the critics. Ulmer then went on to make other ethnic pictures, a host of documentaries and, low budget feature films both here and in Europe. The legacy Ulmer leaves behind is not only over one-hundred films with a strong visual style and flavor all their own, but four Yiddish pictures that brought countless hours of enjoyment to an appreciative Yiddish-speaking audience.

Edgar G. Ulmer passed away in 1972. Yet, in film circles, he still remains at the center of controversy. Some refer to him as "father of the new wave," one who had a genius for producing low budget films in a number of languages all over the world. Others recognize him only as a man who drifted from Hollywood in the early 1930s churning out cheap

"B" movies the remainder of his life. Whichever way one views Ulmer, he stands out in film history as unique and special, a man who made films about Jews, Blacks, Hispanics, Italians, and Ukrainians; a man whose films transcended color, race, language, and place of origin.

Der Vilner Shtot Khazn (The Vilna Cantor, also released as Overture to Glory)

One last "elaborate" production, *Der Vilner Shtot Khazn* (The Vilna Cantor), was begun in 1939. Independent producers Ira Greene and Ludwig Landy wanted to lavish the Yiddish screen with opulence. They used elegant sets, expensive costumes, and a wide variety of scenes and settings on a level unprecendented in Yiddish cinema. As Greene told me, "We wanted faithful reproduction quality!"[20] The producers wanted to emulate a Hollywood picture.

Ossip Dymow undertook writing the story based on the life of Cantor Yoel David Strashunsky. "It was built up right from the ground from facts we found," Greene told me. Strashunsky, known as the "Vilner Balabesl" (the Vilna Petit-Bourgeois), left the Jewish community and his position as "Vilna Cantor," to become a well-known figure in Polish opera. Subsequently, separated from his home and family, he went crazy and died a broken man. Mark Arnstein had immortalized Strashunsky in his 1908 play "Der Vilner Balabesl."

Max Nosseck was hired to assist Dymow with the screenplay and direct the picture. Polish-born Nosseck, whose real name was Alexander Norris, began his film career in Germany. With the rise to power of the Nazis, he worked as both actor and director in a number of countries, including France, Portugal and Spain. Once the screenplay was ready, Yiddish writer Jacob Glatstein was called in to develop the Yiddish dialogue. Alexander Olshanetsky was engaged to write original music and cameraman Larry Williams who had just completed shooting *Tevye* came on as director of photography.

Moishe Oysher was kept in mind from the very start for the lead role. His rich cantorial voice and his previous work in *Dem Khazns Zundl* (1936) and *Der Zinderdiker Shmid* (1938) assured him of the part, and his work in the film turns out to be his finest. The screenwriters took care to write sufficient musical material into the film in order to provide Oysher with singing opportunities. Although Oysher's operatic numbers are well presented, his most evocative moment is the concluding scene when he sings the traditional "Kol Nidre." Arriving "home" at the synagogue on the eve of the Day of Atonement, Oysher's Strashunsky, an emotionally and physically worn being, takes his place at the altar. The Kol Nidre service is a time when it is declared lawful to pray together with those who trans-

Photo: Ira Greene.

Moishe Oysher's magnificent voice can be heard in three Yiddish pictures. Oysher (1907–1958) brought a new musical vitality to Yiddish pictures. The range of his voice is well displayed in *Der Vilner Shtot Khazn* (The Vilna Cantor) (1940), as he easily moves from liturgical music to opera. Oysher with Helen Beverly. The picture was also released as *Overture to Glory*.

gressed. Strashunsky, dressed in black, drapes himself in the white prayer shawl, the tallit, and begins to recite "Kol Nidre" as his personal confession and bid for absolution. Once the beleaguered Strashunsky completes the prayer, he collapses. "For them you sang, for us you prayed," says one congregant. The message to the film viewer is clear: If you bid for success in the "outside" world, should that be what you want, do not forsake your family, your people and your traditions. The moment is matched only by Al Jolson in *The Jazz Singer* (1927) in its vitality and pathos.

Before the picture was even completed, Poland was invaded by Nazi Germany, and a war which would forever disfigure world Jewry was unleashed. With the potential viewing market cut by more than half, promotional funds dried up, and the picture was released with little hoopla. The picture did receive favorable critical reviews but was a financial failure. It has been shown only infrequently during the past forty years.

In 1939, plans were being made for yet another dozen pictures, but growing tensions in Europe and the invasion of Poland by Nazi Germany put an end to that. With Poland at war, a potential commercial market of over three million Yiddish-speaking viewers was closed to American Yiddish filmmakers. In addition, a growing number of assimilated young American Jews were leaving behind their "Yiddish" roots, thus reducing Yiddish film audiences even more. Both these factors, together with a general tightening of money made it unfeasible to produce lavish "large budget" Yiddish pictures. With little money, the classics simply could not be made. Yiddish filmmakers were again forced to produce quickly-made "low cost" pictures. Only these pictures showed any promise of bringing back a profit to the producer.

The Golden Age of Yiddish Cinema would quickly come to an end. True, there would be other Yiddish pictures, but that same high standard toward which filmmakers had aspired would never again be realized. That first Nazi stormtrooper's boot on Polish territory as well as a changing American society were responsible.

Postscript: The Seiden "B" Pictures, 1939-1941

In early 1939, Joseph Seiden decided to put his full energy into making Yiddish pictures. He not only produced and assisted with camerawork as he had done on previous pictures, but he took over direction. Others had failed to capitalize on the "Grade B" Yiddish pictures, so Seiden claimed the territory for himself. The American Yiddish film market was being flooded with so many classics, both domestically produced or from Poland, that Seiden felt that there was still demand for simple melodrama. He reasoned that one of his low-budget "tear-jerkers" dealing with an aspect of contemporary life in America would easily make back its investment. High-budgeted pictures might cater to a larger public, but they also required larger expenditures which might not be recouped.

Seiden had only limited resources. For each film he made, he had to depend on "advance" money. Harold Seiden told how his father made his pictures.

> He would be shooting about four to eight weeks before the holidays and just get the picture finished for the opening. He used to run down to the Clinton theatre [on the Lower East Side] on a Friday to collect money from them as an "advance" against the picture to pay the crew. He worked with no money. He would make enough to start another picture.... It was a hand to mouth existence.[21]

Seiden's first problem was to find a studio where he would have freedom to shoot when he wanted. He rented a loft in Fort Lee, New Jersey, and began making production plans for his first picture, *Der Lebediker Yosem* (The Living Orphan).[22] Working with cameraman J. Burgi-Contner who had shot Ulmer's *Grine Felder* and *Der Zingendiker Shmid*, Seiden hurried to have the picture ready for Passover. He identified Passover and the Jewish New Year as the best dates to exhibit his pictures. *Der Lebediker Yosem* is about a husband and wife, both of whom are actors. The woman's motherly instincts are overshadowed by her desire to achieve fame, and she deserts their child at a time of severe illness. The father takes the child away never to return.

Seiden liked tearful melodrama, plots that involved separation of families and heartache, but he always gave his audience what they wanted at the end, a happy ending. In *Kol Nidre* (1939) a woman about to end her life is reunited with her family as the solemn "Kol Nidre" is chanted, beginning the Day of Atonement. Parents are mistreated by their offspring in *Eli Eli* (My God, My God), but providence brings the family back together. In *Motl Der Operator* (Motel the [Sewing Machine] Operator), a tragedy separates a father and his son; they are reunited when the son unknowingly defends his father in court. In *Ir Tsveyte Mame* (Her Second Mother), a girl and her father are brought together.

Seiden also made two comedies in 1940–1941. *Der Groyser Eytse Geber* (The Great Advisor) is about three friends who attempt to better their lot through luck or marriage and *Der Yidishe Nigun* (The Jewish Melody) is a musical-comedy about teenagers promised to each other who find other mates.

In 1941, Seiden released his last prewar film, *Mazl Tov Yidn* (Mazel Tov, Jews). It is a compilation picture, using film clips from various Seiden short and feature films. Seiden could not afford to produce anything more elaborate. Raw materials and equipment were scarce, money was short and

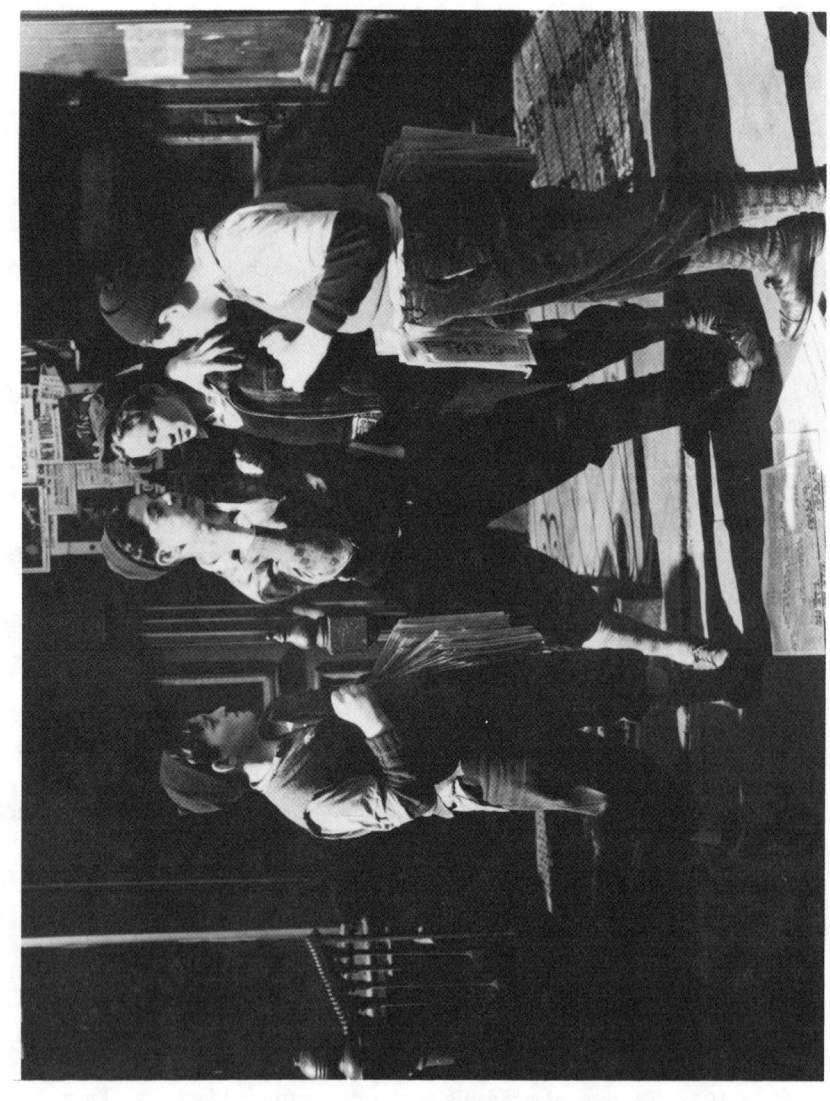

Der Lebediker Yosem (The Living Orphan) (1939). In his later films, director Joseph Seiden tried to tackle difficult issues and bring realism to the Yiddish screen.

Photo: Yiddish Theater Collection, Museum of the City of New York.

Seymour Rechtzeit and Esta Salzman in *Ir Tsveyte Mame* (Her Second Mother) (1940).

Photo: Harold Seiden.

Photo: Harold Seiden.

Michael Rosenberg and Yetta Zwerling in *Mazl Tov Yidn* (Mazel Tov, Jews) (1941).

a war was taking place in Europe that would soon involve America. Shortly afterward, with the bombing of Pearl Harbor, Seiden became involved in wartime production. He did not return to Yiddish filmmaking until the end of the decade.

It is difficult for me, over forty years later, to attempt an evaluation of Seiden's pictures. His films cannot in any way compare with other work produced with higher budgets and greater artistic input both in the United States and Poland, work that was part of the "Golden Age of Yiddish Cinema." But Seiden's sheer perseverance deserves our attention, as he somehow managed to turn out one picture after another. His actors were professionals; surely, with better direction, camerawork, sets and greater opportunity to reshoot scenes, they would have given better performances.

On location. Filming *Eli Eli* (My God, My God) (1940). Joseph Seiden (center, with white shirt and tie) is directing actors Esther Field and Lazar Freed.

Photo: Harold Seiden.

Joseph Seiden (1892–1974) was involved in Yiddish filmmaking in America from 1930 until his death. His passion for Yiddish pictures, not only producing them, but collecting and distributing them has left us with a legacy. Below: Seiden (second from left) directs Chaim Tauber (at sewing machine) in *Motl der Operator* (Motel the [Sewing Machine] Operator) (1939). Opposite page: The scene as the audience saw it.

Photo: Harold Seiden.

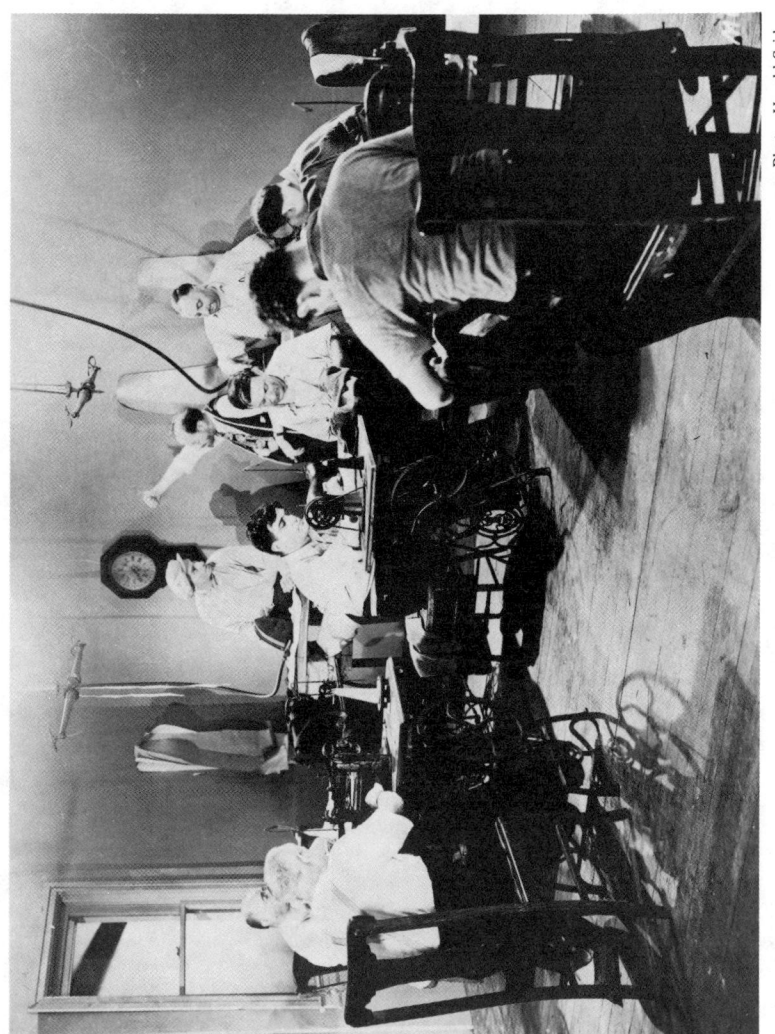
Photo: Harold Seiden.

The cast and crew of *Der Yidishe Nigun* (The Yiddish Melody) (1940). In the center (with top hat and beard) is Isidore Cashier. To his right is Rose Greenfield, Esta Salzman, Yetta Zwerling. On the other side is Chaim Tauber, Lazar Freed, Jacob Zanger, Mae Schoenfeld. Far left is Dave Lubritsky. Far right is Mrs. Seiden. Behind her is Moishe Feder.

Photo: Harold Seiden.

Joseph Seiden could not produce under those circumstances, and given the limited resources he had at hand, he did his best.

Seiden was not an easy man to work with or work for. He pinched every corner, fought for every dollar. He was disliked and respected at the same time. Actors were ashamed of the work that they did for him while at the same time acknowledging that were it not for him there would not have been work. When others quit, Seiden kept on going. He was there at the beginning and he was there at the end. For this, he deserves credit, and an important place in Yiddish film history.

7

After the War: Limited Success, 1946–1950

Germany and Western Europe: The Displaced Person

With the end of World War II in Europe, the task of resettlement of those displaced during the struggle began. Many of these displaced persons were permitted to go home; some returned to their houses only to find them occupied or completely destroyed. Others found it inconceivable to go back to towns or villages that had become burial grounds for their families. Without a home, they were left only with a desire to leave behind the Europe that had tried to annihilate them. These refugees, many of them survivors of Nazi concentration camps, found their way toward "collecting stations" in the American zone of Germany. There, within a year, over 250,000 Jews were gathered together into Displaced Persons Camps, their fate left in limbo.

While the world debated their future, the displaced persons wasted little time in organizing themselves. With the assistance of the American Joint Distribution Committee and the United States military government they organized political, educational and cultural committees to take charge of various aspects of internal camp life. They set up schools, people's universities, newspapers, and drama groups. They also made pleas to the Allied leaders to allow them to make their way to Palestine, which because of Britain's Middle East policies had been cut off to them.

Israel Becker was one of the refugees stranded in Germany, unable to reach a place he could call home. In early 1947, he developed a scenario touching on his life experiences during and after the war. Scenario in hand, Becker approached "Yafo,"[1] the Yiddish Film Organization, a film group created in 1946 with funding from the American Joint Distribution Committee. Yafo's only previous film work had been the dubbing into Yiddish and Hebrew of *Death Factories* (in Yiddish it was called *Toytmiln*[2]), a documentary film about the Nazi concentration camps made by the American Army.³ The organization was most excited with the idea of making a narrative from Becker's story about tragedy during and following the Holocaust. They approached the Information Control Division of the American military, who had worked with them on *Death Factories* for advice and possible funding.

The American government at this time had been strongly committed to the resettlement of displaced Jews in Palestine. Through the Harrison report and the report of the Anglo-American Committee of Inquiry in 1946, an endorsement for the transfer of refugees to Palestine was made; this unfortunately was not implemented by the British. Becker hoped to show in his film not only the atrocities perpetrated by the Nazis but the depressing consequences. Some aspects of pre- and post-Holocaust life were already portrayed in such films as Fred Zinnemann's *The Search* (1947) and Aleksander Ford's 1947 *Border Street* (Ulica Graniczna),⁴ but Becker wished to go beyond what those films had presented by making a plea for the admission of displaced Jews into Palestine.

Yafo received the military endorsement they sought, and with funding from a financial backer,⁵ production was readied at the Munich studios of the Information Control Division. Yiddish actors from the MYKT (Munich Yiddish Art Theatre) were engaged to play lead roles. Berta Litwina who was in Zygmund Turkow/Henryk Szaro's *Tkies Kaf* (1937) and Joseph Green's *Der Purimshpiler* (1937), played the mother and Becker played the son. In addition, German actress Bettina Moissi was hired to play a German Jewish survivor of the camps who speaks German rather than Yiddish.⁶ Other non-professional actors and displaced persons played minor roles. German director H. B. Fredersdorf began the direction of the picture with the assistance of Marek Goldstein. After some difficulties with the cast, Becker himself completed the picture.

Becker's story *Lang Iz Der Veg* (Long is the Road) begins before the War in Warsaw, when the Jelin family witnesses German occupation, restrictions on Jews and ghettoization. Intercut with sequences of life in the troubled city is newsreel footage of the Nazi invasion. When the "transport order" comes, young David Jelin manages to escape from a freight car which leads the rest of his family to Auschwitz. Here, the filmmakers take special care to emphasize that falling into the hands of Polish peasants was no better than being caught by the Germans; young Jelin witnesses this as countrymen take out sticks to beat a Jewish runaway. David avoids the Poles, joins a partisan group and spends the rest of the war fighting the Nazis.

Up to this point, the picture has served to recount the Holocaust in clear narrative form intercut with newsreel footage. There is also occasional metaphor, as with an elderly man reciting the "shma" prayer, an

Lang Iz der Veg (Long Is the Road) (1947) was drawn from events in writer/actor Israel Becker's life, during and after the Holocaust. David Jelin in hiding with his parents. From left to right: Israel Becker, Berta Litwina, Jacob Fischer. Below: Jelin's meeting with his mother after years of separation. L to r: Bettina Moissi, Otto Wernicke, Israel Becker, Berta Litwina.

Photo: David Matis.

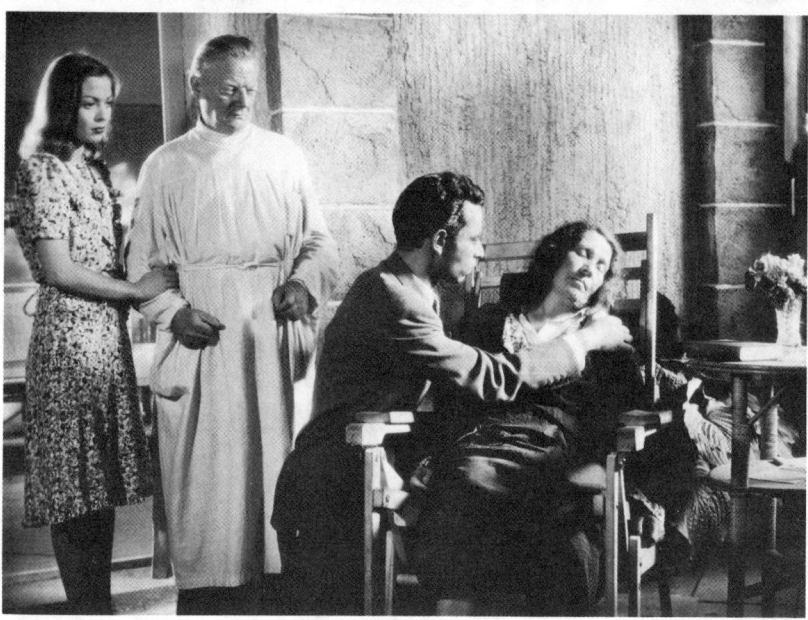

Photo: Israel Becker.

affirmation of faith, juxtaposed against chimney smoke from a crematorium. In the latter part of the picture, Becker, the filmmaker, makes a strong political statement about the futility of refugee life. As if surviving the atrocities of the Holocaust were not enough for these displaced persons, they now had to endure being the "shuttlecock" of humanity.

Lang Iz Der Veg is important because it is an expression of those who survived the horrors of the War, much like Wanda Jakabowska's *The Last Stage* (1947) or Ford's *Border Street* (1947). It is also of interest because its use of documentary-style footage intercut with narrative material set into place a style for the Holocaust film genre. This was developed further by Alfred Radok the following year in his Czech film *Distant Journey*.[7]

Lang Iz Der Veg was criticized at the time of its release as a propaganda film that focuses only on the lives of Jewish DP's.[8] However, the film makes no claim of doing anything else. It is no mistake that Yiddish is chosen as the prominent language—this is a picture about Jews made by Jews. Despite criticism, the film has been used in cinema halls and classrooms alike as an aid for study of the period.[9] The picture meant to show how the Jew suffered and that the future of the Jewish people rested only with a Jewish homeland.[10]

"Yafo" made only two short fund-raising pictures in 1947 and then disbanded. The following year a French documentary-style narrative, *We Live Again*, about children made homeless and orphaned by Nazism was produced. Using a combination of newsreels, actual footage shot of the children receiving aid by the relief agencies, and a few reenacted sequences made by the Central Committee for Child Welfare of the Union of Jews for Resistance and Mutual Aid in France, it was modeled on Aleksander Ford's 1935 *Mir Kumen On*.

Poland

Despite anti-Jewish outrages and scattered incidents in Poland, some Jews found this country whose language they spoke and whose landscape they knew, far more appealing than the Displaced Persons Camp. True, the temporary government, the Polish Committee of National Liberation was under Soviet domination, but the Committee seemed most eager to assist Jews in returning to their homes. There was tremendous hope on the part of many Jews that they could reestablish a center for Jewish life and culture in Poland.

The Polish Committee encouraged the establishment of Jewish self-government, a Central Committee of Polish Jews, as well as many other prewar cultural and religious organizations. To support welfare and reconstruction activities, Jewish organizations from abroad, particularly the

World Jewish Congress and American Joint Distribution Committee, poured in foreign currency, clothing, medical supplies and food.[11] With this assistance and an official position on the part of government supporting Jewish national activity, cultural life flourished. About twenty Jewish periodicals published in Hebrew, Yiddish, and Polish surfaced.[12] Jewish programmes were broadcast over the radio, and Yiddish theater prospered, particularly in Lodz and Wroclaw.

German occupation was so swift at the beginning of the war that the Polish army was effectively defeated on its own soil. Only outside of Poland, in the Soviet Union, could the army regroup. There, in Moscow, the Kosciusko Division was mobilized, and within it was created a film unit. The unit was organized to a great extent through the efforts of Polish documentary filmmakers Jerzy Bossak and Aleksander Ford, and composed in large part of members of the prewar Polish avant-garde film group "Start." The Polish Army film unit photographed and recorded the division's campaigns and by 1944 had grown into a complete production team. As the Soviets and armies-in-exile pushed westward across Poland, captured German film equipment was turned over to the unit, so that by 1945 with the liberation of Warsaw, the unit had a sizable production arsenal.

The Nazis had left the Polish film industry in a state of disarray. With Warsaw leveled, Lodz was chosen as the temporary film center of postwar Poland. To accommodate the new industry, factories were converted, a gymnasium and athletic field were requisitioned for a studio, and equipment was inventoried.[13] With a nationalized Army Film Unit serving as a nucleus, "Film Polski" was organized and Aleksander Ford was placed in charge.

Shaul Goskind and Kinor

In 1946, producer Shaul Goskind returned from refuge in the Soviet Union with hopes of continuing his work in filmmaking. His Sektor studios had been destroyed during the War and there was no immediate hope of reestablishing them under the socialist regime. With the help of Ford, whom he had known well in Warsaw, Goskind got a position as a film library administrator for Film Polski. However, Goskind was not content, and despite an offer by Ford to make him a production department head, Goskind left Film Polski. Still interested in making Jewish films, Goskind chose to set up a film department for the Central Committee of Polish Jews.[14] With Ford's blessing and letter of recommendation, he proceeded to successfully convince the Joint Distribution Committee to fund his operation.

Shaul Goskind had exceptional talents in organizing people, keeping abreast of institutions and in preparing operational groups. This innate perception and imagination always pushed him toward action before words.... It's possible to debate the efficacy of this system, but the fact remains that due to this, Goskind succeeded in filming historic and extremely valuable material.[15]

Goskind persuaded cameramen Adolf and Vladislaw Forbert, sons of Leo Forbert, to assist him in the filming of important Jewish events and activities. The first of these activities was the presentation to Israel's Chief Rabbi Herzog of Torah scrolls found in the ruins of the Warsaw Ghetto. The "El Mole Rakhmim," the traditional memorial prayer chanted on that occasion by the late great cantor David Koussevitsky, became the prologue for Goskind's first postwar documentary feature.

By the end of 1947, Goskind's film unit molded itself into a cooperative called Kinor (Hebrew for harp).[16] The group was entitled to full use of Film Polski facilities and equipment. Members of the group included Goskind, producer Joseph Juszynski, sculptor Natan Rapaport, Adolf Forbert, and Natan Gross. Gross, who had served as an assistant director with Film Polski, was hired as film director. Their first effort, *Mir Lebn Geblibene* (We the Living Remnant), was to document Jewish life in Poland after the war. The film begins with Koussevitsky's prayer and glimpses of Jewish life as it had been before the war. The narrator then tells the story, in "album" format, of resettlement and the cultural, political and religious activity that characterizes postwar Polish Jewry. With music prepared by Saul Brezhuwski and script by Ephraim Kaganovsky, the picture was released with Yiddish narration read by actor Jacob Rotboym.

After completion of work on *Mir Lebn Geblibene,* the group energetically set out to make a number of Yiddish documentary short subjects. Kinor produced the following documentary short films in 1947–48: *Der Yidisher Yishuv in Nider-Slezie* (The Jewish Community in Lower Silesia), *Der Veg Tsum Gezunt* (The Way Toward Health), *Der Finfter Yortsayt fun Oyfshtand in Varshever Geto* (The Fifth Anniversary of the Warsaw Ghetto Revolt), *Der Finfter Yortsayt fun Oyfshtand in Bialistoker Geto* (The Fifth Anniversary of the Bialystok Ghetto Revolt) and a newsreel, *Der Yidisher Yishuv in Poylin* (Jewish Life in Poland).

By summer of 1948, with the creation of the State of Israel, conditions got worse; the new regime began introducing restrictions on Jewish communal life. Ford who had made the Polish film *Ulica Graniczna* (Border Street) about the Warsaw Ghetto Revolt was denounced by Stalin himself for having used a "Jewish instead of a class hero."[17] Ford was also criticized for giving too much credit to the Jews for their part in the Ghetto

Extensive use of non-professional child actors was made in *Unzere Kinder* (Our Children) (1948). Children (most of them survivors of the Holocaust) of the Halnowek Orphans' Home listen to performances by comics Dzigan and Schumacher. The film was produced by Shaul Goskind and directed by Natan Gross.

Photo: Natan Gross.

uprising.[18] As government criticism grew, the Kinor group found it increasingly harder to cover Jewish events, especially those linked with Israel.

"Unzere Kinder" (Our Children) — 1948

The famous comedians Dzigan and Schumacher returned to Poland in 1948. They had joined the Polish army-in-exile in 1942 but were later denounced and shipped off to Soviet labor camps. After being released in 1946, they were again arrested for anti-Soviet activities but were finally able to secure their release and repatriation to Poland. Goskind, learning of their arrival in Poland, launched plans for a picture featuring the two humorists. Goskind had worked well with the two in the prewar years on both *Al Khet* and *Freylekhe Kabtsonim* and deeply wanted to make another film with them. A comedy aloof from reality seemed an improper choice, so they seized on the idea of bringing together the present with the immediate past, the Holocaust. This was to be done through a series of skits, stories and flashbacks. Director Natan Gross recalled the scriptwriting sessions for the new film *Unzere Kinder* (Our Children):

> We sat then, in a resort town in Lower Silesia — Dzigan, Schumacher, and author Rokhl Auerbach, Goskind and I — and we composed the framework for an actual story, keeping in mind the potential of using the Halnowek orphanage for its structure, landscape and occupants.[19]

Dzigan and Schumacher played themselves — traveling comics, who came to perform at the Halnowek children's home and spend the evening listening to the orphans' experiences during the Holocaust. Despite the horrors that were, the childrens' lives continue. The film evolves as a fine narrative, based in part on fact, with non-professional child actors playing themselves.

By mid-1949, any activity not within the framework of communism was outlawed in Poland. The communist coalition in the Central Committee of Polish Jews assumed power of the organization and quickly cut itself off from contact with the World Zionist Congress. With this break with organized World Jewry came an end to the funding of many cultural activities; this included Kinor which had been funded by the American Joint Distribution Committee.

Filming on *Unzere Kinder* was barely finished when the "Joint" was forced to leave Poland and production money disappeared. Goskind, with his dream of an active Yiddish filmmaking cooperative shattered, a large debt on his hands for production of *Unzere Kinder,* and a seeming inability to complete the picture, left for Israel. Gross, Dzigan and Schumacher among others, followed. According to Goskind, the picture's costs were finally covered and the footage was shipped through diplomatic channels to Israel where post-production work took place.[20] The film premiered at the Eden Theatre in Tel Aviv in 1951, with seemingly little interest shown.

With the changes in Polish policy in 1948-1949, the hope for the rejuvenation of Jewish art and culture had been quashed. "Jewish" filmmaking, both in Polish as done by Aleksander Ford with *Border Street,* and in Yiddish came to an abrupt end. Two decades later with pronounced anti-Semitism and an attempted exclusion of Jews from the film industry, it became even worse; this resulted in the emigration of directors like Ford and scholar/teachers like Jerzy Toeplitz. The hope that was shared by a handful of pioneers blossomed for too short a time. Although Yiddish theater in Poland somehow survived, it too was to undergo severe changes. The new goals of the Polish government clearly curtailed Jewish cultural expression.

With the turn of the decade, the Yiddish film form terminated as a creative Jewish means of expression in Europe. (It would be used again in Poland only as a means for recording Yiddish theater.) Many of the artists who had been so much a part of it made their way to Israel, where Hebrew, the language of the land, had become the only acceptable means of cinematic exposition. There, the future of the Yiddish film form looked bleak.

The United States

Joseph Seiden became involved in the production of collapsible masts for rafts during the war, and it was not until 1949 that he again turned his attention to Yiddish filmmaking. With the European market all but closed, the lack of interest, even contempt for Yiddish pictures in Israel, and a new generation of non-Yiddish speakers, the commercial producers who were so enamored with the Yiddish cinema only a few years before dropped out of sight. Seiden's commitment, however, did not waver and in June, 1949, he set about making preparations for his biggest project ever, the filming of Jacob Gordin's *Got, Mentsh un Tayvl* (God, Man and Devil). The play is about the transformation of a traditional Jew into a man of station whose greed destroys everything around him. A reworking of *Faust,* the Devil has overpowered the poor man, causing him to divorce his wife, effect a murder, and bring about his own ruin.

Seiden brought together many of the talents performing on the Yiddish stage at that time: Michel Michalesko, Max Bozyk, Gustav Berger, Berta Gersten who played Mirele in *Mirele Efros* (1939), and Lucy Gehrman who starred in *A Brivele der Mamen* (1938). Each actor had played on stage *Got, Mentsh un Tayvl* many times before. Seiden was paying "exorbitant" salaries of $500 to Gersten and Michalesko and $300

Joseph Seiden attempted to continue, after the War, making films based on Yiddish classics. His first (and last) adaptation was Jacob Gordin's *Got, Mentsh un Tayvl* (God, Man and Devil) (1949). Michal Michalesco (left) with Leon Schechter.

Photo: Harold Seiden.

to Gehrman and Berger; all this for about ten days work. In addition, he hired composer/conductor Sholom Secunda and a seven piece band for $1,000. Seiden really meant to continue the tradition of "Yiddish classics" filmmaking begun twelve years before; he hoped that the professionalism of his cast would accomplish this. However, even though the roles were familiar to the stars, the direction was again lacking. The film, produced in Seiden's West Side New York studios, remains stagebound and only a mere recording of a potentially dramatic picture. Its editing is primitive, with scenes shot in one take and from one angle and broken up only by an occasional cut-away.

Seiden did not wait to see what kind of response *Got, Mentsh un Tayvl* received in theatres. Relentless as he was, he was making preparations for another picture, Abraham Blum's *Dray Tekhter* (Three Daughters) by November. Seiden contracted Michael Rosenberg to play the same role that he played ten years earlier on the stage. Charlotte Goldstein and Max Wilner, Maurice Schwartz's former partner at the Yiddish Art Theater were also engaged; Sholom Secunda took charge of music. *Dray Tekhter* is about three daughters and the various joys and sorrows of childhood. The film was made in a little over a week; Seiden's son, Harold, a professional, did camerawork.

Before post-production on *Dray Tekhter* was completed, *Got, Mentsh un Tayvl* opened to an extremely poor reception at theaters. Seiden, who had always worked on a small, tight budget, was overwhelmed at the failure of his first "big name" production. There seemed to be no longer an interest in Yiddish culture. That same year, 1950, Maurice Schwartz's Yiddish Art Theater closed its doors after thirty-two years of continuous operation. With such frightening realities, Seiden spent little effort or money to prepare the release of *Dray Tekhter*, though he had originally seen it as a "smash" follow-up to *Got, Mentsh un Tayvl.*

Meanwhile, producer Martin Cohen along with actor/composer Hymie Jacobson, who had appeared in *Der Purimshpiler* (1937), came up with the idea of filming a musical revue. They modeled the picture after a television variety show. The picture, *Catskill Honeymoon,* presents the story of a couple celebrating their fiftieth wedding anniversary in the Catskill Mountains. The two enjoy being entertained by ten different acts from comedy routines done by Henrietta Jacobson and Julius Adler to the singing of Bas Sheva or Jan Bart. The picture was directed by Josef Berne, who made *Mirele Efros* (1939); music was written by Jacobson and Alexander Olshanetsky. *Catskill Honeymoon* became an immediate success on the elderly and rehabilitation home circuit.[21] This seemed to be the only audience left for Yiddish pictures.

Seiden watched the "success" of *Catskill Honeymoon* carefully from

Joseph Seiden's last dramatic Yiddish picture and the last Yiddish narrative for a quarter of a century was *Dray Tekhter* (Three Daughters) (1949). On the left is Gertrude Bullman. On the right is Charlotte Goldstein.

Photo: Harold Seiden.

Martin Cohen's Yiddish "variety film" was an attempt to combine a series of theater acts into a film. Julius Adler and Henrietta Jacobson on stage in *Catskill Honeymoon* (1950).

Photo: Yiddish Theater Collection, Museum of the City of New York.

the sidelines. He engaged Michael Rosenberg in September of 1950 to introduce a series of film clips from old Seiden pictures. Seiden used footage he owned of actors like Menashe Skulnick, Leo Fuchs, Michel Michalesko, Max Wilner and Joseph Buloff, and was able to put together a picture at practically no cost. Originally titled *Borsht Belt Follies,* Seiden released the picture as *Monticello, Here We Come.* He exhibited the picture along with a short film, *Singers of Israel* which he made that year of Cantor Samuel Melavsky and his family choir. Seiden soon realized that "borsht belt" musical revues aimed at the elderly Jewish audience could not sustain Yiddish cinema.

The year 1950 witnessed the demise of Yiddish cinema. There were a number of factors that brought this about, from television to high production costs, but most important, the Yiddish-speaking audience was all but gone. What government immigration restrictions had not destroyed in potential audience, the extermination of nearly six million Yiddish-speaking Jews did. No longer could a producer think of sinking twenty, fifty, or a hundred thousand dollars into a Yiddish picture with any hope of meeting costs, let alone bringing in a profit. Seiden tried, but even he, who had witnessed the beginnings of the Yiddish sound film in 1929 and managed to churn out pictures year after year, was unable to succeed.

Epilogue: A Rebirth of Interest, 1974—

The year 1950 marked the end of an era. That Maurice Schwartz's Yiddish Art Theater was to close its doors that year, while Joseph Seiden and his contemporaries were making their last Yiddish picture seems more than coincidence. Indeed, American Jews were beginning to view themselves differently—how they lived, where they lived, what professions they chose, and how they entertained themselves. Having largely recovered from the trauma of the Holocaust, American Jews, both native and foreign born, were finding it easy and comfortable to be just as "American" as their Gentile neighbors. A Yiddish picture, with its language and plot tied to an Eastern Europe of a bygone era, was of little interest. The Holocaust had shattered the illusion of comfort and peace in the "Old Country." American Jews, now more than ever, wanted American culture.

With little interest or potential for Yiddish film production, many of the stars of Yiddish pictures found a place for themselves in American performing arts. Herschel Bernardi, David Opatoshu and Molly Picon succeeded in handling a variety of roles on the stage and screen. Moishe Oysher made a few English language pictures before his untimely death in 1958; others, like Leo Fuchs and Michael Gorin (Goldstein) played character roles on television.

While directors like Edgar G. Ulmer continued to make a variety of pictures in Europe and America, Joseph Seiden turned his attention to the distribution of Yiddish films. Seiden tried to rerelease his pictures to commercial movie theaters wherever possible. He also made 16mm prints for use in schools, community centers and homes for the aged. Though he did not produce any new pictures, he was able to scratch out a meager income from his rental business. Seiden managed to enlarge his film collection by acquiring rights to many of the still extant Yiddish pictures made in America and Poland.

Over the years, the Seiden prints began to deteriorate. Many of the 35mm original nitrate negatives crumbled to powder in their original cans.

158   A Rebirth of Interest

Other films simply fell apart from overuse or were lost in the mails; sometimes there were no negatives for these prints. Seiden's son Harold relates that on one occasion, the only known existing print of a Yiddish picture was left behind in a coffee shop.[1]

Still, it was Seiden's persistence and business acumen that brought together so many of the Yiddish pictures which otherwise would have been scattered in attics and basements across the world, possibly never again to be found. For over twenty years, he distributed the films from his West Side New York home. When Seiden passed away in the early seventies, he left behind a collection of over thirty-three Yiddish pictures.

Several stories appeared in the press during the fifties and sixties about projected films in Yiddish. In 1964, film director Jules Dassin announced that he had acquired film rights to Andre Schwarz-Bart's *Last of the Just* and that he planned to make the picture in Yiddish. The Parisian Yiddish newspaper, *Naye Prese*, quoted Dassin as saying "the reality of the people and the experiences can be evoked only in Yiddish."[2] Later, *Jewish Daily Forward* reported that United Artists had finally "acceded to the director's demand that the original film be made in Yiddish."[3] Despite the publicity, The *Last of the Just* was never made.

It was not until 1974, when Josh Waletzky, a bright and talented film student at New York University, made *Dos Mazl* (Luck) that Yiddish was again used as the language for a narrative film. Waletzky made this 20-minute film, based on a folk-tale, with non-professional actors, the staff and campers of Camp Boyberik; sound was added in post-production. The picture has been shown to Yiddish groups across North America. Waletzky, subsequently made *Image Before My Eyes* (1981), a cinematic account of Polish Jewry between the World Wars. He is presently preparing a film about Jewish resistance in the Lodz ghetto during World War II.

Preservation of Yiddish pictures

In 1973, the Institute for Jewish Life funded a media project that would serve the media-related needs of the North American Jewish community. That same year the associate director of the Media Project, Stuart Fox, developed a proposal for "rescuing" Yiddish films. It was his contention, quite correctly, that the Seiden collection was deteriorating and unless something was done quickly, the rich heritage of Yiddish cinema would be lost to future generations. Attempts were made to elicit funds from a variety of national Jewish organizations in order to purchase the collection from Seiden's estate. Finally in 1976, the Jewish Media Service,[4] in association with the American Jewish Historical Society made an arrangement with Harold Seiden for the transfer of the films; the Rutenberg and Everett

Photo: David Matis/Josh Waletzky.

The first Yiddish film in nearly a quarter of a century was a student film, *Dos Mazl* (Luck) (1974), made by Josh Waletzky. Lila Glogowsky and Matthew Speier.

Yiddish Film Library was established. The Film Library now part of the National Center for Jewish Film, along with the American Film Institute and Library of Congress, has begun the difficult task of rehabilitating and preserving its collection of Yiddish films; to date, over ten pictures have been preserved.

In 1976, the YIVO Institute for Jewish Research began a project to preserve and rehabilitate pictures made in Eastern Europe. I was most fortunate to have been personally involved in this historic period. In the fall of 1976, I was asked to become the curator of film at YIVO. As curator, I was to oversee preservation and rehabilitation work as well as create new avenues for the exhibition of Yiddish film. My first task was to work on preserving one of Joseph Green's four pictures made in Poland between 1936 and 1938, *Mamele* (1938).

Most of the Yiddish motion pictures made before World War II were produced using a highly flammable nitrate film stock. This film stock allowed for the best possible resolution and contrast in black and white film. However, with time, nitrate film begins to disintegrate into powder with almost the same combustibility as gun powder. The person preserving a film must be able to transfer it to a more stable acetate film stock before it is beyond the point where it can be copied. At the same time, great care must be taken as the motion picture is dangerously flammable. I will never forget the experience of driving from New Jersey to New York City, across the George Washington Bridge with the only known existing print (on nitrate stock) of Edgar G. Ulmer's *Amerikaner Shadkhn* (1940). I had visions of a newspaper headlines reading "young researcher perishes with last copy of Yiddish film. Explosion closes bridge down."

Joseph Green's *Mamele* was in fair condition, but the original negative was lost in Poland during the war, and we had to work from 35mm nitrate prints. Assisting me with technical matters was a volunteer veteran filmmaker, Elwood Siegal, and we began our work by transferring 35mm negative film to non-flammable "safety" acetate. The work was timed and retimed until we achieved the desired results. We then began work on the soundtrack which was in desperate need of all the filtering and cleaning up that modern technology could afford. After transferring the sound, we went to a "sound mix" and finished with a fairly clear soundtrack. The picture completed, we deposited the negative and prints for safekeeping and preservation in special vaults of the YIVO Institute archive; rehabilitated prints were made available for release.

While the rehabilitation work on *Mamele* was being undertaken, a meeting was held in mid-February 1977 at YIVO, of representatives of six New York based Jewish organizations for the planning of a New York Yiddish Film Festival. At that meeting and subsequent meetings a plan was formulated for the exhibition over the next year of nine Yiddish pictures in three different New York locations. There was some concern that the program might not work. Yiddish films had continued over the years to be shown, usually under poor conditions, at various locations in New York City. The attendance was fair and the audience was almost entirely made up of senior citizens. Still, we felt that there was a potential interest, and if programmed properly the films would have an audience.

The New York Yiddish Film Festival proved to be a major success, far beyond anyone's hopes. It was repeated in 1978–1979 and 1979–1980 at New York's 92nd Street Y, with audiences from all age groups. Generated by the success of this program, similar Yiddish film festivals have been undertaken across North America and most recently in France, Italy and West Germany.

In the spring of 1978, we began work on the restoration of Joseph Green's *Der Purimshpiler*. Again, we were forced to work with nitrate positive prints, and when we first brought the two copies of the film to the laboratory, we were given only a 50–50 chance for success. The film was in much worse condition than the previous picture, covered with dirt and oil. The laboratory could only remove the dirt; the oil remained. Since we were working with original prints, we feared that extensive cleaning might cause damage to our picture; because it was highly combustible, not everyone would undertake such work. Fortunately, almost miraculously, we found someone who handled the special work, and the laboratory quickly transferred the picture to acetate, providing us with an "answer print."

Once we had a clear answer print, we could begin our work with the sound. When we first listened to the soundtrack, we discovered that somehow during the twenty years the picture lay inactive, it had been re-edited from several existing prints, each one recorded with a different sound system. At this point, the picture had to physically be taken apart, with the sound re-recorded on a standard track. This work was time consuming and costly, but soon a new soundtrack was prepared, re-recorded and mixed. There were also other problems, like shrunken footage, poor sprocket gauging and white sub-titles that could not be read when the background was light; each of these problems was eventually remedied. *Der Purimshpiler* was re-released in March 1979, as part of the Second New York Yiddish Film Festival. Later, Green's other two films were rehabilitated.

Restoration and preservation of Yiddish pictures has continued. In October 1976, a newly rehabilitated print of *Grine Felder* was released by the Rutenberg and Everett Yiddish Film Library of the American Jewish Historical Society in conjunction with the American Film Institute; in December of that year, a new print of *Tevye* was exhibited. Most recently, Edgar G. Ulmer's *Di Klyatshe* (The Dobbin), a.k.a. *The Light Ahead*[5] was shown at the 1982 New York Film Festival as part of a special retrospective. It immediately drew a sell-out crowd.

Yiddish film has drawn a new audience. As American Jewry begins a rediscovery of its Jewish heritage, more and more young Jews are drawn to this film form. The general cinema audience has turned its attention to this creation of an ethnic minority, as one of the more interesting examples of independent cinema. Interest in Europe has also grown, as Yiddish films have been shown on both German and Scandinavian television. Other countries are now exploring innovative approaches to showcasing Yiddish cinema.

New Production, 1980 –

Yiddish has been used in a number of feature films since 1950, but Joan Micklin Silver was the first to film entire sequences in Yiddish in her 1975 film, *Hester Street*. Yet, it was not until 1980, thirty years after Seiden's

Photo: David Matis.

Samy Szlingerbaum's autobiographical *Dakh-Brisel* (Shelter-Brussels/Brussels-Transit) (1980) recounts displacement and homelessness in post-Holocaust Europe. The picture was made in Belgium.

last picture, that a feature-length narrative picture in Yiddish was to again be produced.

Brussels-Transit (also called *Dakh-Brisel* [Shelter-Brussels]) was made by Belgian filmmaker Samy Szlingerbaum who felt the only way he could relate his family's search for refuge was through his mother-tongue, Yiddish. Indeed, his own mother narrates in Yiddish this autobiographical story of how the Szlingerbaum family leaving Poland, makes its way across Europe in 1947 in search of a new home. The story is recounted through a mixture of drama and stark documentary technique. First, there is the uncertainty of travel and what lies ahead. Then we witness the sometimes funny, sometimes painful encounter of these foreigners with a Brussels unknown to them, watching them learn to cope and adapt to their new environment. This film is filled with dark, sometimes surrealistic images, contrasted with the realism of Yiddish language. It is a most fascinating study of postwar European Jewry in search of a new identity. The film was premiered in North America in the fall of 1981 at the Museum of Modern Art in New York as part of the "New Directors, New Films" series. *Brus-*

Photo: David Matis/David Greenwald.

The gypsy well holds a clue for the future in David Greenwald's short film, *Der Brunem* (The Well) (1983). Jeff Nishbal and Helen Perle.

sels-Transit drew positive critical attention, but with the exception of its inclusion in a few film festivals, was never released commercially in America. Whether a market for new Yiddish pictures existed was still unclear.

In 1981, David Greenwald, 24, set out, as had Josh Waletzky seven years earlier, to make a Yiddish film as his master's thesis at New York University. *Der Brunem* (The Well), written by Greenwald, is the story of a Jewish lad who leaves prewar Czechoslovakia for the promise of New York's garment district. At the center of this half-hour film is a Gypsy's tale which Greenwald heard from his parents, that when a local well would run dry, disaster would strike both Jews and Gypsies. The film, released in 1983, is a well-made study in folklore and acculturation.

During the summer of 1982, Jack Garfein, artistic director of New York's Harold Clurman Theater, exhibited a film recording of the E.R. Kaminska Jewish State Theater of Poland's stage production of *Der Dibuk* (The Dybbuk). The cinema recording was originally intended for showing

Photo: Roll Films.

Only fifty years earlier, Yiddish language was banned from Israeli movie houses. But Israeli producers Yair Prudelsky and Israel Ringel sensed a new interest in Yiddish and made *Az Men Git, Nemt Men* (When They Give, Take) (1983), with Yacob Bodo. They drink "Lekhaim—To Life."

on Polish television, a plan never executed after the implementation of martial law in Poland. A similar recording of the Jewish State Theater's rendition of "Mirele Efros" was apparently made in 1973; it has never been shown in the United States. *Der Dibuk* should be seen only as a fine film record in color of the troupe's production; no attempt was made to do anything but film a performance off the stage. As a film, it is slow and boring; as an historic record it is precious. How apropos that this film recording of the E.R. Kaminska theater should be shown exactly seventy years after Esther Rokhl Kaminska herself first appeared before a camera for the film recording of *Mirele Efros*.

In 1983, Israeli producers Israel Ringel and Yair Prudelski chose to adapt their special brand of comic "Borekes" (doughy pastry which contains a "hodge-podge" of ingredients) cinema that appeals to Israeli Jews of oriental origins, for the Eastern European Yiddish-speaking audience. Yiddish as a language was almost completely foreign to Israeli cinema and this effort represented the first Yiddish film to be produced in Israel. The story was meant to draw on the tradition of Yiddish musical comedy, much like the successful Hebrew-language *Kuni Leml* films previously produced by the two.[1] The film, *Az Men Git, Nemt Men* (When They Give, Take) is about a young woman tourist from Brooklyn who falls in love with the "voice" of a singer. Subsequently, a meeting is arranged between the two by a marchmaker and disguise and mistaken identity provide the plot. Plans for release of the picture in America were being made as this book was going to press.

At one point there seemed little future for Yiddish cinema. Yiddish pictures were made for a Yiddish-speaking audience. It seemed that as that audience dwindled in size, it would become less possible or practical to produce Yiddish pictures. Yet, between 1980 and 1983, four Yiddish pictures were produced and two more are in the process of being developed.[2] Five Yiddish film classics, Joseph Green's four films and Ulmer's *Di Klyatshe* were re-released in North American movie theaters, drawing large crowds. A revival seems very much to be in the making.

No one can predict a future for Yiddish cinema. What does seem clear is that in the 1980s this film form has a present. More films are being restored and re-released, others are being produced and interest is stronger than ever. Watching Yiddish pictures can never be just regarded as a phenomenon of the past. Yiddish cinema remains a rich visual record of the culture and lifestyle of a people. Its visions, images and dreams are recaptured every time a Yiddish word is heard on the screen.

Notes

Chapter 1

1. Self-sufficient Jewish market town.
2. The terror arm of the anti-Semitic and pro-monarchy Union of Russian People, organized for the rape and murder of thousands of Jews.
3. *Moving Picture World* 7 (20 August 1910), p. 409.
4. Jay Leyda, *Kino: A History of the Russian and Soviet Film* (New York: MacMillan, 1973), p. 49.
5. *Moving Picture World* 10 (27 September 1913), p. 1424.
6. *Moving Picture World* 10 (13 October 1913), p. 272.
7. Other titles for the film were *Black 107* and *Accused by Darkest Russia*. Films based on the same story followed. The next year the German-made *The Mystery of the Mendel Beilis Trial* was released. Later, there was *The Beilis Case* made in Kiev in 1917. Most recently, John Frankenheimer's *The Fixer* (1968) based on the Bernard Malamud novel tackled the subject.
8. Nahma Sandrow, *Vagabond Stars: A World History of Yiddish Theater* (New York: Harper and Row, 1977), p. 212.
9. Author's interview with Ida Kaminska, Tel Aviv, August 1977.
10. David Matis, "Tsu Der Geshikhte fun Yidishe Films [Toward A History of Yiddish Cinema]," *Ikuf-Almanak* (1961), p. 446.
11. Venyamin Vishnevsky, *Fictional Films of Pre-Revolutionary Russia* (Moscow: Goskinoizdat, 1945), no. 261.
12. Ibid., no. 263.
13. Ibid., no. 1899.

Chapter 2

1. Author's interview with Molly Picon, New York City, August 1977.
2. Author's interview with Seweryn Steinwurcel, Lod, Israel, August 1977.

3. Zygmund Turkow, *Di Ibergerisene Tkufe: Fragmentn Fun Mayn Lebn* [The Discontinuous Period: Fragments from My Life] (Buenos Aires: Central Farband, 1961), p. 92.

4. Ibid., p. 93.

5. Andrzej Wlast, "Dziesiata muza," as quoted in Wladyslaw Banaszkiewics and Witold Witezak, *Historia Filmu Polskiego,* vol. 1 (Warsaw: Wydawnictwa Artystyczne i Filmowe, 1966), p. 175.

6. Ibid.

7. J. M. Neuman, "Plan-Virtshaft in Der Yidisher Film Produksie" [Scheduled for Yiddish Film Production], *Literarishe Bleter* 6 (717), 3 February 1938, p. 91.

8. Turkow, *Di Ibergerisene Tkufe.*

9. Wlast, "Dziesiata muza."

10. Steinwurcel, interview.

11. Jerzy Toeplitz, *Historia Sztuki Filmovcz,* vol. 2 (Warsaw: Filmowa Agencja Wydawnicza, 1956), p. 358.

12. "Opatoshu's *Poylishe Velder* on Film: A Talk with Jonas Turkow," *Literarishe Bleter* 39, 28 September 1928, p. 771.

13. Author's interview with Jonas Turkow, Bat Yam, Israel, August 1977.

14. Jonas Turkow, "Opatoshu in Film," *Literarishe Bleter,* 7 (302), 14 February 1930, p. 136.

15. Ibid.

16. David Denk, *Shvarts Oyf Vays* [Schwartz (Black) on White] (New York: Greenwich Printing, 1963), p. 108.

17. Ibid., p. 123.

18. Mordaunt Hall, "Broken Hearts," *New York Times,* 3 March 1926, p. 26.

Chapter 3

1. B. Chemerinski, "How We Made Sholom Aleichem's *'Mabul'* for film," *Literarishe Bleter* 104, 30 April 1926, p. 286.

2. Raikin Ben-Ari, *Habima,* trans. A. H. Gross and I. Soref (New York: Thomas Yoseleff, 1957), p. 144.

3. Alexander Granovsky, Letter to Mendel Elkin, January 29, 1925, as quoted in Faina Burko, "The Soviet Yiddish Theatre in the Twenties" (Ph.D. dissertation, Southern Illinois University at Carbondale, 1978), p. 80.

4. It seems that Granovsky had originally planned to make the film in the winter of 1926 after the troupe returned from their world tour, but as the trip was postponed, *Yidishe Glikn* was made a year earlier. Needless to say, Habima production of *Der Mabul* spurred Granovsky on. Granovsky also had plans to make a second Jewish film on a "grandiose" scale, but this never materialized. (Granovsky, Letter to Elkin, 19 September 1924, as quoted in Burko).

5. In Yiddish, it also means "Jewish Happiness" and "Jewish Livelihood."
6. G. Riklin, "Menakhem Mendl" *Kino* (Moscow), 36 (1925).
7. S. Deytshedtan, "About Yiddish Films (A Letter to the Editor)" *Der Emes* (Moscow) 63, 15 March 1928, p. 5.
8. Leyda, *Kino,* p. 230.
9. Isaac Babel, *Benya Krik, A Film Novel,* trans. Ivor Montagu and S. S. Nolbandov (London: Collet's 1935).
10. Y. Lubomirsky, "Theater and Film—*Blondzhende Shtern*," *Der Emes* (Moscow) 43, 19 February 1928, p. 4.
11. M. Makotinski, "Through Tears," *Kino* (Kiev) 3/39 (1928), pp. 8-9.
12. Itzik Fefer, "Through Tears, *Kino* (Kiev) 3/39 (1928), p. 3.
13. Itzik Fefer, "Vegn Yidishn Film" [About Yiddish Film], trans. Moishe Rosenfeld, *Kino* (Kiev) 3/39 (1928), p. 2.
14. Author's interview with Grigori Roshal, Moscow, August 1977.

Chapter 4

1. Author's interview with Samuel Kelemer, Los Angeles, November 1978.
2. Harry Potamkin, "Movie: New York Notes," *Close-Up* 6, no. 2 (February 1930), p. 96.
3. "Jewish Films in Own Tongue," *Variety,* 22 January 1930.
4. Morris Freedman, "Contemporary of William Fox Still Making Yiddish Pictures," *New York Herald-Tribune,* 14 November 1948.
5. "A Yiddish Talkie," *Jewish Outlet,* 17 April 1930.
6. "Theater, Movies, Music," *Der Tog,* 18 June 1930.
7. "Yiddish Actors' Union Condemns Yiddish 'Talkies,' " *Tsayt* (London, England), 30 June 1930.
8. "Yiddish Film Starts Rioting in Palestine," *The World,* 26 September 1930.
9. "Compromise Settles Fight over Showing of Initial Yiddish Talkie in Tel Aviv," *Jewish Daily Bulletin,* 30 September 1930.
10. Author's interview with Zvee Scooler, New York City, May 1978, and with Judith Abarbanel, Miami, March 1978.
11. Joseph Greenberg (who changed his name to Green) later marketed this picture in Poland. Soon after, he began making Yiddish pictures.
12. Joseph Buloff was one of a cast of eight who did the narration/framework for the picture.
13. Zygmund Turkow, *Di Ibergerisene Tkufe:* p. 97.
14. Ibid.
15. Wolfe Kaufman, "Shir Hashirim," *Variety,* 23 October 1935.

16. "A People That Shall Not Die," *New York Post*, 1 September 1939.
17. "Movie-maker Joe Seiden Keeps 3 Room Studio Humming," *Brooklyn Daily Eagle*, 7 April 1936.
18. Author's interview with Harold Seiden, New York City, July 1978.
19. "Cantor's Son Dramatizes Life of Star," *New York Post*, 8 January 1938.

Chapter 5

1. Most notable among these films were Julien Duvivier's *David Golder* (1930 – France) and *Le Golem* (1935 – Czechoslovakia); Lothar Mendes' *Jew Suss* and Maurice Elvey's *The Wandering Jew*, both made in Great Britain in 1934.
2. Cholent is a hodgepodge of beans, flanken, and potatoes cooked over twelve hours and traditionally eaten at Sabbath lunch.
3. M. Kitai, *Literarishe Bleter* 19 (626), 8 May 1936, p. 305.
4. Luba Kantorowica-Gilinski, "The Film 'Mir Kumen On' " *Medem Sanatarium Book* (in Yiddish), (Tel Aviv: Menorah Press, 1971), p. 177.
5. Author's interview with Joseph Green, New York City, April 1977.
6. "The New Yiddish Film *Yidl mitn Fidl*," *Literarishe Bleter* 39 (646), 25 September 1936, p. 625.
7. Molly Picon, "Fiddling in Old Kazmierz," *New York Times*, 17 January 1937, 10, p. 5.
8. B. Filmikus, "The Landscape of *Der Dibuk*," *Literarishe Bleter* 29 (688), 16 July 1937, p. 469.
9. B. Tsavion, "From Newspapers and Journals," *Literarishe Bleter* 13 (724), 25 March 1938, p. 229.
10. Parker Tyler, *Classics of the Foreign Film*. (New York: Citadel, 1962), p. 120.
11. "Dr. Goebbels at the Cinema: Excerpts from Diaries," *Sight and Sound*, 19 August 1950, p. 237.
12. "In a Green-Film Shtetl," *Literarishe Bleter* 33 (692), 13 August 1937, p. 533.
13. "A New Yiddish Film: A Talk with Director Aleksander Marten," *Literarishe Bleter* 46/47 (757/8), 16 December, 1938, p. 752.

Chapter 6

1. Robert Sklar, *Movie-Made America* (New York: Random House, 1975), p. 175.
2. Films like *David Copperfield, Anna Karenina, Mutiny on the Bounty, Tale of Two Cities* (all 1935), and *Romeo and Juliet* (1936).
3. Martin Panzer, "Jewish Movies Come of Age; An Interview with Roman Rebush," *The American Hebrew* (New York), 17 November 1939, p. 6.
4. Jacob Fishman, B. Levin, and B. Stabinowitz, *Finf Un Tsvantsik Yor Folksbine* [Twenty-Five Years Folksbienne] (New York: privately published, 1940), p. 95.
5. Author's interview with Jacob Ben-Ami, New York City, March 1975.

6. Author's interview with Herschel Bernardi, California, March 1975.
7. David Matis, "Tsu Der Geshikhte fun Yidishe Films," p. 460.
8. Panzer, "Jewish Movies Come of Age."
9. Peter Bogdanovich, "An Interview: Edgar G. Ulmer," *Film Culture* 58-59-60 (1974), pp. 215-16.
10. Ibid., p. 216.
11. "Freedom in the Newton Hills for Jewish and Ukrainian Actors, Monks, Nudists and Nazis," *New York Daily Mirror,* 18 September 1938.
12. Mendele Mokher Seforim (Mendele the Bookseller), whose real name was S. J. Abramowitz, is known as the "grandfather" of Yiddish literature. He penned his first version of *Fishke der Krumer* in 1869 and *Di Kliatshe* in 1873.
13. Author's interview with David Opatoshu, Long Island, March 1975.
14. Ibid.
15. Thomas Pryor, "Outside of Jericho," *New York Times*, 30 July 1939, 9, p. 3.
16. Schwartz secured film rights to "Tevye der Milkhiker," "200,000" and "Shver Tsu Zayn A Yid" [Hard to Be A Jew] from Mrs. Olga Rabinowitz, widow of Sholom Aleichem.
17. Pryor, "Outside of Jericho."
18. Ibid.
19. Author's interview with Leo Fuchs, Los Angeles, March 1975.
20. Author's interview with Ira Greene, New York City, July 1978.
21. Harold Seiden.
22. Original title was *My Son.*

Chapter 7

1. Acronym for Yidishe Film Organisatsie.
2. Yiddish text by poet David Wolfe and narrated by Yiddish actress Rita Karpinowitz.
3. Norbert Horowitz, "Yidishe Teater fun der Sheyres-Hapleyte" [Yiddish Theatre of the Refugee Remnant], *Fun Noentn Ovar* (1955), pp. 167-68.
4. Also released as *That Others May Live.* The film is about the Warsaw Ghetto uprising in 1943.
5. This, according to accounts, was a Mr. Weinstein.
6. Most of the assimilated Jewish community of Germany spoke German rather than Yiddish, so it was easy to adapt Ms. Moissi into the picture.
7. Originally titled *Ghetto Terezin.*
8. *The New York Times* (12 November 1948) pointing out that it "ignored the majority of DP's in focusing its cameras exclusively on Jews." Joe Pihodna of the *New York Herald Tribune* (12 November 1948) cites it as a "propaganda film (that)...makes a plea to the British to open Israel to the Jewish D.P.'s in Europe."

9. One Austrian periodical, *Illustrierter Film-Kurier* (No. 579, January-February 1949) delves into the various ways that teachers may exploit the film in teaching the Holocaust.

10. Dulio Coletti's Italian language *Il Grido Della Terra* (The Earth Cries Out), made in 1947, picks up where *Lang Iz Der Veg* leaves off—with the illegal immigration into Palestine.

11. Lucjan Dobroszycki, "Post-War Jewish Life in Poland," *Soviet Jewish Affairs* 3, No. 2 (1973), p. 65.

12. Ibid.

13. Christina and Eugene Cenkalski, "Polish Film Builds for the Future," *Hollywood Quarterly* 3/3 (April 1947):295.

14. Natan Gross, "HaSeret HaYehudi B'Polin Acharei Milchemet HaOlam HaShniya" [The Jewish Film in Poland after World War II] *Kolnoa* 2 (May 1974):64.

15. Ibid., p. 65.

16. This brings to mind his Yiddish film group of the late thirties Kinor (or Kino-Or) which was spelled differently in Hebrew and meant "Cinema-Light."

17. Gene Moskowitz, "The Uneasy East," *Sight and Sound* 27/3 (Winter 1957/58):137.

18. Ibid.

19. Gross, p. 70.

20. Goskind.

21. Admiral Records was also enamored with the project. They bought the sound rights for $5,000 and released a record.

Epilogue

1. To date, three *Kuni Leml* films have been made: *Shnai Kuni Leml* (Two Kuni Leml/The Flying Matchmaker) (1970); *Kuni Leml B'Tel Aviv* (Kuni Leml in Tel Aviv) (1977); *Kuni Leml B'Kahir* (Kuni Leml in Cairo) (1983).

2. Two films which explore the Yiddish cinema are in production. One, *Raisins and Almonds* is being coordinated by Russ Karel at Brook Productions in London. A second is being produced for West German television. There is also a group in "pre-production" in Israel.

Filmography

Key to Abbreviations
sc: scenario/screenplay
nar: narrator
adapt: adaptation
cam: cameraman/director of photography
hist adv: historical advisor
art: artistic advisor
dial: dialogue
lit adv: literary advisor
mus: music
ed: editor
prod: producer
dir: director

1911 *A Brivele der Mamen* (A Letter to Mother)
Russia
with sound, refilmed in 1912
cast: Smolensky and Jewish troupe

Di Shtifmuter (The Stepmother)
Polish title: *Macocha*
Sila, Warsaw
cam: Stanislaw Sebel
dir: Andrzej Marek

Lekhaim (To Life)
Pathe Freres, 1230 ft., Moscow,
sc: Alexander Arkatov, from story by Georges Meyer (Mundviller)
cam: Georges Meyer (Mundviller)

       design: Cheslav Sabinsky
       dir: Maurice Maitre, Kai Hansen
       cast: N. Reizen (Rokhele), Nikolai Vasiliev (Moyshe), L. Sychova (mother), Mikhail Doronin (Shlema Matets)

Der Vilder Foter (The Harsh Father)
Polish title: *Okrutny Ojciec*
Sila, 4100 ft., Warsaw
- sc: from Jacob Gordin drama
- cam: Stanislaw Sebel
- prod: M. Towbin
- dir: Andrzej Marek
- cast: Zina Goldstein, Herman Sieracki

1912

Der Yeshive-Bokher (The Yeshiva Student)
Mintus Company, Riga
- sc: based on play by I. Zolatarefsky
- cam: A. Slavinsky
- dir: A. Slavinsky

Di Farshtoysene (The Forgotten)
Polish title: *Wydziedziczeni*
Sila, 3 acts, 3300 ft., Warsaw
- sc: from a play by E. Weissman
- cam: Stanislaw Sebel
- dir: Avrom Yitskhok Kaminsky

Dos Pintele Yid (The Essential Spark of Jewishness)
Mintus Company, 3937 ft., Riga
- sc: from work by Thomashefsky and Zeifert
- cam: A. Slavinsky
- dir: A. Slavinsky
- cast: traveling troupe of Jewish players

Got Fun Nekome (God of Vengeance)
Russian title: *Bog Mesti*
Pathe Freres, 2740 ft., Moscow
- sc: Alexander Arkatov, from Sholom Asch play
- cam: Georges Meyer (Mundviller)
- design: Cheslav Sabinsky
- dir: Alexander Arkatov
- cast: Israel Arko (Yankele Shepshovich), Braginskaya (Sara), Brandesco (Rivkele), Kundinskaya (Gindl), Misha Fishzon (Shloymele)

Got, Mentsh un Tayvl (God, Man and Devil)
  Polish title: *Bog, Czlowiek I Szatan*
  Sila, 2 acts, 1800 ft., Warsaw
  sc: from Jacob Gordin play
  cam: Stanislaw Sebel
  prod: M. Towbin
  dir: Avrom Yitskhok Kaminsky
  cast: Rudolf Zaslawski, Wolska

Khasye di Yesome (Khasye the Orphan)
  Dvinsk
  sc: Nahum Lipovsky, from Jacob Gordin play
  dir: Nahum Lipovsky
  cast: A. Kaminsky, Pivnik, Eisenberg, N. Lipovsky, Sokol, Volskaya, Shriftzetser

Khasye di Yesome (Khasye the Orphan)
  Vilna
  dir: Mark Arnstein

Mirele Efros
  Sila, 3380 ft., Warsaw
  sc: based on Jacob Gordin play
  cam: Stanislaw Sebel
  dir: Andrzej Marek
  design: Lewenhardt
  cast: Regina Kaminska (Sheyndl), Esther Rokhl Kaminska (Mirele Efros), Ida Kaminska (Shloymele), Gershon Weissman (Nukhemtse), Jacob Libert (Shalmen), Rudolf Zaslawski (Yosele), Avrom Yitskhok Kaminsky

Rachel
  Russian title: *Krasavitsa-Naturshchitsa*
  Pathe Freres, 2822 ft., Moscow
  sc: Alexander Arkatov
  cam: Georges Meyer (Mundviller)
  design: Cheslav Sabinsky
  dir: Alexander Arkatov
  cast: N. Reizen (Rachel), L. Sychova (mother), Nikolai Vasiliev (father), B. Pyasetsky (Belsky)

Vu Iz Mayne Khasye (Where Is My Khasye)
  Russia
  with sound
  cast: S.L. Akarski

Yom Hakhupa (The Wedding Day)
Mintus Company, Riga
sc: from play by Jacob Gordin
cam: A. Slavinsky
dir: A. Slavinsky
cast: traveling troupe of Jewish players

1913 *Dem Khazns Tokhter* (The Cantor's Daughter)
Polish title: *Corka Kantora*
Kosmofilm, 3 acts, 3150 ft., Warsaw
sc: from Z. Libin's "Broken Hearts"
cam: Stanislaw Sebel
dir: Avrom Yitskhok Kaminsky
cast: Shmuel Landau (Cantor Nukhem), Regina Kaminska (Gitn), Sonia Shlosberg, Lea Kompaniejec

Der Unbekanter (The Stranger)
Polish titles: *Nieznajomy/Milosc d Smierc*
Kosmofilm, 3300 ft., Warsaw
sc: based on play by Jacob Gordin
cam: Stanislaw Sebel
prod: Henryk Finkelstein
dir: Nahum Lipovsky
cast: Regina Kaminska, Jacob Libert, Gershon Weissman, Vera Zoslovsky

Di Shkhite (The Slaughter)
Polish title: *Uboj*
Kosmofilm, 4 acts, 3250 ft., Warsaw
sc: based on play by Jacob Gordin
cam: Stanislaw Sebel
dir: Avrom Yitskhok Kaminsky
cast: Esther Rokhl Kaminska, Gershon Weissman, Jacob Libert, Shmuel Landau

Gots Shtrof (God's Punishment)
Polish title: *Kara Boza*
Kosmofilm, 3 acts, 2950 ft., Warsaw
sc: from play by Jacob Gordin
cam: Stanislaw Sebel
prod: Henryk Finkelstein
dir: Avrom Yitskhok Kaminsky
cast: Regina Kaminska (Adele), Shmuel Landau (Gindman, her husband), Ida Kaminska, Gershon Weissman, Jacob Libert, Helena Gotlib, Tea Izraelis, Mark Meyerson

Hercele Mejuches
  Polish title: *Fatalna Klatwa*
  Kosmofilm, 5 acts, 4900 ft., Warsaw
  sc: from Richter's "The Oath"
  cam: Stanislaw Sebel
  prod: Henryk Finkelstein
  dir: Avrom Yitskhok Kaminsky
  cast: Regina Kaminska, Gershon Weissman, Isaac Samberg, Mordkhe Fiszelewicz, Shmuel Landau

Leybe Der Shuster (Leybe the Shoemaker)
  Mintus Company, Riga
  sc: from work by P. Prylucki
  cast: actors of Warsaw Jewish theater

Mirele Efros
  Gaumont, 2428 ft., Moscow
  sc: from Jacob Gordin play
  dir: V. Krivtsov
  cast: Russian cast

Shma Yisroel (Hear O Israel)
  Mintus Company, Riga
  sc: from play by Ossip Dymow
  dir: Avrom Yitskhok Kaminsky

Sorrow of Sarah
  Russian title: *Gore Sarri*
  Khanzhonkov, 2625 ft., Russia
  sc: V. Tody (Verberg)
  cam: Alexander Rillo
  dir: Alexander Arkatov
  cast: T. Shornikova (Sarah), A. Bibikov (father), P. Maximova (mother), Ivan Mozhukhin (Isaac), V. Turzhansky (Borekh)

Vu Iz Emes (Where Is Truth)
  Mintus Company, Riga

Yidl mitn Fidl (Yidl with a Fiddle)
  Filma Company, 330 ft., Russia
  with sound

Zayn Vaybs Man (His Wife's Husband)
  Polish title: *Bigamistka*
  Kosmofilm, 3940 ft., Warsaw
  sc: from Meisel's play

cam: Stanislaw Sebel
dir: Avrom Yitskhok Kaminsky
cast: Vera Zoslovsky (Roza), Misha Fishzon (Yosef Gutman), Israel Arko, Isaac Samberg, Helena Gotlib, Ida Kaminska

1914 *Beser Dem Toyt Eyder Aza Shand* (Better Death Than Such Shame)
Russia
with sound
cast: N.B. Leonov

Kiddush Hashem (Sanctification of God's Name)
2 reels, Russia
with sound
prod: Reznikov
cast: M.D. Fachler, R. Fachler

Leah's Suffering
Russian title: Kaznennyi Zhiznyu
Svetoten, 3117 ft., Kiev
cam: V. Vurm
dir: Joseph Soifer
cast: Solovets (David Glazman), M. Leorov (Eva), J. Soifer (Emmanuel), A. Lukovsky (Hersh), E. Malkevich-Khodakovskaya (Lisa)

Di Shtifmuter (The Stepmother)
Polish title: *Macocha*
Kosmofilm, 5250 ft., Warsaw
sc: based on play by Jacob Gordin
cam: Stanislaw Sebel
prod: Henryk Finkelstein
dir: Avrom Yitskhok Kaminsky
cast: Lea Kompaniejec, Shmuel Landau, M. Shlosberg

The War and the Jew
Mizrekh, Russia
sound added in 1915
sc: I. Teneramo
cast: G.M. Kalik-Gramov

1915 *Di Farshtoysene Tokhter* (The Repudiated Daughter)
Polish title: *Wykleta Corka*
Kosmofilm, Warsaw
sc: from a Goldfaden play

cam: Stanislaw Sebel
prod: Henryk Finkelstein
dir: Avrom Yitskhok Kaminsky
cast: Helena Gotlib, Mordkhe Fiszelewisz, Vera Kamiewska Adolf Berman

1916 *Zayn Vaybs Man* (His Wife's Husband)
Polish title: *Malzenstwo Na Rozkrozu*
Kosmofilm, 4 acts, Warsaw
sc: from Meisel's play
prod: Henryk Finkelstein
cast: Isaac Samberg (Israel Baskin), Ida Kaminska (Beyle), Helena Gotlib (Khaye), Shmuel Landau (Yosef Gutman)

1917 *The Beilis Case*
Russian title: *Delo Beilisa*
Svetoten, 6 reels, Kiev
sc: N. Breshko-Breshkovsky
cam: N. Toporkov
dir: Josef Soifer
cast: Y. Yakovlev (Mendel Beilis), Malkevich-Khodakovskaya (Vera Chibiryak), S. Kuznetsov (Krasovsky), S. Tsenin, A. Lundin

Der Blutiker Shpas (The Bloody Jest)
Odessa
sc: V. Voldo, from Sholom Aleichem
dir: Alexander Arkatov

1918 *Aziade*
Khabsayev, Russia
sc: Josef Soifer
cam: A. Stanke
dir: Josef Soifer
cast: Mikhail Mordkin, Margarita Froman

Ven Ikh Bin Roytshild (If I Were Rothschild)
Odessa
sc: from Sholom Aleichem
dir: Alexander Arkatov

Judge, People
Mizrekh, 5 acts, Russia
sc: from I.L. Peretz's "The Broken Tablets"
dir: Alexander Arkatov

1923 *Mizrekh un Mayrev* (East and West)
Austrian title: *Ost und West*
Listo-Picon Film, 6 acts, 7800 ft., Austria
dir: Sidney M. Goldin
cast: Molly Picon, Jacob Kalich, Eugen Neufeld, Johannes Roth, Sigi Hofer
(later re-released with sound as *Mazel Tov*)

1924 *Tkies Kaf* (The Vow)
Polish title: *Slubowanie*
Leo Forbert (Meteor), 12 acts, Poland
sc: Henryk Bojm
cam: Seweryn Steinwurcel
hist adv: Meyer Balaban
prod: Leo Forbert
dir: Zygmund Turkow
cast: Esther Rokhl Kaminska (Mrs. Kronenberg), Moyshe Lipman (Borekh Mandel), Ida Kaminska (Rokhl Kronenberg), Zygmund Turkow (Elijah and 7 other parts), Henryk Tarlow, Shmuel Landau, Wladyslaw Godik, David Lederman, Diana Blumenfeld, Jonas Turkow, Simche Balanoff, Adam Domb, Lev Mogilov
re-released in 1932 with sound as *A Vilna Legend*, later as *Dem Rebens Koyekh* (The Rabbi's Strength)

Yisker (Remembrance)
Austrian title: *Jiskor (Gedenket)*
Judische Kunstfilm, prologue with 6 acts, 8240 ft., Austria
dir: Sidney M. Goldin
cast: Maurice Schwartz, Oskar Beregi, Karl Gotz, Dagny Servaes, Fran Abromowitz
(later re-released with sound as *The Prince and the Pauper*)

1925 *Der Lamedvovnik* (One of the Thirty-Six Just Men)
English title: *The Secret Saint*
Polish title: *Jeden Z 36*
Leo Forbert, 10 acts, Poland
sc: Henryk Bojm
cam: Seweryn Steinwurcel
sets: Ferdynand Vlassak, M. Weintraub, A. Tenenbaum
dir: Henryk Szaro
cast: Jonas Turkow, Moyshe Lipman, Helena Gotlib, Irma Green, Klara Segalowicz, Aleksander Maniecki, Michal Halicz, Chaim Sandler, David Lederman

Der Mabul (The Deluge)
Sovkino, 7736 ft., U.S.S.R.
- sc: D. Rudensky, V. Popova-Khanzhonkova, from Sholom Aleichem
- cam: Alphonse Winkler, A. Solodkov, G. Yegiazarov
- dir: Yevgeni Ivanov-Barkov, Boris Vershilov, Ivan Pyriev
- design: R. Falk, Dmitri Kolupayev
- cast: A. Dzuybina (Tamara Shestopol), D. Chechik-Efrati (Yashke Vorona), J. Vinyan-Kager (Nekhame), D. Itkin (Itsik Shestopol), Hanna Rovina (Anna Zubova), E. Bertonov (Lipa Bashevich), I. Varshana, N. Viniar, Raikin Ben-Ari, Benno Schneider, Ben-Chayim, A. Baratz, Nahum Zemach

Yidishe Glikn (Jewish Luck)
also released as *Menakhem Mendl*
Soviet title: *Yevreiskoye Shchastye*
Goskino, 7880 ft., U.S.S.R.
- sc: G. Gricher-Cherikover, I. Teneramo, L. Leonidov, from Sholom Aleichem
- intertitles: Isaac Babel
- cam: Edward Tisse with Vasili Khvatov, N.S. Strukov
- sets: Natan Altman
- music: Lev Pulver
- dir: Alexander Granovsky
- cast: Solomon Mikhoels (Menakhem Mendl), Tamara Adelheim (Beyle), T. Hazak (Kimbak), M. Goldblatt (Zalmen), Y. Shidlo (Klyachkin), E. Rogaler (Usher), S. Epstein (Yosele)

(re-released in 1933 with sound as *The Matchmaker*)

1926 *Tsebrokhene Hertser* (Broken Hearts)
also released as *Di Umgliklekhe Kale* (The Unfortunate Bride)
Jaffa Art Film, 8 reels, U.S.
- sc: Frances Taylor Patterson, from play by Z. Libin
- cam: Frank Zucker
- dir: Maurice Schwartz
- cast: Maurice Schwartz (Benjamin Rezanov), Lila Lee (Ruth Esterin), Wolf Goldfaden (Cantor Esterin), Bina Abromowitz, Isidore Cashier, Anna Appel, Morris Strassberg

1927   *Benye Krik* (Bennie the Howl)
VUFKU, 7250 ft., U.S.S.R.
sc: Isaac Babel, from his short stories
cam: A. Kalivzhny
dir: Vladimir Vilner
cast: M. Leorov (Mendl Krik), Yu. Shumski (Benye Krik), A.D. Goricheva (Dvoyre), A. Vabnik (Her fiance), N. Nademsky (Kolka Pakovsky), T. Brainin (Levka Byk), G. Astafev (the Tartar), A. Sashin (Savelii Butsis), M. Smolensky (Marantz)

Blondzhende Shtern (Wandering Stars)
Soviet title: *Blushdayushtchi Sviosdy*
VUFKU, 7080 ft., U.S.S.R.
sc: Isaac Babel, based on Sholom Aleichem
cam: F. Verigo-Darovsky
dir: G. Gricher-Cherikover
cast: M. Leorov (Vittorio Maffi), I. Dubravim (Levushka), R. Rami-Shor (Rachel Monko), A. Leorov (Baroness Green), N. Barsov (Retti), Tamara Adelheim (ward), A. Tsesapskaya (Ellen Green), Bri (Reb Ratkovich), Berokhson (Herr Galnishker)

1928   *Durkh Trern* (Through Tears)
Soviet title: *Skvoz Slezy*
VUFKU, 8000 ft., U.S.S.R.
sc: I. Skvirski and G. Gricher-Cherikover, from Sholom Aleichem
cam: N. Farkash, F. Verigo-Darovsky
dir: G. Gricher-Cherikover
cast: J. K. Kovenberg (Shimen-Elye), A. D. Goricheva (Beyle), B. Silberman (Elye's mother), D. Cantor (Elye), M. Leorov (Dodye), A. Vabnik (Pinye), M. D. Sen-Elnikova (Freyde), S. J. Silberman (Motl), F. A. Soslovsky
(re-released in 1933 with sound as *Laughter Through Tears*)

In Poylishe Velder (In Polish Woods)
Polish title: *W Lasach Polskich*
Forbert-Film, 9 acts, Poland
sc: Henryk Bojm, from a novel by Joseph Opatoshu
cam: Ferdynand Vlassak
sets: Leo Forbert
dir: Jonas Turkow
cast: Diana Blumenfeld, Silven Rich, Moyshe Lipman,

Helena Gotlib, S. Prisament, A. Ajzenberg, Klara Segalowicz, Shmuel Landau, Aleksander Maniecki, David Lederman

Motele Shpindler (Motele the Weaver)
also released as *The Simple Tailor*
Soviet title: *Glaza Katorye Videli* (The Eyes that Saw)
VUFKU, 6240 ft., U.S.S.R.
- sc: S. Lazorin
- cam: B. Zavelev
- dir: Vladimir Vilner
- cast: M. Leorov (Shklansky), A. D. Goricheva (his wife), Y. Mindler (Motele Shpindler), J. K. Kovenberg (Meyer), Y. Razomovskaya (Dvoyre), Yu. Solntseva (Rosa), A. Siminov (the General), A. Vabnik

Zayn Ekstselents (His Excellency)
American title: *Seeds of Freedom*
Soviet title: *Yevo Prevoshoditelstvo*
Belgoskino, 5900 ft., U.S.S.R.
- sc: Sofya Roshal, Vera Stroeva
- cam: N. Kozlovski
- sets: Y. Makhlis
- editor: Mark Donskoy
- dir: Grigori Roshal
- cast: Leonid Leonidov (Governor Von Wahl and the Rabbi), J. Untershlak (Hirsh Lekert), Tamara Adelheim (Rivele), M. Sinelnikova (Miriam), A. Sandel (Shpis), A. Grinfeld (Lemzer), A. Nenyukov (Peter)

1929   *Ad Mosay* (Until When)
also released as *The Eternal Prayer*
Metropolitan Studios, 36 min., U.S.
- music: Abe Ellstein
- prod: Max Cohen
- dir: Sidney Goldin
- cast: Shmulikel (Samuel Kelemer), Lucy Levine, Anna Appel, Lazar Freed, Mark Schweid

East Side Sadie
Worldart Films, 6 reels, U.S.
- sc: Isidor Frankel, from story by Sidney Goldin
- cam: Frank Zucker
- music: Sholom Secunda
- ed: Sam Citron

	dir:	Sidney M. Goldin
	cast:	Bertina Goldin, Jack Ellis, Boris Rosenthal, Lucia Backus Seger, Abe Sinkoff, Mark Schweid

1930   *A Mentsh fun Shtetl* (A Man from the Shtetl)
American title: *A Jew at War*
Soviet title: *Chelovek Iz Mestechka*
VUFKU, 71 min., U.S.S.R.

sc:	Sofya Roshal, Vera Stroeva
cam:	Michael Belsky
dir:	Grigori Roshal
cast:	Vinyamin Zuskin (David Gorelik), S. Petrov (Brandt), E. Pinikova (Rivele), N. Leonov (her father), A. Nademsky (tailor), B. Shelestov-Zauze (officer), S. Svashenko, Leske

Eybike Naronim (Eternal Fools)
Judea Films, 6120 ft., U.S.

sc:	H. Kalmonowitz
cam:	Charles Levine, Sam Rosen
ed:	Louis Schwartz
prod:	Joseph Seiden
dir:	Sidney Goldin
cast:	Yudel Dubinsky, Yehuda Bleich, Seymour Rechtzeit, Bella Gudinsky, Isidore Meltzer, Charlotte Goldstein, Beatrice Miller, Gertie Krause

Mayne Yidishe Mame (My Jewish Mother)
Judea Films, 4000 ft., U.S.

sc:	Isidore Lillian
cam:	Don Malcames
prod:	Joseph Seiden
dir:	Sidney Goldin
cast:	Mae Simon, Bernice Simon, Seymour Rechtzeit, Helen Blay

★   ★   ★   ★   ★   ★

The Broken Doll
Judea Films, 1 reel (short), U.S.

sc:	Ivan Bussat
prod:	Joseph Seiden
dir:	Sidney Goldin
cast:	Sadie Banks, Celia Person

Ets Khaim (Tree of Life)
    Judea Films, short film, U.S.
    prod: Joseph Seiden
    dir: Sidney Goldin

An Evening in a Jewish Camp
    Judea Films, 1 reel (short), U.S.
    mus/sc: Sholom Secunda
    prod: Joseph Seiden
    dir: Sidney Goldin
    cast: E. Miller

The Jewish Day Hour
    Judea Films, 2 reels (short), U.S.
    sc: Z. Rubinstein
    prod: Joseph Seiden
    dir: Sidney Goldin

The Jewish Gypsy
    Judea Films, 2 reels (short), 21 min., U.S.
    sc: Hymie Jacobson
    prod: Joseph Seiden
    dir: Sidney Goldin
    cast: Hymie Jacobson, Miriam Kressyn

Kol Nidre
    Judea Films, 1 reel (short), 11 min., U.S.
    mus/sc: Leibele Waldman
    prod: Joseph Seiden
    dir: Sidney Goldin
    cast: Leibele Waldman

Kol Nidre
    Judea Films, 1 reel (short), 10 min., U.S.
    mus/sc: Samuel Gottesman
    prod: Joseph Seiden
    dir: Sidney Goldin
    cast: Shmulikel (Samuel Kelemer)

Land of Freedom
    Judea Films, 2 reels (short), U.S.
    sc: Seymour Rechtzeit
    prod: Joseph Seiden
    dir: Sidney Goldin
    cast: Seymour Rechtzeit

Mai-Ko Mashma-Lon (What Does It Mean)
Judea Films, 1 reel (short), U.S.
- sc: from poem by Abraham Reisen
- prod: Joseph Seiden
- dir: Sidney Goldin
- cast: Harry Peld

Natasha
also released as *Shvartse Natasha* (Black Natasha)
Judea Films, 2 reels (short), U.S.
- sc: Pinchus Lavenda
- prod: Joseph Seiden
- dir: Sidney Goldin
- cast: Mildred Block, Pinchus Lavenda, Hymie Jacobson

Oy Doctor
Judea Films, 2 reels (short), 20 min., U.S.
- sc: Isidore Lillian
- prod: Joseph Seiden
- dir: Sidney Goldin
- cast: Menashe Skulnick

Sailor's Sweetheart
Judea Films, 2 reels (short), U.S.
- sc: Hymie Jacobson
- prod: Joseph Seiden
- dir: Sidney Goldin
- cast: Hymie Jacobson, Miriam Kressyn

Shuster Libe (Shoemaker's Romance)
Judea Films, 1900 ft. (short), U.S.
- sc: Leon Kadison
- art: Robert Van Rosen
- prod: Joseph Seiden
- dir: Sidney Goldin
- cast: Joseph Buloff, Liuba Kadison, Leah Noemi, Leon Kadison

Style and Class
Judea Films, 2000 ft. (short), U.S.
- sc: Marty Baratz
- mus: Harry Lubin
- art: Robert Van Rosen
- prod: Joseph Seiden
- dir: Sidney Goldin

    cast: Marty Baratz, Goldie Eisman, Boris Rosenthal, Ida Goldstein

Unsane-Toykef (Judgment)
    Judea Films, 1 reel (short), U.S.
    mus/sc: Sholom Secunda
    prod: Joseph Seiden
    dir: Sidney Goldin
    cast: Leibele Waldman

Yidishe Nigun (Jewish Melody)
    Judea Films, 1 reel (short), U.S.
    mus/sc: Sholom Secunda
    prod: Joseph Seiden
    dir: Sidney Goldin
    cast: Leibele Waldman

1931   *Zayn Vaybs Lubovnik* (His Wife's Lover)
    High Arts Pictures Corporation, 77 min., U.S.
    sc: from a play by Sheyne Rokhl Semkoff
    cam: Frank Zucker
    prod: Nathan Hirsh and Morris Kleinerman
    dir: Sidney Goldin
    cast: Ludwig Satz (Yankl/Mr. Ritz), Michael Rosenberg (Moishe), Isidore Cashier (Uncle Harry), Lucy Levine (Taybele), Jacob Frank (Peysekh), Lillian Feinman (Breyndl), Zita Maker, Zero Zazi, Moshe Silberstein, Sam Levenworth, William Epstein, Annie Shapiro, Sidney Goldin

★   ★   ★   ★   ★   ★

A Cantor on Trial
    Jacob Berkowitz, 1 reel (short), U.S.
    sc: Isidore Lillian
    prod: Jacob Berkowitz
    dir: Sidney Goldin

Eli, Eli (My God, My God)
    Judea Films, 1 reel (short), 10 min., U.S.
    mus/sc: Sholom Secunda
    prod: Joseph Seiden
    dir: Sidney Goldin

The Feast of Passover
    Jacob Berkowitz, short film, U.S.

      sc: M. Schorr, Mark Schweid
      prod: Jacob Berkowitz
      dir: Sidney Goldin
      cast: Leibele Waldman, Noah Nachbush, Mark Schweid

Shulamis
Judea Films, 5 reels, U.S.
    sc: from play by Goldfaden
    prod: Joseph Seiden
    dir: Sidney Goldin

The Voice of Israel
Judea Films, 10 reels, 8439 ft., U.S.
later 1377 ft. (1950)
    prod: Joseph Seiden
    cast: Cantors Seidel Rovner, David Roitman, Josef Schlisky, Adolph Katchko, Yossele Rosenblatt, Mordechai Herschman, Joseph Shapiro, Leibele Waldman, Shaile Engelhardt

1932

Joseph in the Land of Egypt
Guaranteed Picture Co., Inc., 80 min., U.S.
footage taken in part from 1914 Italian film, *Joseph in Egypt*, with sound, prologue and epilogue added
    sc: Michael Goldstein, from bible stories
    mus: I. J. Hochman
    prod: Samuel Goldstein, Mortimer D. Sikawitt
    ed/dir: George Roland
    cast: Ben Adler, Joseph Greenberg (Green), Sigmund Zuckerberg, Herman Sarotsky, Wolf Goldfaden, Joseph Schwartzberg, Wolf Barzell, Ida Adler, Gertrude Levitan, Sonya Adler

Noson Beker Fort Aheym (Nathan Becker Is Going Home)
English title: *The Return of Nathan Becker*
Belgoskino, 72 min., U.S.S.R.
    sc: Peretz Markish, Boris Shpis, R. Milman
    cam: E. Mikhailov
    mus: E. Brusilovski
    dir: Boris Shpis and R. Milman
    cast: Solomon Mikhoels (Tseyle Becker), David Gutman (Nathan Becker), Elena Kashnitzkaya (Meyke), Boris Bobochkin (Mikulitch), V. Yablonski (party secretary), Kadler Ben-Salem (Jim)

Uncle Moses
  Yiddish Talking Pictures, 80 min., U.S.
  sc: from play by Sholom Asch
  prod: Louis Weiss and Rubin Goldberg
  dir: Sidney Goldin and Aubrey Scotto
  cast: Maurice Schwartz (Uncle Moses), Zvee Scooker (Charlie), Judith Abarbanel (Masha), Mark Schweid (Aaron), Rubin Goldberg (older Melnick), Sally Schor (Rosie), Rebecca Weintraub (Gnendl), Jacob Mestel (Berel), Sam Gertler (Sam), Leon Seidenberg (Mannes), Wolf Goldfaden (Nakhmen)

1933 *Avrom Ovinu* (Abraham Our Patriarch)
  also released as *The Eternal Jew*
  footage taken from various bible films
  Lefco Productions, 62 min., U.S.
  sc: Jacob Mestel
  supervisor: Sam Rosen
  ed/dir: George Roland
  cast: Ruben Wendroff, Morris B. Samuylow, Ben Adler, Jacob Mestel, Abraham Teitelbaum, Leibele Waldman

Gelebt un Gelakht (Live and Laugh)
  Jewish Talking Pictures, 5400 ft., U.S.
  sc: Max Wilner
  ed: Sam Rosen
  sound: Murray Dichter
  prod: Joseph Seiden
  dir: Max Wilner
  cast: Menashe Skulnick, Joseph Buloff, Pinchus Lavenda, Seymour Rechtzeit, Yudel Dubinsky, Boris Rosenthal, Hymie Jacobson, Jack Shargel, Chaim Tauber, Max Wilner, Sadie Banks, Mae Simon

A Vilna Legend
  also released as *Dem Rebins Koyekh* (The Rabbi's Strength)
  footage taken primarily from *Tkies Kaf* (1924) with sound, prologue and epilogue added
  Quality Pictures, 68 min., U.S.
  dial: Joseph Buloff
  ed/dir: George Roland
  cast: Joseph Buloff, Benjamin Fishbein, Ben Besenko,

Leon Kadison, Jacob Mestel and original cast of *Tkies Kaf*

Yidishe Tokhter (Jewish Daughter)
  also released as *Daughter of Her People*
  footage taken in part from 1921 German *Judith Trachtenberg* with sound, prologue and epilogue added
  Quality Films, 75 min., U.S.
  dial: Jacob Mestel
  prod: Harry Brown
  ed/dir: George Roland
  cast: Chaim Shneier, Joseph Greenberg (Green), Michael Rosenberg, Ben Besenko, Helen Blay, Jacob Mestel

1934 *Yidishe Foter* (Jewish Father)
  also released as *Youth of Russia*
  Sov-Am Productions, feature-length, U.S.
  sc: Henry Lynn
  dir: Henry Lynn
  cast: Wolf Goldfaden, Gertrude Bullman, Sam Gertler, Boas Young, Dora Kashinskaya, Rose Wallerstein, Morris Marcus, Moishe Silberstein, Dave Feffer, Morris Strassberg, Esta Salzman, Morris Silberkasten

1935 *Bar Mitsve*
  S & L Film Company, 85 min., U.S.
  sc: Henry Lynn, from a story by Boris Thomashefsky
  cam: Robert J. Marshall and George H. Wicke Jr.
  mus: Jack Stillman
  prod: Jack Stillman and Henry Lynn
  cast: Boris Thomashefsky, Regina Zuckerberg, Anita Chayes, Peter Graf, Gertrude Bullman, Leah Noemi, Morris Strassberg, Sam Colton, Morris Tarlowsky, Benjamin Schechtman

Mir Kumen On (We Are On Our Way)
  American title: *Children Must Laugh*
  Polish title: *Droga Mlodych*
  Medem Sanatorium Committee, 70 min., Poland
  sc: Wanda Wasilevska, with Jacob Pat, S. Mendelson and H. S. Kazdan
  cam: Stanislaw Lipinski
  mus: Henikh Kahn with Yankl Trowpianski
  dir: Aleksander Ford
  cast: children of Medem Children's Sanatorium

Shir Hashirim (Song of Songs)
  Henry Lynn Productions, feature-length, U.S.
  sc: Henry Lynn, from a story by Anshel Schorr
  mus: Joseph Rumshinsky
  prod: Henry Lynn
  dir: Henry Lynn
  cast: Samuel Goldenberg, Dora Weissman, Max Kletter, Mirele Gruber, Seymour Rechtzeit, Yudel Dubinsky, Ruben Wendroff, Anna Toback

Yidishe Kinig Lir (Jewish King Lear)
  Jewish Talking Pictures, 80 min., U.S.
  sc: A. Armband, from play by Jacob Gordin
  cam: Joe Freeman
  sound: Murray Dichter
  art: Robert Van Rosen
  prod: Johnnie Walker and Jack Riegel
  supervisor: Joseph Seiden
  dir: Harry Thomashefsky
  cast: Maurice Krohner (David Moshele), Fannie Levenstein (Hanna, his wife), Jacob Bergreen (Joffe), Miriam Grossman (Taybele), Eddie Pascal (Shamay), Rose Schwartzberg (Diener), Morris Weissman (Abraham Chariff), Esther Adler (Gitl), Morris Tarlowsky (Moses Choris), Janet Paskevitch (Estelle)

1936 *Al Khet* (For the Sin/Confession)
  English title: *I Have Sinned*
  Polish title: *Za Grzechy*
  Kinor, 93 min., Poland
  sc: J. M. Neuman
  cam: Stanislaw Lipinski
  mus: Henikh Kahn
  design: Yankl Adler and Czeslaw Piaskowski
  prod: Shaul Goskind and W. Tenenbaum
  dir: Aleksander Marten
  cast: Rokhl Holzer (Esther), Avrom Marevsky (her father), Shimen Dzigan (comedian), Yisroel Schumacher (comedian), Ruth Turkow (adopted daughter), Kurt Katch (professor), Khevel Buzgan (lieutenant), Herbert Scherzer, Isaac Samberg, Dina Halpern, Fania Rubina, Klara Segalowicz

Libe un Laydnshaft (Love and Passion)

released as *Love and Sacrifice*
Jewish Talking Pictures, 75 min., U.S.
sc: based on novel by Isidore Zolatarefsky
mus: Abe Ellstein
prod: Joseph Seiden
dir: George Roland
cast: Lazar Freed, Rose Greenfield, Leibele Waldman, Anna Thomashefsky, Louis Kramer, Morris Silberkasten, William Schwartz, Jacob Wexler, Esta Salzman, Ray Schneier, Anna Loeb, Arthur Winters, Sam Kravitz

Yidl mitn Fidl (Yidl with a Fiddle)
English title: *Yiddle With His Fiddle*
Polish title: *Judel Gra Na Skrzypcach*
Green Film, 92 min., Poland
sc: Konrad Tom
cam: Jacob Janilowicz
design: Jacek Weinreich
art: Jacob Kalich and Czeslaw Piaskowski
mus: Abe Ellstein
lyrics: Itzik Manger
prod: Edward Hantower and Josef Frankfurt with Joseph Green
dir: Joseph Green and Jan Nowina-Przbylski
cast: Molly Picon (Yidl), Simchi Fostel (Aryeh), Max Bozyk (Isaac), Leon Liebgold (Froym), Shmuel Landau (Gold), Dora Fakiel (Taybele), Chaya Levin (Mme. Flaumbaum), Basia Liebgold, S. Nathan, A. Kurc
(re-released in English in 1955 as *Castles In The Sky*)

1937 *Dem Khazns Zundl* (The Cantor's Son)
Eron Films, 90 min., U.S.
sc: Mark Schweid, based on a story by Louis Freiman
cam: Frank Zucker
mus: Alexander Olshanetsky
art: Robert Van Rosen
prod: Arthur Block and Samuel Segal
dir: Sidney Goldin and Ilya Motyleff
cast: Moishe Oysher (Sol), Florence Weiss (Helen), Judith Abarbanel (Rivke), Michael Rosenberg (Yosel), Isidore Cashier (Rossevitch), Yehuda Bleich (Zonvel, his father), Bertha Guttenberg (Malke, his mother), Irving Honigman (Ben), Rose Wallerstein (Clara), Lorraine

Abarbanel (Rivke as a child), Vicki Marcus (Shloymele)

Der Dibuk (The Dybbuk)
   Polish title: *Dybuk*
   Phoenix Film, 125 min., Poland
   sc: Alter Kacyzna and Mark Arnstein, assisted by Anatol Stern, from the play by S. Anski
   cam: Albert Wywerka
   hist. adv.: Meyer Balaban
   design: Jacek Rotmil and Steffan Norris
   mus: Henikh Kahn
   dance: Judith Berg
   asst. prod.: Zygfryd Mayflaner
   prod: Ludwig Prywes
   ritual songs: Gershon Sirota
   dir: Michal Waszynski
   cast: Avrom Marevsky (Rabbi of Miropol), Isaac Samberg (Meshulleh), Lili Liliana (Leah), Leon Liebgold (Khonen), Moyshe Lipman (Sender), Dina Halpern (Freyde), Max Bozyk (Nute), Shmuel Landau (Zalmen), David Lederman (Meyer), S. Branecki (Nakhman), Abraham Kurc (Michael), M. Messinger (Menashe), G. Lamberger (Nissen)

Der Purimshpiler (The Purim Player)
   American title: *The Jester*
   Polish title: *Blazen Purymowy*
   Green Film, 90 min., Poland
   sc: Chaver-Pahver and Joseph Green (Joseph Victor)
   cam: Seweryn Steinwurcel
   design: Jacek Weinreich
   mus: Nicholas Brodsky, assisted by Henryk Wars
   lyrics/dial: Itzik Manger
   prod: Joseph Green and Edward Hantower
   dir: Joseph Green and Jan Nowina-Przybylski
   cast: Hymie Jacobson (Dick), Zygmund Turkow (Getsl), Miriam Kressyn (Esther), Isaac Samberg (Nukhem), Max Bozyk (grandfather), Berta Litwina (Tsippe), Eni Liton (Leah), Max Brin (Shames), Jacob Rajnglas

(shoemaker's helper), Shmuel Landau (rich man), Jacob Fisher (matchmaker)

Di Freylekhe Kabtsonim (Jolly Paupers)
Polish title: *Weseli Biedacy*
Kinor, 62 min., Poland
- sc: Moshe Broderson
- cam: Adolf Forbert
- mus: Henikh Kahn
- prod: W. Tenenbaum and Shaul Goskind
- dir: Zygmund Turkow
- cast: Jennie Lovie, Shimen Dzigan, Yisroel Schumacher, Ruth Turkow, Chana Lewin, Max Brin, Max Bozyk, Menashe Oppenheim, Simche Natan, S. Goldstein, Zygmund Turkow

Grine Felder (Green Fields)
Collective Film Producers, 120 min., U.S.
- sc: George Moskov and Peretz Hirschbein, based on Hirschbein's play
- cam: J. Burgi-Contner, William Miller
- mus: Vladimir Heifetz
- prod: Roman Rebush and Ludwig Landy
- dir: Edgar G. Ulmer and Jacob Ben-Ami
- cast: Michael Goldstein (Leyvi-Yitskhok), Helen Beverly (Tsine), Isidore Cashier (David-Noyakh), Anna Appel (Rokhl), Leah Noemi (Gitl), Dena Drute (Stere), Max Vodnoy (Elkhune), Saul Levine (Hersh-Ber), Herschel Bernardi (Avrum-Yankev)

Ikh Vil Zayn a Mame (I Want to be a Mother)
Jewish Talking Pictures, 75 min., U.S.
- sc: Isidore Lillian
- cam: Joe Freeman
- prod: Joseph Seiden
- dir: George Roland
- cast: Leo Fuchs (Khaim Bok), Hanna Hollander (Tante), Yetta Zwerling (Brinye), Leibele Waldman (cantor), Muni Serebroff (Aaron Waldman), Dave Lubritsky (Sol), Esta Salzman (Celia), Moishe Feder (Jacob Goodman), Sam Gertler (Eugene Guggenheim), Rose Greenfield (Bas Sheva)

Tkies Kaf (The Vow)
Polish title: *Slubowanie*
Leo-Film, 97 min., Poland

sc: Henryk Bojm
dial: H. Bojm, J. M. Neuman
cam: Stanislaw Lipinski
mus: Iso Szajewicz
design: Jacek Weinreich
dir: Henryk Szaro
artistic
dir: Zygmund Turkow
cast: Zygmund Turkow (Elijah), Kurt Katch (Mendl), Dina Halpern (Rokhl), Moyshe Lipman (Khaim), Shmuel Landau (Esmul Weber), E. Perlman (Mirele), Itskhok Grudberg (Jacob), Berta Litwina (Esther), Menashe Oppenheim (David), Max Bozyk (matchmaker), Simche Fostel (administrator), Max Brin

Vu Iz Mayn Kind (Where Is My Child)
Menorah Pictures, 80 min., U.S.
sc: S. Siegel, S. Steinberg and Henry Lynn, from a story by Louis Freiman
cam: J. Burgi-Contner
ed: George Roland
mus: Jack Stillman
prod: Abraham Leff
dir: Henry Lynn
cast: Celia Adler (Esther Liebman), Anna Lillian (Alice Gross), Morris Strassberg (Dr. Reisner), Ruben Wendroff (Alek), Morris Silberkasten (Morris Gross), Blanche Bernstein (Malke), Mischa Stutchkoff (Victor), Ceril Arnon (Julia), Leon Schechtman, Solomon Steinberg, Esther Gerber

★ ★ ★ ★

Ikh Vil Zayn A Pansyoner (I Want to be a Boarder)
Jewish Talking Pictures, 1525 ft. (short), U.S.
prod: Joseph Seiden
dir: George Roland
cast: Leo Fuchs, Yetta Zwerling

1938 *A Brivele der Mamen* (A Letter to Mother)
Polish title: *List Do Matkl*
Green Film, 100 min., Poland
sc: Mendel Osherowitz
cam: Seweryn Steinwurcel
design: Jacek Rotmil and Steffan Norris
mus: Abe Ellstein

lit. asst:	J. M. Neuman
asst. prod.	Edward Hantower and Benjamin J. Weinberg
prod:	Joseph Green
dir:	Joseph Green and Leon Trystan
cast:	Lucy Gehrman (Dobrish), Misha Gehrman (Mr. Shine), Edmund Zayenda (Irving Bird), Max Bozyk (Shimen), Gertrude Bullman (Miriam), Alexander Stein (David), Itskhok Grudberg (Meyer), Simche Fostel (Cantor), Shmuel Landau (merchant), Chana Lewin (Shimen's wife), Irving Bruner, Gustav Berger

Der Zingendiker Shmid (The Singing Blacksmith)
Collective Film Producers, 110 min., U.S.

sc:	Ossip Dymow, Ben-Zvi Baratoff and David Pinski, based on Pinski's play
cam:	William J. Miller
mus:	Jacob Weinberg
prod:	Roman Rebush
dir:	Edgar G. Ulmer
cast:	Moishe Oysher (Yankl), Miriam Riselle (Tamare), Ben-Zvi Baratoff (Bendl), Florence Weiss (Rivke), Anna Appel (Khaye-Peshe), Michael Goldstein (Refuel), Leah Noemi (Mariashe), Max Vodnoy (Simkhe), Yudel Dubinsky (Aaron), Benjamin Fishbein (Froyke), Ruben Wendroff (Elye), Herschel Bernardi (Yankl as child)

Di Kraft fun Lebn (The Power of Life)
Henry Lynn, 74 min., U.S.

sc:	from a story by Isidore Zolatarefsky
dir:	Henry Lynn
cast:	Michel Michalesko (Nathan Rabinowitz), Morris Strassberg (Simon Schrinder), Charlotte Goldstein (Leah), Bertha Hart (Mrs. Rabinowitz), Morris B. Samuylow (Mr. Blitzer), Sam Josephson (Julius), Frank Schechtman (Max), Saul Josephson (Sam Schrinder), MIke Wilensky (Mr. Feinberg), Abe Lax

Mamele (Little Mother)
Polish title: *Mateczka*
Green Film, 100 min., Poland

sc:	Konrad Tom, based on a play by Meyer Schwartz
cam:	Seweryn Steinwurcel
design:	Jacek Rotmil and Steffan Norris
lit. asst:	J. M. Neuman

mus: Abe Ellstein
lyrics: Molly Picon
art: Jacob Kalich
asst.
prod: Edward Hantower and Benjamin J. Weinberg
prod: Joseph Green
dir: Joseph Green and Konrad Tom
cast: Molly Picon (Mamele-Khavtshi), Edmund Zayenda (Schlesinger), Max Bozyk (Berel Samet), Simche Fostel (Naderman), Gertrude Bullman (Bertha), Menashe Oppenheim (Max Katz), Ola Shlifko (Yetke), Max Perlman (David), Ruth Turkow (Beyltshi), Shmuel Landau, Lew Schriftzetzer, Carl Latowich, Max Brin, Adam Domb, Edward Steinback

Shkheynim (Neighbors)
originally: *Pietro Wyzej* (The Apartment Above)
dubbed into Yiddish
Best Film Company, 72 min., Poland
sc: J. Fethke and N. Snodek
adapt: Joseph Tunkel
art: Jacek Rotmil and Steffan Norris
mus: Henry Wars
dir: Leon Trystan
cast: Helen Gross (Sonia), Eugene Bodo (Henry), Joseph Orwid (Hershel), L. Sempolinsky (Radel)

Tsvey Shvester (Two Sisters)
Graphic Picture Productions, 79 min., U.S.
sc: Samuel H. Cohen
cam: George F. Hinners
art: William Saulter
mus: Joseph Rumshinsky
dir: Ben K. Blake
cast: Jennie Goldstein (Betty Glickstein), Sylvia Dell (Sally Glickstein), Muni Serebroff (Dr. Max Feinberg), Michael Rosenberg (Chymitcha), Celia Budkin (Mrs. Glickstein), Betty Bialis (Betty as child), Joan Carroll (Sally as child), Harvey Kier (Dr. Jack Glickstein), Jack Wexler (Leybish Glickstein), Betty Jacobs (Dubrish), Abe Teitelbaum (Gershon Glickstein), Rebecca Weintraub (Khane Glickstein), Yudel Dubinsky, Anna Levine, Ida Adler, Anita Hoffman

1939 *Der Lebediker Yosem* (The Living Orphan)
also released as *My Son*

Jewish Talking Pictures, 90 min., U.S.
sc: Chaim Tauber
cam. J. Burgi-Contner
mus: Alexander Olshanetsky
dir: Joseph Seiden
cast: Gustav Berger (Muni Berger), Fania Rubina (Freda Berger), Jerry Rosenberg (Benny), Harry Feld, Yetta Zwerling, Ida Dworkin

Di Klyatshe (The Dobbin)
also released as *The Light Ahead* and *Fishke der Krumer*
Ultra Films, 80 min., U.S.
sc: Chaver-Pahver based on novels by Mendele Mokher Seforim
cam: J. Burgi-Contner, Edward Hyland
design: Robert Benney
prod: Edgar G. Ulmer
dir: Edgar G. Ulmer
cast: Isidore Cashier (Mendele Mokher Seforim), Helen Beverly (Hodl), David Opatoshu (Fishke), Yudel Dubinsky (Isaac), Rosetta Bialis (Drabke), Tillie Rabinowitz (Mekhe), Misha Fishzon (Aaron), Leon Seidenberg (Alter Yaknehose), Anna Giskin (Gitl), Celia Budkin (Khaye), Jennie Cashier (Dobe), Wolf Mercur (Getsl), Leon Schechter (Frechman), Wolf Goldfaden (Wecker)

Kol Nidre
Jewish Talking Pictures, 82 min., U.S.
sc: Ben Gitlitz
mus: Sholom Secunda
dir: Joseph Seiden
cast: Lili Liliana, Leon Liebgold, Leibele Waldman, Joel Feig Double Choir, Menashe Oppenheim, Bertha Hart, Mischa Stutchkoff, Chaim Tauber, Yetta Zwerling, David Lederman

Mirele Efros
Credo Pictures, 91 min., U.S.
sc: Ossip Dymow and Joseph Berne, from Jacob Gordin's play
cam: J. Burgi-Contner
mus: Vladimir Heifetz
prod: Roman Rebush
dir: Joseph Berne
cast: Berta Gersten (Mirele Efros), Michael Rosenberg

(Nukhemtse), Ruth Elbaum (Sheyndl), Albert Lipton (Yosele), Sarah Krohner (Khane-Dvoyre), Moishe Feder (Shalmen), Louis Brandt (Donya), Jerry Rosenberg (Shloymele), Ruben Wendroff (Badkhn), Jacob Mestel (Pogerelsky), Paula Walter (Makhle), Moishe Schorr (coachman), Eugene Sigaloff (peasant), Clara Deutchman (barwoman)

Mothers of Today
Apex Productions, 75 min., U.S.
sc: Henry Lynn, from a play by Simon Wolf
dir: Henry Lynn
cast: Esther Field (Esther Waldman), Max Rosenblatt (Solomon), Gertie Krause (Anna), Paula Lubelska (Evelyn), Vera Lebedoff (Brendl), Arthur Winters (Izzie), Simon Wolf, Jack Shargel, Leon Seidenberg, Louis Goldstein

Motl der Operator (Motel the Operator)
Jewish Talking Pictures, 89 min., U.S.
sc: Chaim Tauber
cam: Don Malcames, Charles Levine
mus: Sholom Secunda
dir: Joseph Seiden
cast: Chaim Tauber (Motl), Malvina Rappel (his wife), Yetta Zwerling, Seymour Rechtzeit, Joseph Schoengold, Maurice Krohner, Isidor Frankel, Leibele Waldman, Gertie Krause, Jacob Zanger, Michel Gibson

On a Heym (Without a Home)
Polish title: *Bezdomni*
Alma Film, 90 min., Poland
sc: Alter Kacyzna, from a play by Jacob Gordin
cam: Jacob Janilowicz, David Eisenstadt
design: Jacek Weinreich
mus: Iso Szajewicz
prod: Adolph Mann
dir: Aleksander Marten
cast: Adam Domb (Jacob Elkhonon), Aleksander Marten (Avreyml), Ida Kaminska (Bas Sheve), Ben Zuker (Khonokh), Shimen Dzigan (Motl), Yisroel Schumacher (Fishl), Vera Gran (Bessie), Dora Fakiel (Lina), Mirele Gruber

A People That Shall Not Die
segments taken from 1934 British *Jud Suss* and dubbed

into Yiddish
Feature-length, U.S.
- narr: Julius Adler
- dir: Henry Lynn
- cast: Ben Adler, Zina Goldstein, Lillian Blum, Leon Schechter, Herman Zorotzsky, Miriam Torlofsky, Max Rosenblatt, A. Timyanow, Morris Bilofsky, with original *Jud Suss* cast.

Tevye der Milkhiker (Tevye the Milkman)
Maymon Films, 80 min., U.S.
- sc: Maurice Schwartz, from stories by Sholom Aleichem
- cam: Larry Williams
- mus: Sholom Secunda
- prod: Harry Ziskin
- dir: Maurice Schwartz
- cast: Maurice Schwartz (Tevye), Miriam Riselle (Khave), Rebecca Weintraub (Golde), Paula Lubelska (Tsaytl), Leon Liebgold (Fedya), Vicki Marcus (Shloymele), Julius Adler (Priest), Morris Strassberg (Starasta), Boas Young (Vradnik), Helen Grossman (Mikita's wife), Betty Marcus (Perele), David Makarenko (Mikita), Louis Weisberg (Shtarsina), Al Harris (Zazulya)

1940 *Amerikaner Shadkhn* (American Matchmaker)
Fame Films, 87 min., U.S.
- sc: S. Castle, from an original story by G. Heimo
- cam: J. Burgi-Contner, Edward Hyland
- dial: B. Ressler
- art: W. Saulter
- mus: Sam Morgenstern
- lyrics: William Mercur
- dir: Edgar G. Ulmer
- cast: Leo Fuchs (Nat Silver), Judith Abarbanel (Judith Aarons), Rosetta Bialis (Mrs. Aarons), Yudel Dubinsky (Morris Zucker/Moishe Pipik), Abe Lax (Simon P. Schwalbenrock), Anna Guskin (Elvie), Celia Budkin (Nat's mother), William Mercur, Esther Adler

Der Groyser Eytse Geber (The Greater Advisor)
Jewish Talking Pictures, 70 min., U.S.
- sc: Isidor Frankel
- dir: Joseph Seiden
- cast: Irving Jacobson, Yetta Zwerling, Sol Dickstein, Max

Baden, Muni Serebroff, Abe Lax, Mae Schoenfeld, Chaim Tauber, Helen Blay, Isidor Frankel, David Yanover, Dora Weissman, Rose Greenfield, Lazar Freed, Leibele Waldman

Der Vilner Shtot Khazn (The Vilna Cantor)
also released as *Overture to Glory* and *Der Vilner Balabesl*
G & L Motion Picture Corporation, 85 min., U.S.
sc: Ossip Dymow, from a play by Mark Arnstein
cam: Larry Williams
dial: Jacob Glatstein
mus: Alexander Olshanetsky
prod: Ira Greene and Ludwig Landy
prod.
dir: George Moskov
dir: Max Nosseck
cast: Moishe Oysher (Yoel-David Strashunsky), Helen Beverly (Wanda), Florence Weiss (Khane Strashunsky), Baby Winkler (Perets Strashunsky), Maurice Krohner (Aaron), Lazar Freed (Rabbi), Benjamin Fishbein (Nute), Jack Mylong Munz (Moniuszko), Ossip Dymow (Count Parnofsky), Leonard Elliot (Tilchinsky), Luba Wesoly (countess), Ivan Busatt (director of opera), Erika Zaranova (Prima Donna)

Der Yidishe Nigun (The Jewish Melody)
Jewish Talking Pictures, 89 min., U.S.
sc: Chaim Tauber
mus: Sholom Secunda
dir: Joseph Seiden
cast: Isidore Cashier, Lazar Freed, Chaim Tauber, Seymour Rechtzeit, Dave Lubritsky, Moishe Feder, Yetta Zwerling, Mae Schoenfeld, Esta Salzman, Rose Greenfield, Jacob Zanger

Eli Eli (My God, My God)
Jewish Talking Pictures, 89 min., U.S.
sc: Isidor Frankel
mus: Sholom Secunda
dir: Joseph Seiden
cast: Esther Field, Lazar Freed, Irving Jacobson, Mae Schoenfeld, Muni Serebroff, Rose Greenfield, Max Baden, Isidor Frankel, Herman Rosen, Paula Lubelska, Eddie Friedlander

Ir Tsveyte Mame (Her Second Mother)
Jewish Talking Pictures, feature-length, U.S.

mus: Sholom Secunda
dir: Joseph Seiden
cast: Esta Salzman, Muni Serebroff, Yetta Zwerling, Max Baden, Jacob Zanger, Rose Greenfield, Seymour Rechtzeit, Isidor Frankel, Herman Rosen

1941 *Mazl Tov Yidn* (Mazel Tov, Jews)
Jewish Talking Pictures, 89 min., U.S.
mus: Alexander Olshanetsky, Sholom Secunda
dir: Joseph Seiden
cast: Michael Rosenberg, Leo Fuchs, Yetta Zwerling, Chaim Tauber, Leibele Waldman, Esta Salzman, Hanna Hollander, Lili Liliana, Jacob Zanger, Menashe Oppenheim, Gustav Berger, Seymour Rechtzeit, Anna Thomashefsky

1947 *Lang Iz der Veg* (Long Is the Road)
International Film Organization, 77 min., West Germany
sc: Karl-Georg Kulb and Israel Becker, from a story by Becker
cam: Franz Koch
mus: Lothar Bruhne
art: C. L. Kirmse
prod: Abraham Weinstein
dir: Herbert B. Fredersdorf and Marek Goldstein, Israel Becker
cast: Israel Becker (David Jelin), Bettina Moissi (Dora Berkowitz), Berta Litwina (Hanna Jelin), Jacob Fischer (Jakob Jelin), Alexander Bardini (Farmer), David Hart (Liebermann), Mischa Nathan (Partisan), Otta Wernicke (older Doctor), Paul Dahlke (Doctor), Hans Leo Fischer (Chodetzki)

Mir Lebn Geblibene (We the Living Remnant)
Kinor, 50 min., Poland
sc: Ephraim Kaganovsky
cam: Adolf Forbert
mus: Saul Brezhuwski
narr: Jacob Rotboym
prod: Shaul Goskind and Joseph Juszynski
art: Natan Rapaport
dir: Natan Gross

1948 *Unzere Kinder* (Our Children)
also released as *It Will Never Happen Again*
Kinor, feature-length, Poland

sc: Rokhl Auerbach
prod: Shaul Goskind
dir: Natan Gross
cast: Shimen Dzigan, Yisroel Schumacher, Nusia Gold

We Live Again
Jewish Film Distributors, 50 min., France
prod: M. Bahelfer, O. Fessler, A. Hamza, I. Holodenko, J. Weinfeld

1949 *Dray Tekhter* (Three Daughters)
Cinema Service Corp., feature-length, U.S.
sc: from a play by Abraham Blum
cam: Harold Seiden
mus: Alexander Olshanetsky
lyrics: Chaim Tauber
dir: Joseph Seiden
cast: Michael Rosenberg, Sacha Shaw, Rebecca Weintraub, Charlotte Goldstein, Max Wilner, Jacob Shachter, Anatole Winogradoff

Got, Mentsh un Tayvl (God, Man and Devil)
Aaron Films, 100 min., U.S./Canada
sc: Isidor Frankel, from a Jacob Gordin play
cam: Harold Seiden
mus: Sholom Secunda
prod: Daniel Silver and Sol C. Rynd
dir: Joseph Seiden
cast: Michel Michalesco (Hershele Dubrovner), Berta Gersten (Pesenyu), Gustav Berger (Mizek), Lucy Gehrman (Dobe), Max Bozyk (Lazar), Shifra Lehrer (Freydenyu), Leon Schechter (Khaskl), Esta Salzman (Tsipenyu), Joshua Zeldis (Motl)

1950 *Catskill Honeymoon*
Pictorial Ventures, feature-length, U.S.
cam: Charles Down
mus: Hymie Jacobson and Alexander Olshanetsky
prod: Martin Cohen and Jack Lamont
dir: Josef Berne
cast: Henrietta Jacobson, Julius Adler, Bas Sheva, Jan Bart, Dina Goldberg, Irving Grossman, Bobby Colt, Michel Michalesco, Abe Lax, Mary La Roche, Feder Sisters

Monticello, Here We Come
also released as *Borsht Belt Follies*

Cinema Service Corporation, 83 min., U.S.
narr: Michael Rosenberg
cam: Harold Seiden
dir: Joseph Seiden
cast: Michel Michalesco, Leo Fuchs, Maneshe Skulnick, Max Wilner, Joseph Buloff

Singers of Israel
Cinema Service Corporation, 10 min., U.S.
cam: Harold Seiden
dir: Joseph Seiden
cast: Cantor Samuel Melavsky and his family choir

1974 *Dos Mazl* (Luck)
New York University Film Department, 20 min., U.S.
sc: from folktale
cam: Sally Heckel
mus: Josh Waletzky
narr: Fishl Kolko
dir: Josh Waletzky
cast: Lili Glogowsky, Matthew Speier

1980 *Dakh-Brusil* (Shelter-Brussels)
released as *Brussels-Transit*
Paradise-Films, 80 min., Belgium
sc: Samy Szlingerbaum
cam: Michel Houssiau
prod: Marilyn Watelet
dir: Samy Szlingerbaum
cast: Helene Lapiower, Boris Lehman, Jeremy Wald, Micha Wald, Suzy Falk, Jean-Paul Connard, Lucien Charbonnier, Jean Pascal, Adeline Liebman, Simone Duriev

Der Dibuk (The Dybbuk)
E. R. Kaminska Jewish State Theater of Poland
feature-length, Poland
sc: Simon Szurmiej, from the play by S. Anski
dir: Stephan Szlachtycz
cast: Golda Tencer (Leah), Jan Szurmiej (Khonon), Hersz Hercher (Rabbi of Miropol), Simon Szurmiej Meshulleh), Symche Daleki (Sender), Stefana Straszewsaka (Freyda), Chaim Rajfer, Joachim Reknitz, Mosze Szwejlich, Josef Adelson, Witokd Gruca

1983 *Der Brunem* (The Wall)
David Greenwald Productions, 30 min., U.S.

sc: David Greenwald
cam: Paul Ziller
mus: Leon Odenz
prod: Paula Pevzner
dir: David Greenwald
cast: Jeff Nishball, Moishe Rosenfeld, Raquel Yossifson, Itzik Gottesman, Avram Malowicki, Jacob Axelrod, Helen Perle, Helen Rubinstein

Az Men Git Nemt Men (When They Give, Take)
English title: *Giveaway*
Hebrew title: *K'shenotnim, Kach*
Roll Films, 90 min., Israel
sc: Michael Greenstein
cam: Nissim Leon
mus: Martin Moskowitch
prod: Yair Prudelski and Israel Ringel
dir: Alfred Steinhardt
cast: Yacob Bodo, Rachel Dayan, Karol Feldman, Irit Meiry

Bibliography

Books

Arosev, Alexander Vokovlevich, ed. *Soviet Cinema.* Moscow: VOKS, 1935.
Babel, Isaac. *Benya Krik, A Film-Novel.* Translated by Ivor Montagu and S. S. Nolbandov. London: Collet's, 1935.
Babitsky, Paul and Rimberg, John. *The Soviet Film Industry.* New York: Frederick A. Praeger, 1955.
Banaszkiewics, Wladyslaw, and Witezak, Witold. *Historia Filmu Polskiego.* Warsaw: Wydawnietwa Artystyezne i Filmowe, Vol. 1, 1966.
Baron, Salo W. *The Russian Jew Under the Tsars and Soviets.* New York: MacMillan, 1964.
Belton, John. *Howard Hawks, Frank Borzage, Edgar G. Ulmer.* New York: A. S. Barnes, 1974.
Ben-Ari, Raikin, *Habima.* New York: Thomas Yoseloff Inc., 1957.
Brownlow, Kevin. *The Parade's Gone By.* New York: Alfred A. Knopf, 1968.
Burko, Faina. "The Soviet Yiddish Theatre in the Twenties." Ph.D. dissertation, Southern Illinois University at Carbondale, 1978.
Cantacuzino, Ion, ed. *Contributii La Istoria Cinematografiei in Romania, 1896-1948.* Bucherest: Editura Academiei Republicii Socialiste Romania, 1971.
Copyright Office of Library of Congress. *Catalog of Copyright Entries Cumulative Series Motion Pictures 1912-1939.* Washington, D.C.: Copyright Office of Library of Congress, 1951.
Cripps, Thomas. *Slow Fade to Black.* New York: Oxford University Press, 1977.
Denk, David. *Shvarts Oyf Vays.* New York: Greenwich Printing, 1963.
Dobroszycki, Lucjan, and Kirshenblatt-Gimblett, Barbara. *Image Before My Eyes: A Photographic History of Jewish Life in Poland, 1864-1939.* New York: Schocken, 1977.
Dubnov, Simon. *History of the Jews.* New York: Thomas Yoseloff, Vol. 5, 1973.
Dzigan, Shimen. *Der Koyakh fun Yidishn Humor.* Tel Aviv: Orly, 1974.
Eisner, Lotte H. *The Haunted Screen.* Berkeley: University of California Press, 1973.
Encyclopedia Judaica, First Edition, S. v. "Motion Pictures," by Nachman Ingbar.
Encyclopedia Shel Galuyot. S. v. "Jews in Film Production (Warsaw)," by J. M. Neuman.
Fishman, Jacob, Levin, B. and Stabinowitz, B. *Finf Un Tsvantsik Yor Folksbine.* New York: privately published, 1940.
Fox, Stuart, comp. *Jewish Films in the United States: A Comprehensive Survey and Descriptive Filmography.* Boston: G. K. Hall & Co., 1976.
Friedman, Lester D. *Hollywood's Image of the Jew.* New York: Frederick Ungar, 1982.
Gilboa, Yehoshua. *The Black Years of Soviet Jewry.* Boston: Little, Brown and Co., 1971.

Gorin, B. *Di Geshikhte Fun Yidishn Teater.* 2 vols. New York: Max N. Mayzel, 1923.
Greenberg, Eliezer, and Howe, Irving. *A Treasury of Yiddish Stories.* New York: Schocken Books, 1973.
Heller, Celia. *On the Edge of Destruction.* New York: Columbia University Press, 1977.
Howe, Irving. *World of Our Fathers.* New York: Simon and Schuster, 1976.
Howe, Irving and Greenberg, Eliezer. *Ashes Out of Hope: Fiction by Soviet-Yiddish Writers.* New York: Schocken, 1977.
Interviews with Soviet Artists. Moscow: Press Department. VOKS, no date.
Kaminska, Ida. *My Life, My Theatre.* Translated by Curt Leviant. New York: MacMillan, 1973.
Kochan, Lionel, ed. *The Jews in Soviet Russia Since 1917.* London: Oxford University Press, 1972.
Kohansky, Mendel. *The Hebrew Theatre.* Jerusalem: Israel Universities Press, 1969.
Kracauer, Siegfried. *From Caligari to Hitler: A Psychological History of the German Film.* Princeton: Princeton University Press, 1974.
Levaco, Ronald, ed. *Kuleshov on Film.* Berkeley: University of California Press, 1974.
Leyda, Jay. *Kino: A History of the Russian and Soviet Film.* New York: Collier, 1973.
Lifson, David. *The Yiddish Theatre in America.* New York: Thomas Yoseloff, 1965.
Liptzin, Sol. *The Flowering of Yiddish Literature.* New York: Thomas Yoseloff, 1963.
Macheret, Alexander, et. al., eds. *Soviet Fictional Films, An Annotated Catalog.* Vol. 1: *Silent Film (1918-1935),* compiled by Gosfilmofond. Moscow: Iskusstvo, 1961.
Medem Sanatorie Bukh. Tel Aviv: Menorah Press, 1971.
Mellen, Joan. *The Waves At Genji's Door.* New York: Pantheon, 1976.
Miron, Dan. *A Traveler Disguised.* New York: Schocken, 1973.
Munden, Kenneth W., ed. *The American Film Institute Catalog, Feature Films 1921-1930.* New York and London: R. R. Bowker Co., 1971.
Paimann's Filmlisten [Vienna], 1923-1924.
Picon, Molly. *Molly!* New York: Simon and Schuster, 1980.
Picon-Vallin, Beatrice. *Le Theatre Juif Sovietique Pendant Les Années Vingt.* Lausanne: La Cité-L'Age d'Homme, 1973.
Pratt, George C. *Spellbound in Darkness: A History of the Silent Film.* Greenwich, Connecticut: New York Graphic Society, 1973.
Richie, Donald. *Japanese Cinema.* New York: Anchor, 1971.
Rosenfeld, Lulla. *Bright Star of Exile: Jacob Adler and the Yiddish Theatre.* New York: Crowell, 1977.
Rotha, Paul, and Griffith, Richard. *The Film Till Now.* Norwich: Fletcher & Son Ltd., 1967.
Rumanian Film Reviews. Bucharest: Rumanian National Film Archive, no date.
Sachar, Howard Morley. *The Course of Modern Jewish History.* New York: Delta, 1963.
Sadoul, Georges. *Historire du Cinéma Mondial: Des Origines A Nos Jours.* Paris: Flammarion, 1949.
Sandrow, Nahma. *Vagabond Stars: A World History of Yiddish Theater.* New York: Harper & Row, 1977.
Sklar, Robert. *Movie-Made America.* New York: Random House, 1975.
Slonim, Marc. *Russian Theatre from the Empire to the Soviets.* New York: Collier Books, 1961.
Toeplitz, Jerzy. *Historia Sztuki Filmovcz.* Warsaw: Filmowa Agencja Wydawnicza, Vol. 2, 1956.
Turkow, Zygmund. *Di Ibergerisene Tkufe: Fragmentn fun Mayn Lebn.* Buenos Aires: Central Farband, 1961.
Tyler, Parker. *Classics of the Foreign Film.* New York: Citadel, 1962.

Vishnevsky, Venyamin. *Fictional Films of Pre-Revolutionary Russia*. Moscow: Goskino Izdat, 1945.
Wright, Basil. *The Long View*. New York: Alfred A. Knopf, 1974.
Zborowski, Mark, and Herzog, Elizabeth. *Life Is With People: The Culture of the Shtetl*. New York: Schocken, 1973.
Zylbercweig, Zalmen, comp. ed., *Leksikon fun Yidishn Teater*. New York: Hebrew Actor's Union of America, Vols. 1-6, 1931-1969.

Periodicals

Basshe, Em Jo. "Three Films." *New Masses* 5 (November 1929), pp. 14-15.
Bogdanovich, Peter. "Edgar G. Ulmer, An Interview." *Film Culture* 58-59-60 (1974), pp. 206-35.
Cenkalski, Christina and Eugene. "Polish Film Builds for the Future." *Hollywood Quarterly* 3/3 (April 1947), pp. 294-96.
"Der Nayer Yidisher Film *Yidl Mitn Fidl*." *Literarishe Bleter* [Warsaw] (1936), p. 625.
Deytschedtan, S. "Vegn Yidishn Film." *Der Emes*. [Moscow] 63, 15 March 1928, p. 5.
Dobroszycki, Lucjan. "Post-War Jewish Life in Poland." *Soviet Jewish Affairs* 2/3 (1973), pp. 58-72.
"Dr. Goebbels at the Cinema: Excerpts from Diaries." *Sight and Sound* 19 (August 1950).
Dreyer-Sfard, Regina. "HaBa'aya HaYehudit B'Kolnoa Ha-Sovyeti." *Kolnoa* 3/4 (September 1974), pp. 122-26.
Erens, Patricia. "Mentshlekhkayt Conquers All: The Yiddish Cinema in America." *Film Comment,* January-February 1976, pp. 48-53.
———. "Rescuing Surrender." *Velvet Light Trap* (1975), pp. 1-6.
Fefer, Itzik. *"Skvoz' Slezy."* *Kino* [Kiev] 3/39 (1928), p. 3.
———. "Vegn Yidishn Film." *Kino* [Kiev] 3/39. (1928), p. 2.
Filmikus, B. "Oyf Landshaft-Oyfnames Tsum *'Dibuk'*-Film." *Literarishe Bleter* [Warsaw] (1937), p. 469.
"Fun Tsaytungen Un Zhurnaln." *Literarishe Bleter* [Warsaw] (1938), p. 229.
Granach, Alexander. "Granovsky, Mikhoels un Zuskin—a yesher koakh aykh." *Literarishe Bleter* [Warsaw] (1928), p. 390.
Granovsky, Alexei. "Unzer Teater." *Literarishe Bleter* [Warsaw] (1938), pp. 317-18.
Gross, Natan. "HaSeret HaYehudi B'Polin Acharei Milchemet HaOlam HaShniya." *Kolnoa* 2 (May 1974), pp. 53-71.
Horowitz, Norbert. "Yidishe Teater fun der Sheyris-Hapleyte." *Fun Noentn Ovar* (1955), pp. 167-68.
"In Shtetl fun Grin-Film." *Literarishe Bleter* [Warsaw] (1937), p. 533.
Kitai, M. "Ershter Yidisher Klangfilm *Al Khet*." *Literarishe Bleter* [Warsaw] (1936), p. 305.
Klein, Albert. "HaNoseh HaYehudi B'Kolnoa HaSovyeti." *Kolnoa* 1 (March 1974), pp. 78-92.
———. "HaNoseh HaYudi B'Kolnoa HaSovyeti: Tshuva L'Mamara Shel Dr. Regina Dreyer-Sfard B'Choveret 3/4." *Kolnoa* 5 (April-May 1975), pp. 80-84.
Kon, Henikh. "In Film Atelye." *Literarishe Bleter* [Warsaw] (1937), p. 485.
Lubomirsky, Y. "Teater un Kino-*Blondzhende Shtern*." *Der Emes* [Moscow] 43, 19 February 1928, p. 4.
Makotinski, M. *"Skvoz' Slezy."* *Kino* [Kiev] 3/39 (1928), pp. 8-9.
Matis, David. "Tsu Der Geshikhte fun Yidishe Films." *Ikuf-Almanak* (1961), pp. 439-65.
Meizel, Nakhman. "Perets Hirshbeyns *Grine Felder* In Film." *Literarishe Bleter* [Warsaw] (1938), pp. 143-45.

———. "Moris Shvarts bay der Arbet." *Literarishe Bleter* [Warsaw] (1938), pp. 197–99.
———. "Mikhoels." *Literarishe Bleter* [Warsaw] (1928), pp. 881–82.
Miron, Dan. "HaDimui HaSifruti HaClasi Shel HaAyara." Unpublished article, no date.
Moskowitz, Gene. "The Uneasy East." *Sight and Sound* 27/3 (Winter 1957–58), pp. 136–40.
"A Nayer Yidisher Film." *Literarishe Bleter* [Warsaw] (1938), p. 752.
Neuman, J. M. "Plan-Virtshaft in der Yidisher Film-Produksie." *Literarishe Bleter* [Warsaw] (1938), p. 91.
"Opatashus *Poylishe Velder* oyfn Film." *Literarishe Bleter* [Warsaw] (1928), p. 771.
Potamkin, Harry Alan. "Movie: New York Notes." *Close-Up* 6 (February 1930), pp. 98–104.
Riklin, G. *"Evreiskoe Schaft'e. Kino* [Moscow] 36 (1925).
Roskies, David. "The Celluloid Jew." *Response* 7 (Spring 1970), 13–19.
Rothman, N. L. "The Jew on the Screen." *Jewish Forum* XI (October 1928), pp. 527–28.
Senff, Felix. "Rudolph Schildkraut Tells How." *Cinema Art* 5 (February 1926), p. 52.
Shnior, M. "Henikh Kon-Un Zayn Muzikalishe Tetikayt." *Literarishe Bleter* [Warsaw], (1937), p. 305.
"*Tkies Kaf.*" *Literarishe Bleter* [Warsaw] 2 (1924), p. 6.
Tsavion, B. "Fun Tsaytungen un Zhurnaln." *Literarishe Bleter* [Warsaw] (1938), p. 229.
Tshemerinski, B. "Vi Mir Hobn Oyfgefirt Sholem Aleykhms *Mabul* farn Film." *Literarishe Bleter* [Warsaw] (1926), pp. 286–87.
Tsintsinatus, A. "Vegn Yidishn Film In Poyln." Unknown journal, Private collection of Shaul Goskind.
Turkow, Jonas. "Opatashu in Film," *Literarishe Bleter* [Warsaw] (1930), p. 136.
"Vegn Klangfilm *Mir Kumen On.*" *Literarishe Bleter* [Warsaw] (1936), p. 318.
"Yidisher Klangfilm *On A Heym.*" *Literarishe Bleter* [Warsaw] (1939), p. 145.

Newspapers

Bart, Peter. "How to Be a Loner in Hollywood." *New York Times,* 13 March 1966.
"Broken Hearts: An All Jewish Cinema of Jewish Immigrant Life." *American Hebrew,* 26 February 1926, p. 497.
"Cantor's Son Dramatizes Life of Star." *New York Post,* 8 January 1939.
Cheavens, David. "26 Yiddish Talkies Planned by Judea." *Telegraph,* 13 June 1930.
———. "All Yiddish Film Theatre to Open." *Telegraph,* 25 August 1930.
"Compromise Settles Fight Over Showing of Initial Yiddish Talkie in Tel Aviv." *Jewish Daily Bulletin,* 30 September 1930.
"First All-Yiddish Talking Film Here." *Evening Telegram,* 24 September 1930.
"First Yiddish All-Talking Picture Given Preview." *American Hebrew,* 5 September 1930, p. 423.
Freedman, Morris, "Contemporary of William Fox Still Making Yiddish Pictures." *New York Herald-Tribune,* 14 November 1948.
"Freedom in the Newton Hills for Jewish and Ukrainian Actors, Monks, Nudists and Nazis." *New York Daily Mirror,* 18 September 1938.
Golden, Herb. "Negro and Yiddish Film Boom." *Variety,* 3 January 1940.
Hamilton, Maxwell. "Movie Maker Joe Seiden Keeps 3 Room Studio Humming." *Brooklyn Daily Eagle,* 7 April 1936.
Hall, Mordaunt. "Broken Hearts." *New York Times,* 3 March 1926, p. 26.
"Jennie Goldstein Signed for Jewish Talker Series." *Film Daily,* 18 March 1930.
"Jennie Goldstein to Make Talkies." *New York American,* 17 March 1930.
"Jewish Films In Own Tongue." *Variety,* 22 January 1930.

"'Judea Film Company' and its First Talkies in the Yiddish Language." *Jewish Daily Forward*, 1 June 1930.
"Judea Films' First Two Shorts Ready." *Exhibitors Daily Review and Motion Pictures Today*, 24 February 1930.
"Judea Ready to Release First Two Talkers." *Film Daily*, 10 March 1930.
Kaufman, Wolfe. "Shir Hashirim." *Variety*, 23 October 1935.
Mandelbaum, A. "Khazeray Deluks." *Morning Freiheit*, 3 July 1930.
"New Company to Produce Motion Picture Film." *Motion Picture News*, 25 January 1930.
"New Yiddish Film Producing Outfit A La Group Theater." *Variety*, 27 October 1937.
"New York to Have Three Houses Devoted to Yiddish Talkies." *Jewish Post* (Paterson, N.J.), 24 May 1930.
Panzer, Martin. "Jewish Movies Come of Age." *American Hebrew*, 17 November 1939, p. 6.
Picon, Molly. "Fiddling in Old Kazmierz." *New York Times*, 17 January 1937, 10, p. 5.
"A People That Shall Never Die." *New York Post*, 1 September 1939.
Pryor, Thomas. "Outside of Jericho." *New York Times*, 30 July 1939, 9, p. 3.
"Raymond L. Schrock, The Man Who Makes Hebrew Comedies." *Moving Picture World*, 1 January 1927, p. 50.
"Screen Director to be Paid Homage." *Jewish Journal*, 16 July 1930.
"Seiden Producing." *Daily Review*, 6 February 1930.
"Teater, Muvis, Muzik." *Der Tog*, 18 June 1930.
"Three Theatres in New York Nucleus of National Yiddish Talkie Chain." *Intermountain Jewish News*, 30 May 1930.
"12 Features, 24 Shorts Planned by Judea Films." *Film Daily*, 6 May 1930.
"'Shuster Libe' in Beneson Teater." *Jewish Daily Forward*, 23 March 1930.
"Union Yiddish Actors Barred From Appearing in Yiddish Talkies." *Daily World* (Philadelphia), 1 July 1930.
"Yiddish Film Starts Rioting in Palestine." *The World*, 26 September 1930.
"A Yiddish Talkie." *Jewish Outlet*, 17 April 1930.
"Yiddish Talkies Started by Judea Films." *Jewish Times*, 30 May 1930.
"Yiddish Theatre becomes Picture House." *Moving Picture World*, 5, 18 September 1909, p. 376.
"Yidishe Aktyorn Yunyon Gegn Yidishe 'Tokies.'" *Tsayt* (London), 30 June 1930.

Interviews

Abarbanel, Judith. Miami, 6 March 1978.
Ben-Ami, Jacob. New York, 16 March 1975.
Bernardi, Herschel. Los Angeles, 22 March 1975.
Dzigan, Shimen. Tel Aviv, 31 August 1977.
Fuchs, Leo. Los Angeles, 30 March 1975.
Goskind, Shaul. Tel Aviv, August 1976.
Green, Joseph. New York, 14 April 1977.
Greene, Ira. New York, 10 July 1978.
Gross, Natan. Tel Aviv, August 1976.
Kaminska, Ida. Tel Aviv, 2 September 1977.
Kaminska-Turkow, Ruth. New York, 6 May 1978.
Kelemer, Samuel. Los Angeles, 13 November 1978.
Kressyn, Miriam. New York, 19 July 1977.
Liebgold, Leon. New York, 13 June 1977.

Liliana, Lili. New York, 13 June 1977.
Malcames, Don. New York State, 13 October 1978.
Opatoshu, David. Long Island, 20 March 1975.
Picon, Molly. New York, 10 August 1977.
Rechtzeit, Seymour. New York, 19 July 1977.
Riselle Orloff, Miriam. Philadelphia, 24 January 1978.
Roshal, Grigori. Moscow, 19 August 1977.
Scooler, Zvee. New York, 16 May 1978.
Seiden, Harold. New York, 11 July 1978.
Steinwurcel, Seweryn. Lod, Israel, 8 September 1977.
Turkow, Jonas. Bat Yam, Israel, 9 September 1977.
Zucker, Frank. Miami, 16 October 1978.

Listing of Yiddish Films Available for Rental (16mm)

Jewish Media Service/JWB
15 East 26th Street
New York, NY 10010

or

Films Incorporated
1144 Wilmette Avenue
Wilmette, Illinois 60091

    A Brivele der Mamen (A Letter to Mother)(1938)
    Dem Khazns Zundl (The Cantor's Son)(1937)
    Laughter through Tears (From Durkh Trern—1927)(1933)
    Mamele (Little Mother)(1938)
    Der Purimshpiler (The Purim Player)(1937)
    Yidl mitn Fidl (Yidl with a Fiddle)(1936)

Rutenberg and Everet Yiddish Film Library
National Center for Jewish Film
Lown Building/102
Brandeis University
Waltham, Massachusetts 02254

    Amerikaner Shadkhn (American Matchmaker)(1940)
    Catskill Honeymoon (1949)
    Got, Mentsh un Tayvl (God, Man and Devil)(1949)
    Grine Felder (Green Fields)(1937)
    Di Klyatshe (The Dobbin/The Light Ahead)(1939)

Mir Kumen On (We Are On Our Way/Children Must Laugh)(1936)
Mirele Efros (1938)
Mizrekh un Mayrev (East and West)(1923)
Tevye der Milkhiker (Tevye the Milkman)(1939)
A Vilna Legend (From Tkies Kaf — 1924)(1933)
Vu Iz Mayn Kind (Where Is My Child)(1937)
Der Zingendiker Shmid (The Singing Blacksmith)(1938)

Index

Listings in boldface type refer to photographs

"A Bletl Geshikhte." *See Durkh Trern*
A Brivele der Mamen (1911), 9, 173
A Brivele der Mamen (1938), 30, 90, 102-4, **104**, 151, 195-96
A Jew At War. See A Mentsh fun Shtetl
A Mentsh fun Shtetl, 46-49, 184
Abarbanel, Judith, 67, **68**, **69**, 81, 129, **129**
Abarbanel, Lorraine, **80**
Abramovitz, S.J. *See* Mendele Mokher Seforim
Actors, films about, 40
Ad Mosay, 56, 183
Adler, Ben, 70
Adler, Celia, 74, **75**, 112
Adler, Julius, 153, **155**
Adler, Yankl, 87, 109
"The Adolescent," 46
Agudath Israel, 27, 29-30
Akarski, S.L., 6-7, 9
Al Khet, 86, 87, **88**, 92, 100, 109, 150, 191
Alcoholism, treatment of, 116
Aleichem, Sholom. *See* Sholom Aleichem
Alexander III, Czar, 1
Alexandrov, Grigori, 40, 49
American Film Institute, 159, 161
American Jewish Historical Society, 122, 158, 161
American Joint Distribution Committee, 143, 147, 150
American Matchmaker. See Amerikaner Shadkhn
Amerikaner Shadkhn, 127, **129**, 160, 200
Anglo-American Committee of Inquiry, 144
Anski, S. (Solomon Zaynwil Rapaport), 60-61, 92, 95
Appel, Anna, 56, **117**
Arbatov, Nikolai Nikolevich, 23
Arkatov, Alexander, 1-2, 6, 9, 10
Arko, Israel, 6

Arnstein, Mark, 6, 96, 118, 130
Artistishe Vinkele. *See* Dos Artistishe Vinkele
Asch, Sholom, 6, 67, 87
Ashmidai, 61
Audience, examination of viewing, 127
Auerbach, Rokhl, 150
Auschwitz, 144
Austria, film production in, 11-16
Avrom Ovinu, 70, **71**, 189
Axelbank, Herman, 121-22
Azarkh, Abraham. *See* Granovsky, Alexander
Aziade, 9, 179
Az Men Git, Nemt Men, 64, 164, **164**, 205

Babel, Isaac, 36, 37, 48, 51
Balaban, Meyer, 96
Banks, Sadie, 57
Bar Mitsva, **73**, 74, 83, 190
Baratoff, Ben-Zvi, 118, 120
Baratz, Marty, 57, **58**
Bart, Jan, 153
Bas Sheva, 153
The Battleship Potemkin, 36
Becker, Israel, 144, **145**, 146
The Beilis Case, 179
Beilis, Mendel, 3
Belgium, film production in, 162
Belgoskino, 46
Ben-Ami, Jacob, 81, 113, 114, 120
Ben-Ari, Raikin, 34
Benye Krik, 37-40, 44, 182
Berg, Judith, 97, **98**, **99**
Berger, Gustav, 151
Berkowitz, Jacob, 64
Berliner, Sam, 56
Bernardi, Herschel, **114**, 115, 157
Berne, Josef, 122, 153
Besenko, Ben, 70
Beser Dem Toyt Eyder Aza Shand, 9, 178
Beverly, Helen, **114**, 120, **121**, **131**
Bialik, Chaim Nachman, 96

216   Index

Biograph Studios, 126
Birobidjan, film production in, 50
The Black Cat, 113-15, 121
Black Hundreds, 1, 34
The Black Hundreds. See The Terrors of Russia
Blake, Ben K., 77, 78, 112
Blay, Heln, **59**
Bleeding Hearts, 3
Bleich, Yehuda, 64, **80**
Block, Mildred, 61
Blondzhende Shtern, 40, 44, 48, 182
Blum, Abraham, 153
Blumenfeld, Diana, 18, 27, 30
Bodo, Eugene, 107
Bodo, Yacob, **163**
Bojm, Henryk, 17, **19**, 22, 23-27
Border Street. See Ulica Graniczna
Borsht Belt Follies. See Catskill Honeymoon
Bossak, Jerzy, 147
Boyberik camp, 158
Bozyk, Max, **91**, **93**, 95, 100, **101**, 104, **106**, 151
Bredschneider, Bruon, 18
Brezhuwski, Saul, 148
Broderson, Moshe, 92, 100, 109
Brodsky, Nicholas, 90, 100, 109
The Broken Doll, 57, 184
Broken Hearts. See Tsebrokhene Hertser
Bronx, film production in, 126
Bruner, Irving, **105**
Brussels-Transit. See Dakh-Brisel
Brzeziny, film production in, 102
Bullman, Gertrude, 104, **105**, **106**, **154**
Buloff, Joseph, 70, 100, 156
Burgi-Contner, J., 61, 115, 120, 133
Burstyn, Joseph, 44, 70
Buzgan, Khevel, **88**

A Cantor on Trial, 64, 187
The Cantor's Son. See Dem Khazns Zundl
cantorial film recordings, 56, 60, 64, 79, 130-32, 148, 156
cantors, films about, 81, 130-32
Cashier, Isidore, **66**, 120, **121**, 140
Casimir III, King, 3, 92
Castles in the Sky. See Yidl Mitn Fidl
Catherine II, Czarina, 1
Catholic Legion of Decency, 111
Catskill Honeymoon, 153, **155**, 203
censhorship of film, 27-30
Central Committee for Child Welfare, Union of Jews for Resistance and Mutual Aid in France, 146
Central Committee of Polish Jews, 146, 147, 150
Chalutzim, 84
Chaplin, Charles, 13, 36

Chaver-Pahver (Gershon Einbinder), 97, 119
Child desertion, film about, 133
Ciechocinek, film production in, 104-7
Cobb, Lee J., **114**, 120
Cobbler Love. See Shuster Libe
Cohen, Martin, 153, 155
Cohen, Max, 55
Cohen, Sam, 77
Collective Film Producers, 116
Come Blow Your Horn, 12
Confession, 86. *See also Al Khet*
Cracow, film production in, 100

Dakh-Brisel, 162, **162**, 204
Das Judenmadel, 12
Dassin, Jules, 158
A Daughter of Her People. See Yidishe Tokhter
Dawn to Dawn, 122
Day of Atonement. *See* Yom Kippur
Death Factories, 144
Dem Khazns Tokhter, 176
Dem Khazns Zundl, 4, 80, 81, 116, 130, 192-93
Dem Rebins Koyekh. See Tkies Kaf (1923)
Denk, David, 32, **59**
Der Blutiker Shpas, 9, **10**, 179
Der Brunem, 163, **163**, 204-5
Der Dibuk, 61, 92-96, 97, **98**, **99**, 193; Israeli production in Hebrew, 97, **98**, **99**; Polish theater film recording, 97, 163-64, 204
Der Finfter Yortsayt fun Oyfshtand in Bialistoker Geto, 148
Der Finfter Yortsayt fun Oyfshtand in Varshever Geto, 148
Der Groyser Eytse Geber, 133, 200-201
Der Lamedvovnik, 23, **26**, 91, 95, 180
Der Lebediker Yosem, 133, **134**, 197-98
Der Mabul, 33, 35, 181
Der Purimshpiler, 30, 90, 92, 97-100, **101**, 102, 103, 104, 119, 144, 153, 160-61, 193-94
Der Unbekanter, 176
Der Veg Tsum Gezunt, 148
Der Yeshive-Bokher, 174
Der Vilder Foter, 5, 174
Der Vilner Balabesl. See Der Vilner Shtot Khazn
Der Vilner Shtot Khazn, 116, 118, 130-32, **131**, 201
Der Yidishe Nigun (1940), 133, **140**, 201. *See also Yidishe Nigun* (1930)
Der Yidishe Tokhter. See Yidishe Tokhter
Der Yidisher Yishuv in Nider Slezie, 148
Der Yidisher Yishuv in Poylin, 148
Der Zingendiker Shmid, 113, 116, **117**, 119, 122, 126, 127, 130, 133, 196
Di Farshtoysene, 6, 174

Di Farshtoysene Tokhter, 178
Di Freylekhe Kabtsonim, 92, 100-2, **103**, 109, 150, 194
"Di Kishufmakhern," 90
Di Klyatshe, 119-22, **121**, 161, 165, 198
Di Kraft fun Lebn, 74, 196
Di Shkhite, 176
Di Shtifmuter (1911), 5, 173
Di Shtifmuter (1914), 178
Displaced persons, film production by, 144, 146-47
Distant Journey, 146
Divorce Racket, 67
Domb, Adam, **20**, **21**, 104
Dos Artistishe Vinkele, 18
Dos Mazl, 158, **159**, 204
Dos Pintele Yid, 6, 174
Dovzhenko, Alexander, 40
Dray Tekhter, 153, **154**, 203
Dubinsky, David, 86
Dubinsky, Yudel, 64
Durkh Trern, 40-44, **42**, **43**, 70, 182
Dvinsk, film production in, 6
The Dybbuk. See Der Dibbuk
Dymov, Ossip, 6, 118, 122, 130
Dzigan, Shimen, 84, 86, 102, 103, **108**, 109, 149, 150

E.R. Kaminska Jewish State Theater of Poland, 163
East and West. See Mizrekh un Mayrev
East Side Sadie, 56, 183-84
Easton, Pennsylvania, film production in, 81
Egypt and Palestine, 7
Eisenstein, Sergei, 37, 38, 39, 40, 49
Eisman, Goldie, 57, **58**
"El Mole Rakhamim," 56, 148
Eldad, Ilan, 97
Eli Eli (1931), 64, 187
Eli Eli (1940), 133, **135**, 301
Elijah the prophet, depiction of, 18, **20**, **21**, 92
Ellstein, Abe, **66**, 90, 104, 109
Engelhardt, Shaile, 65
Equitable Film, 61
Escaped from Siberia, 3
The Essential Spark of Jewishness. See Dos Pintele Yid
Eternal Fools. See Eybike Naronim
The Eternal Jew. See Avrom Ovinu
The Eternal Prayer. See Ad Mosay
Ets Khaim, 61, 185
An Evening in a Jewish Camp, 61, 185
Eybike Naronim, 64, 184
The Eyes That Saw. See Motele Shpindler

"Far Unzer Gloyben," 87

"Faust," 151
The Feast of Passover, 64, 187-88
Feder, Moishe, **140**
Fefer, Itzik, 44, 51
Feuchtwanger, Lion, 48-49, 52, 53
fidelity in marriage, exposition on, 116
Fiddler on the Roof, 12, 127
Field, Esther, 74, **77**, **135**
Film d'Art, 5, 7
Film Polski, 147
Filma Company, 9
Finkelstein, Henryk, 7
First Cavalry Army, 37
Fischer, Jacob, **145**
Fishbein, Benjamin, 119
Fisher, Jacob, **19**
Fishke der Krumer. See Di Klyatshe
Fishman, Jacob, 112
Fishzon, Misha, 6
Folksbine, 112
Fonvizin, Denis, 46
Forbert, Adolf, 148
Forbert, Leo, 17, 18-19, **19**, 23, 92, 148
Forbert, Vladislaw, 148
Ford, Aleksander, 84, 85, 144, 147-48, 151
Fort Lee, New Jersey, film production in, 133
Fostel, Simche, **91**, **93**, 104, **106**
Fox Pictures, 61, 84
Fox, Stuart, 158
France, Yiddish Film Festival in, 160
Fredersdorf, H.B., 144
Freed, Lazar, 56, **135**, **140**
Freiman, Louis, 74, 81
Frey, Leonard, **128**
Freylekhe Kabtsonim. See Di Freylekhe Kabtsonim
Fuchs, Leo, 79, 127, **129**, 156, 157

Gabel's Public Theater, 57
Gangsters, film about, 37-40
Garfein, Jack, 163
Gaumont Films, 6-7
Gehrman, Lucy, **105**
Gelebt un Gelakht, 77, 189
Gelekhter Durkh Trern, 44. *See also Durkh Trern*
Germany, film production in, 143-46
United States military government in, 143
Yiddish film festival in West Germany, 160
See also Nazi Germany
Gersten, Berta, 112, 122, **123**, 151
Ghetto life, exposition of, 87
Gibson, Michel, **68**, **69**
Gilinski, Shlomo, 84
Giveaway. See Az Men Git, Nemt Men
Glatstein, Jacob, 130

218   Index

Glogowsky, Lila, **159**
God, Man and Devil. See Got, Mentsh un Tayvl
God of Vengeance. See Got fun Nekome
Goebbels, Joseph, 97
Golan, Menachem, 127
Goldberg, Rubin, 67
Goldfaden, Avrom, 5, 70, 90
Goldfaden, Wolf, 70
Goldin, Sidney, 3-5, **4**, 10, 12-17, **14**, 18-19, 31, 55-56, 58, **59**, 61, **63**, 67, **80**
Goldman, Moe, 56, **59**
Goldstein, Charlotte, 153, **154**
Goldstein, Jennie, 57, 77, 112, 122
Goldstein, Marek, 144
Goldstein, Michael, **114**, 157
The Golem, 35, 61
Gordin, Jacob, 5, 6, 77, 107, 113, 118, 151, 153
Goricheva, A.D., 44
Gorin, Michael. *See* Goldstein, Michael
Gorky, Maxim, 40
Goskind, Shaul, 84, 86, 87, 102, 104, 149, 150
Goskind, Yitskhok, 84
Got fun Nekome, 6, 174
Got, Mentsch un Tayvl, (1912), 6, 175
Got, Mentsh un Tayvl, (1949), 151, **154**, 203
Gots Shtrof, 176
Granovsky, Alexander, 33, 35, 37, 40
The Great Advisor. See Der Groyser Eytse Geber
Green, Annette, **91**
Green Fields. See Grine Felder
Green, Joseph, 12, 70, 81, 89-92, **91**, 97-107, **100**, **105**, 111, 119, 129, 144, 165
   preservation of films, 157-58, 160-61
   profile, 89-92
The Green Millionaire, 55
Greenberg, Joseph. *See* Green, Joseph
Greene, Ira, 130
Greenfield, Rose, 79, **140**
Greenwald, David, 163
Gricher-Cherikover, Grigori, 36, 37, 40
Grine Felder, 112-16, **114**, 120, 127, 133, 161, 194
Gross, Helen, 107
Gross, Natan, 148, 150
Gruber, Muriel, **108**
Grudberg, Itskhok, **94**, **105**
"The Guardsman," 64
Guskin, Reuben, 61
Gustkov, Karl, 5
Guttenberg, Bertha, **80**

Habima Theater, 33, 35, 46, 95
Hall, Mordaunt, 32
Halnowek orphanage, **149**, 150
Halpern, Dina, 95, 109
Harold Clurman Theater, 163

Harris, Rosalind, **128**
Hefer, Haim, 127
Her Second Mother. See Ir Tsveyte Mame
Hercele Mejuches, 177
Herschman, Mordechai, 65
Herzl, Theodor, 11
Herzog, Chief Rabbi Isaac, 148
Hester Street, intro, 161
High Arts Pictures Corporation, 64
Hirsch, Baron Maurice de, 36
Hirschbein, Peretz, 112, 113, 116
The Hirschbein Troupe, 113
Hirsh, Nathan, 64
His Wife's Lover. See Zayn Vaybs Lubovnik
Holocaust, films dealing with the, 144-46, 150, 157, 162, 164
Holzer, Rokhl, **88**
Hoover, Herbert, 61
Horizon, the Wandering Jew, 50
How The Jews Take Care of Their Poor, 3
Hütet Eine Töchter, 12

I Want to be a Boarder. See Ikh Vil Zayn A Pansyoner
Ikh Vil Zayn A Mame, 79, 81, 194
Ikh Vil Zayn A Pansyoner, 79, 195
I Have Sinned. See Al Khet
Image Before My Eyes, 158
In Poylishe Velder, 23-30, **28**, **29**, 86, 182-83
In The Czar's Name, 2
"The Initiative of Jewish Actors and Artists," 84
Insanity, exposition of, 74
Institute for Jewish Life, 159
Intermarriage, exposition on, 126
International Ladies Garment Workers' Union, 86
Ir Tsveyte Mame, 133, **138**, 201-2
Israel, Film exhibition in, 64, 151
   Film production in, 64, 164
Italy, Yiddish Film Festival in, 160
Ivanov-Barkov, Yevgeni, 34, 35

Jacobson, Henrietta, 153, **155**
Jacobson, Hymie, 57, 61, **63**, 100, 153
Jakubowska, Wanda, 146
Janilowicz, Jacob, **91**
The Jazz Singer, 55, 89, 132
Jericho, Long Island; film production in, 124
The Jester. See Der Purimshpiler
Jew Süss, 77
Jewish Art Theater. *See* Naye Teater
Jewish Day Hour, 61, 185
Jewish Freedom Under King Casimir of Poland. See Bleeding Hearts
The Jewish Gypsy, 57, 185
Jewish King Lear. See Yidishe Kinig Lir

Jewish Life in Poland. See Der Yidisher Yishuv in Poylin
Jewish Luck. See Yidishe Glikn
Jewish Media Service, 158
The Jewish Melody. See Der Yidishe Nigun
Jewish Talking Pictures Company, 77
Jewish Types in Russia, 1
Jewison, Norman, 127
Joint Distribution Committee. *See* American Joint Distribution Committee
Jolly Paupers. See Di Freylekhe Kabtsonim
Jolson, Al, 132
Joseph in Egypt, 70
Joseph in the Land of Egypt, 70, 83, 188
Judea Pictures, 56-64, 74, 77
Judge, People, 179
Judith Trachtenberg. See Yidishe Tokhter
Juszynski, Joseph, 148

Kabbalistic practice, 96
Kacyzna, Alter, 96, 107
Kadison, Liuba, 57
Kadison, Louis, 57
Kahn, Henikh, 87, 96, 100, 109
Kalich, Jacob, 12-13, **15**, 91, **91**, 104
Kalmonowitz, H., 64
Kaminska, E.R. Theater. *See* E.R. Kaminska Jewish State Theater of Poland
Kaminska, Esther Rokhl, 5, 6, 18, **19**, 22, **24, 25**, 70, 122, 164
Kaminska, Ida, 6, 17, **19**, **24, 25**, 70, 109
Kaminska, Regina, 6
Kaminsky, Avrom Yitskhok, 5, 6
Kaminsky Troupe, 5, 6, 17
Karloff, Boris, 115
Katch, Kurt, 87
Katchko, Adolph, 64, 65
Kaufman, Wolfe, 74
Kazimierz nad Wisla, film production in, 23, 91, 92, 97
Kelemer, Cantor Samuel, 56, **60**
Kessler, David, 102
Khasye di Yesome, 6, 175
The Kid, 13
Kiddush Hashem, 9, 178
Kiev Group, 49
"King Lear," 77
Kinor Film Group; pre-war, 84, 92, 10 post-war, 148
Kirschner Studios, 23
Kitai, M., 83
Kleinerman, Morris, 64
Klezmorim, depiction of, 91, 93
Kaganovsky, Ephraim, 148
Kol Nidre (1930), 60, **60**, 185
Kol Nidre (1939), 133, 198
Korsh-Sablin, Vladimir, 50

Kosciusko Polish Division of Soviet Army, 147
Kosmofilm, 7
Kotzk dynasty, 27
Kotzk, Film production in, 27
Koussevitsky, David, 148
Krause, Gertie, **76**
Kreisler, Otto, 11, 12
Kressyn, Miriam, 57, 61, **63**, 100, **101**
K'Shenotnim, Kach. See Az Men Git, Nemt Men
Kuleshov, Lev, 50
Kursk, Film production in, 9

la Vida Bohemia, 122
Land of Freedom, 61, 185
Landau, Shmuel, 7, 95, 100
Landy, Ludwig, 130
Lang Iz Der Veg, 144, **145**, 146, 202
"Last of the Just," 158
Laughter Through Tears, 42, 43, 70. *See also Durkh Trern* and *Gelekhter Durch Trern*
Lavenda, Pinchus, 61
Leah's Suffering, 178
Lebedoff, Vera, **76**
Lederman, David, **19**
Leff, Abraham, 74, 75
Leivick, H., 61
Lekert, Hirsh, 46
Lekhaim, 1, 2, 173-74
Leningrad, Film production in, 34, 46
Leo-Film, 17, 23, 92
Leonidov, Leonid, 46
Leonov, N.B., 9
Leorov, M., 37, 44
Levine, Lucy, 56
Leybe der Shuster, 6, 177
Leyda, Jay, 37
Libe Un Laydnshaft, 79, 191-92
Libert, Jacob, 6
Libin, Zalmen, 31
Library of Congress, 159
Liebgold, Leon, **91**, **93**, 96, 126
The Light Ahead. See Di Klyatshe
Liliana, Lili, 96, **98**, **99**
Lipinski, Stanislaw, 87
Lipman, Moyshe, *20*, **21**, 23, 70, 95, **98**, **99**
Lipovsky, Nahum, 6
Liptzen, Kenni, 122
Little Girl with Big Ideas, 12
Litwina, Berta, **101**, 144, **145**
Live and Laugh. See Gelebt un Gelakht
The Living Orphan. See Der Lebediker Yosem
Love and Sacrifice. See Libe un Laydnshaft
Lower East Side of New York, 67
Lubitsh, Ernst, 96
Lubormirsky, Y., 40
Lubritsky, Dave, **140**

Index

Lugosi, Bella, 115
Lynn, Henry, 72-77, 112

MGM, 31, 84, 100
Mabul. See Der Mabul
Machtenberg, Choir Director, **65**
Mai-Ko Mashma-Lon, 57, 186
Makotinski, M., 41
Malcames, Don, **59**, 61, **63**
Mamele, 12, 30, 90, 104, **106**, 159, 196-97
Manger, Itzik, 90, 100, 109
Mann, Adolph, 107
Marcus, Betty, **125**
Marcus, Vicki, **80, 125**
Marek, Andrzej, 5, 6
Marevsky, Avrom, 96, 109, 112
Markish, Peretz, 49-50, 51
   profile, 49
Marten, Aleksander, 102, 107, 109
   profile, 87
Masters and Workers, 6
The Matchmaker, 70. *See also Yidishe Glikn*
Mayne Yidishe Mame, 57, **59**, 74, 184
   showing in Tel Aviv, 61
Maymon Film Company, 124
Mazel Tov, 83. *See also Mizrekh un Mayrev*
Mazl Tov Yidn, 133, **139**, 202
Medem Sanatorium, 84, 85
Meir Ezofowicz, 7, **8**
Melavsky, Cantor Samuel, 156
Menakhem Mendl. See Yidishe Glikn
Mendel of Kotzk, Rabbi, 27
Mendele Mokher Seforim (S.J. Abramovitz), 119, 121
Mendes, Lothar, 77
Menorah Pictures, 74
Menschen am Sonntag, 113
mental illness, exposition on, 74
Mentsh Fun Shtetl. See A Mentsh Fun Shtetl
Mestel, Jacob, 70
Meteor Studio, 17, 18
Metropolitan Studios, 55
Meyerhold, Vsevolod, 23
Michalesco, Michel, 74, 151, **152**, 156
Miedzeszyn, film production in, 84
Mikhoels, Solomon, 33, 36, **38, 39,** 48, 51, **52, 53**
   profile, 36
Milman, Mark, 50, 51
Minkin, Adolf, 51
Mintus Company, 6
Mir Kumen On, 84-86, **85,** 87, 146, 190
Mir Lebn Geblibene, 148, 190
Mirele Efros (1912), 7, 175
Mirele Efros (1913), 177
Mirele Efros (1939), 113, 118, 119, 122, **123,** 151, 164, 198-99

Mirele Efros (1973), 164
Mizrekh Company, 9
Mizrekh Un Mayrev, 12, 13, **14, 15,** 31, 83, 180
Moissi, Bettina, 144, **145**
Molière, 31
Monticello, Here We Come, 156, 203-4
Moscow Yiddish State Art Theater, 33, 36, 46
Motele Shpindler, 44-45, **45,** 183
Moteleff, Ilya, 81
Mothers of Today, 74, **76,** 199
Motl der Operator, 133, **136, 137,** 199
"Motl Peyse dem Khazns." *See Durkh Trern*
Mozhukhin, Ivan, 7
Muni, Paul, 102
Munich, film production in, 144
Murnau, F.W., 113
Museum of Modern Art, 162
My Son. See Der Lebediker Yosem

National Center for Jewish Film, 122, 159
   See also Rutenberg and Everett Yiddish Film Library
Natalka Poltavka, 113, 115
Natasha, 61, 186
Nazi Bund, 119
Nazi Germany, 130, 144
Neighborhood Playhouse, 112
Neighbors. See Shkheynim, 107
Neuman, J.M., 22, 86-87, 104
   profile, 86-87
New York City, film exhibition in, 81
   film production in, 153
   production on Lower East Side, 67
New York Film Festival, 122, 161
New York Motion Picture Company, 61
New York University, 158, 163
New York Yiddish Art Theater, 13, 31, 89, 124, 153, 157
New York Yiddish Film Festival, 90, 161
Newton, New Jersey, film production in, 118
Nikolas II, Czar, 9
Ninety-Second Street YM-YWHA, 160
Nishbal, Jeff, **163**
Nitrate film stock, 79, 157, 160-61
Noemi, Leah, 57, **73, 117**
Norris, Alexander. *See* Nosseck, Max
Norris, Steffan, 96
Noson Becker fort Aheym, 9, 50, **51, 52, 53,** 83, 188
Nossack, Max, 118, 130
Nowina-Przybylski, Jan, 91, **91,** 100

Odessa, film production in, 9
"Odessa Stories," 37
Olshanetsky, Alexander, 130, 153
On A Heym, 107-9, **108,** 199

Index 221

Opatoshu, David, **98, 99**, 120, **121**, 157
Opatoshu, Joseph, 27, 120
The Oppenheim Family, 48, 50-51, **52, 53**
Oppenheim, Menashe, **103**
Orzeszkowa, Eliza, 7
Osherowitz, Mendel, 102
Overture to Glory. See Der Vilner Shtot Khazn
Oy Doctor, 57, 58, 186
Oysher, Moishe, **80**, 81, 112, 116, **117**, 130, **131**, 157
   profile, 116

Pale of Settlement, Yiddish theater in, 5, 6
   Film production in, 6
Palestine, film exhibition in, 61
Panzer, Martin, 116
Passover, 102, 105
   Exhibition on, 133
Pathè Film Company, 1
Pavlova, Tatiana, 23
Pearlman, Joseph. *See* Dymow, Ossip
Peld, Harry, 57
A People Eternal. See A People That Shall Not Die
A People That Shall Not Die, 77, 199-200
Peretz, I.L., 9
Perle, Helen, **163**
Perlman, Max, **106**
Person, Celia, 57
Petrograd, Yiddish theater in, 36
Phoenix Film, 92
Pinski, David, 113, 116, 118
Picon, Molly, 12, **14, 15**, 90-91, **91, 93**, 104, **106**, 109, 112, 157
   profile, 12
Pietro Wyzej. See Shkheynim
Pilsudski, General Joseph, 17, 23-27
Poland, film production in, 3, 16-30, 83-109, 146-51
   Theater in, 17, 19-22
Polish Army Film Unit, 147
Polish cities, films about, 148
Polish Committee on National Liberation, 146
Potamkin, Harry, 56
The Power of Life. See Di Kraft fun Lebn
Preservation of Yiddish film, 159-61
The Prince and the Pauper. See Yisker
Producers' Service Studio, 115
Professor Mamlock, 51
Prudelski, Yair, 164
Pryor, Thomas M., 124
Prywes, Ludwig, 96
Prywes, Naftal, 96
Pudovkin, Vsevolod, 49
Purim, 100, 104
Purim play, 104

The Purim Player. See Der Purimshpiler
Purimshpiler. See Der Purimshpiler

RCA Sound Studios, 57
Rabinowitz, Sholom. *See* Sholom Aleichem
Rachel, 2, 175
Radok, Alfred, 146
Rajnglas, Jacob, **101**
Rapaport, Natan, 148
Rapoport, Solomon Zeynwil. *See* Anski, S.
Rappoport, Herbert, 51
Rebush, Roman, 111-19, 122-24
Rechtzeit, Seymour, **59**, 61, **138**
Reinhardt, Max, 87, 113
Reisen, Abraham, 57
The Return of Nathan Becker. See Noson Beker fort Aheym
Reznikov, M. 9
Rich, Silven, 27
Riga, Film production in, 6
Riklin, G., 36
Ringel, Israel, 164
Riselle, Miriam, 118, **125**, 126
Rivlin & Company, 61
Rodensky, Shmuel, **128**
Roitman, Cantor David, 64, 65
Roland, George, 70, 74, 79
Roosevelt, Franklin D., 111
Rosenberg, Michael, 44, **66**, 70, **139**, 153
Rosenblatt, Cantor Yossele, 64, 65
Rosenblatt, Max, 64, **76**
Rosh Hashanah, exhibition on, 133
Roshal, Grigori Lvovich, 45-46, **47**, 49, 50-51
   profile, 45-46
Roshal, Sofya, 46
Rotboym, Jacob, 148
Rotmil, Jacek, 96
Rovner, Cantor Seidel, 64, 65
Rubinstein, Z., 61
Rumshinsky, Joseph, 12, 74
Russia, films about, 1-3, 9-10
   films attacking, 3
Russia, The Land of Oppression, 2
Rutenberg and Everett Yiddish Film Library, 158-59, 161
Rywale, 23

Sabra. See Chalutzim
Sabbath, 83-84
Sackler, Harry, 13, 61
Sailor's Sweetheart, 61, **63**, 186
St. Petersberg, film production in, 6
Salzman, Esta, 79, **138, 140**
Samberg, Isaac, 7, 100, **101**
Sandomierz, film production in, 23
Satz, Ludwig, 64, 67

Schechter, Leon, **152**
Schildkraut, Joseph, 11, 89
Schildkraut, Rudolf, 11, 89
Schildkraut Theater, 89
Schlisky, Josef, **65**
Schoenfeld, Mae, **140**
Schomer, Abraham, 55
Schorr, Anshel, 74
Schumacher, Yisroel, 84, 86, 102, 103, **108**, 109, 149, 150
Schwartz-Bart, André, 158
Schwarz, Maurice, 12, 13, **16**, 31, 67, **68, 69**, 83, 89, 104, 112, 124-27, **125**, 153
  profile, 31
Schweid, Mark, 56, 67
Scooler, Zvee, 67
Scotto, Aubrey, 67
The Search, 144
Sebel, Stanislaw, 5
The Secret Saint. *See Der Lamedvovnik*
Secunda, Sholom, 60, 61, **63**, 70, 153
Seder for Passover, 104, 105
Seeds of Freedom (1928). *See Zayn Ekselents*
Seekers of Happiness (1936), 50
Seiden Films, 61
Seiden, Harold, 81, 133-41, 153, 158
Seiden, Joseph, 56-64, **59**, **60**, **63**, **65**, 74, 77-81, 133, 134, **135, 136, 137**, 151-56, 157
  distribution of Yiddish films, 157
Seiden, Mrs., **140**
Sektor Film, 84
Sektor Studios, 147
Semkoff, Sheyne Rokhl, 64
Shakespeare, adaptation of, 77
Shapiro, Henryk. *See* Szaro, Henryk
Shapiro, Joseph, 65
Shir Hashirim, 72, 191
Shkheynim, 107, 197
Shma Yisroel, 6, 177
Shmulewitz, S., 102
Shmulikel. *See* Kelemer, Samuel
Shneier, Chaim, 70
Shoemaker's Romance. *See Shuster Libe*
Sholom Aleichem (Sholom Rabinowitz), 9, 10, 31, 34, 36, 40, 42, 43, 44, 48, 49, 90, 124, 125, 127, 128
Shpis, Boris, 50, 51
Shtetl, recreation of, 100, 127
Shtetl life, exposition of, 41, 127
Shulamis, 64, 188
Shumski, V., 37
Shuster Libe, 57, 186
Siegel, Elwood, 160
Single-Parent family, depiction of, 104
Sila Film Company, 5, 6
Silberman, S.J., **42, 43**

Simon, Bernice, **59**
Simon, Mae, 57, **59**
The Simple Tailor. *See Motele Shpindler*
Singers of Israel, 204
The Singing Blacksmith. *See Der Zingendiker Shmid*
Singing in the Dark, 118
Siodmak, Robert, 113
Sklar, Robert, 111
The Skotilins, 46
Skulnick, Menashe, 57, 77, 156
Skvirski, I., 40
Soifer, Josef, 9-10
Song of Songs. *See Shir Hashirim*
The Sorrows of Israel, 3, 4
Sorrow of Sarah, 6-7, 177
Sov-Am Productions, 72
Soviet Union. *See* Union of Soviet Socialist Republics
Speier, Matthew, **159**
Stalin, Joseph, 49, 51
Stanczyk, S., 23
Stanislavsky, Konstantin, 95
"Start" Film Group, 84, 147
Stein, Joseph, 127
Steinwurcel, Seweryn, 18-19, 23, 30, 100, 104
  profile, 18
Strashunsky, Yoel David, 130
Strassberg, Morris, **73**
Stroeva, Vera, 46
Sukkot, 104
Style and Class, 57, **58**, 186-87
Szapiro, Henryk. *See* Szaro, Henryk
Szaro, Henryk, 23, 92-96, 144
  profile, 23
Szlingerbaum, Samy, 162

Talmadge Studios, 57
Tannenbaum, Marek. *See* Martin, Aleksander
Tauber, Chaim, **136**, **137**
Tel Aviv, film exhibition in, 61, 151
Television, showing of Yiddish films on
  Germany, 161
  Scandanavia, 161
The Terrors of Russia, 3
Tevye der Milkhiker, 90, 124-27, **125**, 161, 200
The Theater of Youth, 46
Theodor Herzl, der Bannerträges des Jüdischen Volkes, 11
Thomashefsky, Boris, 6, 72, **73**, 83, 112, 116
Thomashefsky, Harry, 77
Three Daughters. *See Dray Tekhter*
Tisse, Edward, 36, 38, 39
Tkies Kaf (1924), 7, 17-18, **19, 20, 21**, 23, **24, 25**, 70, 87, 95, 102, 124
Tkies Kaf (1937), 30, 92-95, **94**, 100, 144, 194-95

Toeplitz, Jerzy, 23, 92, 151
Tolstoy, Lev, 6
Tom, Konrad, 104
Topol, Haim, **129**
Towbin, Mojzesz Mordka, 5
Toytmiln. See Death Factories
Trachtenberg, Judith. *See* Judith Trachtenberg
Tradition, film expositions dealing with, 104, 125-26
Trystan, Leon, 90, 107
Tsvey Shvester, 57, 77, **78**, 112, 197
Tsavion, B., 97
Tsebrokhene Hertser, 31-32, 124, 181
Tunney-Dempsey Fight, 61
Turkow, Itskhok. *See* Grudberg, Itskhok
Turkow, Jonas, 17, 23, **24, 25, 26,** 27, **29,** 86, 91, 94
Turkow, Ruth, 103
Turkow, Zygmund, 17, 19, **19, 20, 21,** 30, 70, 92, **94,** 100, **101, 103,** 109, 112, 144
Tuvya V'Shiva B'notav, 127, **128**
Two Sisters. See Tsvey Shvester
Two Women, 46
Tyler, Parker, 97

Ukraine, film production in, 9, 33, 37-45
Ukrainian film production, 113, 119
Ulica Graniczna, 144, 146, 148, 151
Ulmer, Edgar George, 81, 113-21, **114, 121,** 127, 133, 157, 160, 161, 165
  profile, 113-15
  Ukrainian Pictures, 113, 119
Ulmer, Shirley, 119, 127
Uncle Moses, **66,** 67, 81, 83, 189
Underhill Farm, 124
Union of Soviet Socialist Republics (U.S.S.R.)
  films about Soviet ideology, 46
  film production in, 33-51
  Socialist realism, 49-50
  films attacking, 72
Unions. *See* Yiddish Actors' Union
United Artists, 158
United States of America, film production in, 30-32, 55-81, 111-41, 151-56, 165
United States Military, Information Control Division, 144
  Government, 143-44
Unsane-Toykef, 61, 187
Unzer Teater, 89
Unzere Kinder, **149,** 150-51, 202-3
Uriel Acosta, 5

Vakhtangov, Yevgeni, 33
Ven Ikh Bin Roytshild, 9, 179
Vershilov, Boris, 35
Vilna Circle Theater, 6
Vienna, film production in, 11-12

Vilna, film production in, 22
A Vilna Legend, 22, 70, 83, 189-90
  See also Tkies Kaf (1924)
Vilna Troupe, 89, 95
Vilner Balabesl. See Der Vilner Shtot Khazn
Vilner Shtot Khazn. See Der Vilner Shtot Khazn
Vilner, Vladimir, 37, 45
Vladek, Barney, 86
Vodnoy, Max, **114, 117**
The Voice of Israel, 77, 188
Von Wahl, Governor-General, 46
The Vow. See Tkies Kaf
Vu Iz Emes, 6, 177
Vu Iz Mayn Kind?, 74, **75,** 195
Vu Iz Mayne Khasye, 6, 9, 175
Vufku Studios, 37-45, **45,** 49
The Voice of Israel, 64, **65**
Voldo, V., 9

Waldman, Cantor Leibel, 60, 64, 65, 79
Waletzky, Josh, 158, 159, 163
The Wandering Jew. See Avrom Ovinu
Wandering Stars. See Blondzhende Shtern
Warner Brothers Pictures, 55, 79, 84
The War and the Jew, 9, 178
Warsaw, film production in, 5, 17, 22, 92, 97
Warsaw Ghetto Revolt, 148
Warsaw Yiddish Art Theater, 17
Wasilevka, Wanda, 84
Waszynski, Michal, 96
We Live Again, 146, 203
Weinreich, Jacek, 91, 109
Weintraub, Rebecca, **78**
Weisman, Gershon, 6
Weiss, Florence, 81, **117,** 118, 119
Weiss, Louis, 67
The Well. See Der Brunem
Wendroff, Ruben, **117**
Wernicke, Otto, 145
Where is My Child? See Vu Iz Mayn Kind?
Wilder, Billy, 113
Williams, Larry, 130
Wilner, Max, 77, 153
Without a Home. See On A Haym
Wlast, Andrzej, 22
Working conditions, films dealing with, 67, 68, 69, 133, 136, 137
Wolf, Simon, 74, **76**
World Film, 61
World Jewish Congress, 147
World Zionist Congress, 150
Worldart Film, 56
Worldkino, 70

Yafo Film Organization, 143, 146

Yiddish, use of language in Palestine, 64
Yiddish Literature, adaptation of, 111
Yiddish Actors' Union, 61
Yiddish Art Theater. *See* New York Yiddish Art Theater; Moscow Yiddish State Art Theater; and Warsaw Yiddish Art Theater
Yiddish Compilation Film, 67-68
Yiddish Film Organization. *See* Yafo Film Organization
Yiddish Talking Pictures Company, 67
Yidishe Foter, 72, 190
Yidishe Glikn, 33, 35-37, **38**, **39**, 40, 70, 181
Yidishe Kinig Lir, 77, 191
Yidishe Nigun (1930), 60, 187. *See also Der Yidishe Nigun* (1940)
Yidishe Tokhter, 70, 190
Yidl Mitn Fidl (1913), 9, 177
Yidl Mitn Fidl (1936), 12, 81, 90-92, **91**, **93**, 97, 104, 111, 126, 192
Yidn In Poylishe Velder. See In Poylishe Velder

Yisker, 12, 13, **16**, 19, 31, 180
YIVO Institute for Jewish Research, 159
Yom Hakhupa, 6, 176
Yom Kippur, 87, 130-32, 133
A Youth of Russia. See Yidishe Foter

Zamenhoff, Ludwig, 87
Zanger, Jacob, **140**
Zaporesh sa Dunayem, 119
Zayenda, Edmund, 104, **106**
Zayn Ekselents, 46, 183
Zayn Vaybs Lubovnik, 64-67, **66**, 187
Zayn Vaybs Man (1913), 177-78
Zayn Vaybs Man (1916), 17, 179
Zeifert, Moyshe, 6
Zinnemann, Fred, 144
Zolatarefsky, Isidore, 6, 74
Zuckerberg, Regina, 72
Zuskin, Vinyamin, 33, 46-48, 50
Zwerling, Yetta, 79, **139**, **140**